African American Voic
from Iwo Jima

African American Voices from Iwo Jima

Personal Accounts of the Battle

CLARENCE E. WILLIE

With forewords by
Lieutenant General Frank E. Petersen, USMC (Retired)
Major General John R. Piatak, USA (Retired)

McFarland & Company, Inc., Publishers
Jefferson, North Carolina, and London

LIBRARY OF CONGRESS CATALOGUING-IN-PUBLICATION DATA

Willie, Clarence E., 1945–
    African American voices from Iwo Jima : personal accounts of the
battle / Clarence E. Willie ; with forewords by Frank E. Petersen,
John R. Piatak.
        p.   cm.
    Includes bibliographical references and index.

    ISBN 978-0-7864-4158-7
    softcover : 50# alkaline paper ∞

    1. Iwo Jima, Battle of, Japan, 1945—Personal narratives,
American.   2. World War, 1939–1945—Participation, African
American.   3. World War, 1939–1945—Personal narratives,
American.   I. Title.
D767.99.I9W56   2010
940.54'2528—dc22   2010021586

British Library cataloguing data are available

Front cover: top Mt. Surabachi; DUKW drivers attempting to get their
cargo and personnel ashore in the middle of continuous enemy fire

Manufactured in the United States of America

McFarland & Company, Inc., Publishers
    Box 611, Jefferson, North Carolina 28640
    www.mcfarlandpub.com

To all of the men and women who
supported and participated in World War II
both at home and abroad.
And particularly to those who
would not return and have the opportunity
to see the extraordinary results of their sacrifices.

Acknowledgments

THE RESEARCH AND COMPLETION of this work could not have happened without the assistance and valuable information provided by others. I want to express my sincerest appreciation to the 11 men highlighted in this work and to their families for allowing me to come into their homes and for sharing their recollections and memoirs of personal experiences and significant events from their generation that changed the course of American history forever.

Significant events of their time have been very well recorded in history, but there are very few accounts of their service in the Battle of Iwo Jima. Without the interviews so graciously offered by them, the photographs I have been able gather from the National Archives of the United States, literary holdings from several libraries too numerous to mention and those who were willing to share their research holdings in support of this effort, this work could not have been completed. I particularly appreciate the support of Frank E. Petersen, Lieutenant General, United States Marine Corps (Retired), and John R. Piatak, Major General, United States Army (Retired), for their written support of this project.

In conclusion, I wish to express my gratitude to my family and some very special friends for their steady, persistent support and encouragement throughout the writing of this book.

Table of Contents

Foreword

Frank E. Petersen
Lieutenant General, United States Marine Corps (Ret.)

BOTH DR. WILLIE AND I have walked in the shadows of the men you will come to know in this book, *African American Voices from Iwo Jima*. He has captured their accounts of the life and times of a period in American history when the United States clearly emerged as a world leader. The oral histories that the men provide in this book include their service in one of the fiercest battles of World War II, the Battle of Iwo Jima. When the barriers to military service for African Americans began to fall in the early 1940s, these men answered the call. They all agreed that they believed it was their duty to serve, even though they knew they would be required to do so in segregated units. That was the policy for the service of African Americans during World War II. There were some exceptions, but most were assigned to support units, which were generally located in rear areas, rather than on the front lines. A presidential Executive Order issued in 1948 began the process of desegregating the military, and in 1954 the last segregated unit was disbanded.

The interviewees share with readers their personal experiences from the time they were born in the early 1900s, growing into adulthood during the Great Depression, the pre–World War II years, their military training, the thirty-six-day battle for Iwo Jima, coming home and the civil rights struggles that occurred during the 1950s and 1960s. One of them would be awarded the third highest award given for valor in the face of the enemy, the Silver Star Medal, and another would remain in the military after World War II, participate in the Korean and Vietnam conflicts and retire from

1

active duty with twenty-six years of service. Most would be discharged, return to their families and pursue careers as civilians. Segregation and racial discrimination continued to be a way of life for them until the passage of the Civil Rights Act in 1964. They all believed that they would never live to see that happen or to see the election of an African American president.

Dr. Willie's educational and military background has clearly prepared him for the task of preserving the oral histories included in this book. He was reared in a military family and graduated from high school on a military installation in Germany. His surroundings during those years nurtured a keen interest in the military, world history and World War II. In college, he pursued those interests by majoring in social studies and history. When he graduated from college, he entered the United States Marine Corps and became intrigued with the service of African Americans in the military. After twenty-two years of service, he retired from the Marine Corps as a lieutenant colonel, became a high school history teacher, earned a doctoral degree in educational leadership and retired from the profession of education as a school district superintendent.

He has now developed a keen interest in documenting the service of African Americans in the military. In that regard, he initiated an effort which culminated in the production of a documentary that has aired on national television and introduced its viewers to the first African Americans to serve as United States Marines. And now, by way of this book, Dr. Willie has recorded and preserved for history some new perspectives to add to that body of knowledge about the Battle of Iwo Jima and the service of eleven African Americans who participated in that conflict, perspectives that could otherwise have been lost forever.

Lieutenant General Frank E. Petersen became the first African American aviator to serve in the Marine Corps and in 1979 became the first African American to be promoted to the rank of brigadier general in the Marine Corps. He flew more than 350 combat missions in the Korean and Vietnam conflicts.

Foreword

John R. Piatak
Major General, United States Army (Ret.)

I HAVE HAD THE PLEASURE of reading and re-reading Lt. Col. Clarence E. Willie's manuscript entitled "African American Voices from Iwo Jima." I commend it to the reader as it sheds significant light on the hard work and heroics of African American military men in support of the fighting forces at Iwo Jima. In today's business vernacular they would be described as a significant part of the supply chain management of that great battle. His effort is an opening into the hearts and minds of eleven African American Marines and soldiers and their experiences growing up in the 1930s and '40s; entering the military as new recruits; deploying to a far-off battle; and sustaining a positive attitude throughout difficult racial times.

What most impressed me about these eleven men was their acceptance of responsibility as citizens of our country during a period when they were not always treated fairly. When I entered the United States Army at Fort Eustis, Virginia, in 1958, race relations had improved since their service in the military. Executive Order 9981 (1948) and the *Brown vs. Board of Education* (1956) decision would prove to be the catalyst that would make a significant impact on race relations both in the military and in our greater society. In a discussion with an African American Army captain shortly after I reported to military service early in my career, I became very aware that the country as a whole, in spite of initiatives at the highest levels of government, was not willing to recognize members of all ethnic groups as quickly as it was happening in the military services. The captain revealed to me that

3

on a trip from Fort Hood, Texas, to Fort Eustis, he could not find a motel that would rent him a room for the night.

Although the military is generally recognized by many as the vanguard of the integration movement in the United States, the memoirs of the men in this book also clearly indicate that during the post–World War II era, they too recall that the military was slow in realizing the essence of the intent of Executive Order 9981. Most of those interviewed for this book returned to civilian life after World War II but remained in government service, and during their careers as civil servants witnessed the intent of President Truman's Executive Order gradually take hold in the military. From the time of their military service until recent years, discrimination continued to be an issue with regard to assignments for minorities. They were frequently assigned to positions of lesser stature than their white counterparts.

The number of minority officers, senior enlisted members and civilians serving the military when they were on active duty is a fraction of the large number of minorities serving at all ranks from private to general officer in today's military. One of the clearest indications of that significant change was the election of an African American as our president and commander-in-chief of our military forces. Both the veterans whose personal accounts are in this book and I agree that tremendous strides have been made in the military, in government initiatives and legislation, and at national and state levels to satisfy the intent of President Truman's Executive Order, but also that we are not quite there yet.

Major General John R. Piatak is a veteran of two tours of duty in Vietnam and directed the deployment of United States and Allied forces to the Persian Gulf in support of Operation Desert Storm. His Army career includes service and leadership responsibilities at all levels of command within the continental United States and abroad.

Preface

SHORTLY AFTER ENTERING the Marine Corps, I became aware of the fact that African Americans had only begun to serve as Marines in 1942 and only then as enlisted men. Those first African American Marines trained near Jacksonville, North Carolina, at a segregated training camp known as Montford Point, until 1949. Their service was one of perseverance, honor and dedication in the face of racial discrimination. For several years, I sought funding to document their experience. Through the efforts of Dr. Thomas Shuster, CEO of Spectrum Consulting of North Logan, Utah, and Dr. Melton McLaurin, professor of history emeritus at the University of North Carolina at Wilmington, a federal grant was awarded that funded the production of a documentary to tell the story of those first African American Marines. The documentary, on which I served as consultant and interviewer, was completed in 2006 and it is entitled *The Marines of Montford Point: Fighting for Freedom*. The documentary has aired on the Public Broadcasting System and other broadcast markets nationally, and it provides an account of those first African Americans recruited and trained to be United States Marines. Some of the Marines interviewed during the production of the documentary acknowledged the fact that they had actually participated in the Iwo Jima invasion. That piqued my interest and I began to explore the participation of African Americans in one of the most significant armed conflicts of World War II in the Pacific, the Battle of Iwo Jima.

In addition to the Marine Corps veterans, I found that African Americans serving with the United States Army also played a very significant role in the Iwo Jima invasion. I have located 11 of these Marine and Army veterans, interviewed them, and based this book on accounts of their experiences during that historical battle. The African Americans interviewed for

The island of Iwo Jima was the site of one of the fiercest battles of World War II. Its close proximity to Japan would put American forces within striking distance of the Japanese mainland. (National Archives)

this book served in the U.S. Marine Corps' 8th Ammunition Company, 33rd and 36th Depot Companies and the U.S. Army's 476th Amphibian Truck Company during the Iwo Jima campaign. The African American Marines would support the shore party of the Fifth Amphibious Corps, unloading and stockpiling ammunition and other supplies and moving the cargo inland. The African American soldiers would provide valuable support to ground troops by operating the amphibian vehicle known as the DUKW (pronounced "duck"). The DUKW is a six-wheel-drive vehicle designed for transporting supplies, troops, and equipment over land or water during amphibious attacks. It was developed in the United States and would be usually found in the inventory of amphibious craft designated for use in most of the amphibious operations conducted in World War II in the Atlantic and Pacific. Its driver had the capability to inflate its tires so that it could travel on solid ground or deflate them for movement in the water; with the assistance of a rudder attached to the rear of the vehicle, the driver also had the ability to steer the vehicle while maneuvering in the water.

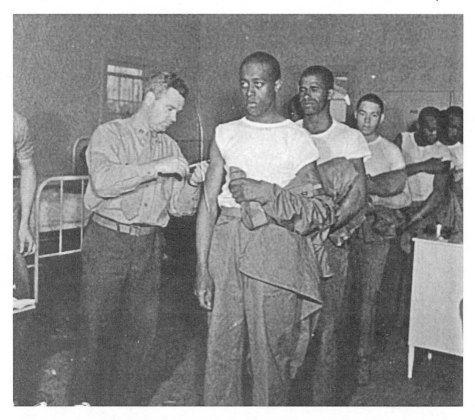

Two and a half million African Americans registered for the military during World War II, and for the first time in U.S. history, nearly 20,000 of them served as U.S. Marines. (National Archives)

The secretary of the Navy issued the following commendation to all of the support units of the Fifth Amphibious Corps, United States Fleet Marine Force:

> For extraordinary heroism in support of Military Operations during the seizure of enemy Japanese-held Iwo Jima, Volcano Islands, February 19–28, 1945. Landing against resistance which rapidly increased in fury as the Japanese pounded the beaches with artillery, rocket and mortar fire, the Support Units of the FIFTH Amphibious Corps surmounted the obstacles of chaotic disorganization, loss of equipment, supplies and key personnel to develop and maintain a continuous link between thousands of assault troops and supply ships. Resourceful and daring whether fighting in the front lines of combat, or serving in the rear areas or on the wreck of obstructed beaches, they were responsible for the administration of operations and personnel; they rendered effective fire support where Japanese

pressure was greatest; they constructed roads and facilities and maintained communications under the most difficult and discouraging conditions of weather and rugged terrain; they salvaged vital supplies from craft lying crippled in the surf or broached on the beaches; and they ministered to the wounded under fire and provided prompt evacuation to the hospital ships. By their individual initiative and heroism, and their ingenious team work, they provided the unfailing support vital to the conquest of Iwo Jima, a powerful defense to the Japanese Empire.

John L. Sullivan
Secretary of the Navy

The commendation also states, "All personnel attached to and serving with the following Support Units of Fifth Amphibious Corps, United States Fleet Marine Force, during the Iwo Jima Operation from February 19 to 28, 1945, are authorized to wear the Navy Unit Commendation Ribbon." Among the personnel authorized to receive this commendation were the nearly 900 African Americans who served with Army, Navy and Marine Corps Units during the battle at Iwo Jima.

This book offers a glimpse into the diverse backgrounds from which these men came. The majority of them were born and reared in the South. Some had not completed high school when they were called to service; some of them were called to service from college; some of them were drafted; some volunteered; and some of them were employed when they were called. They were all willing to serve in defense of the United States and all of them are proud of their service.

Legislative activity at the national level, strong civil rights activity and the need to pull together all of the human resources of our country as the United States began to emerge as a world power prior to World War II would become catalysts that would eventually remove barriers to service for African Americans in the armed forces. The men interviewed for this book were among the 34 million American men between the ages of 18 and 37 who would register for the draft. The Marine Corps had never recruited or trained African Americans to serve as Marines. The office of the Secretary of the Navy announced on May 20, 1942, that on June 1, 1942, the Navy would begin recruiting 1,000 African Americans a month and that during June and July a complete battalion of 900 African Americans would be formed by the Marine Corps. Their training would take place not at Parris Island, South Carolina, with their white counterparts, but at a location adjacent to the sprawling Marine Corps Base Camp Lejeune located near Jacksonville, North Carolina, known as Montford Point. The green huts constructed there would serve as barracks and training facilities for the new recruits. More than

20,000 recruits would train there. The camp was originally constructed to serve 1200 African American recruits but was expanded as that number increased. The four Marine veterans included in this book were among the first group of the more than 20,000 Marines who trained there between 1942 and 1949. All of the African Americans who served in any branch of the military trained and served under segregated conditions during World War II. African Americans were usually found in support units, while front line units were all white. Racial segregation was the policy observed by all branches of the military. In that regard, life was no different in the military than it was in the greater society. Some of the veterans were very vocal about the fact that that they were channeled into support activities and did not have the option or opportunity to truly fight for their country. Under battlefield conditions, some of them did come into contact with the enemy, and some of them did die for their country.

When the men whose interviews are included in this book shipped out, there were indications that they would more than likely be serving in or close to a combat zone. Combat equipment was issued, additional training was conducted and new units were formed. The men believed that they were going to war, but they did not know where. Some who followed the patterns of activity were able to make reasonable assumptions, but they really did not find out where they were headed until their transport ships moved into the waters surrounding the island of Iwo Jima in the Pacific. Their descriptions of the activity aboard ship in the waters off shore of Iwo Jima, the massive movement of troops and supplies in the battle area before going ashore, and the ultimate confrontation with a determined enemy were vividly descriptive. Hearing bombs exploding constantly, taking cover in the face of incoming mortar, and small-arms fire 24 hours a day was a way of life for them when they went ashore for the 36-day battle. They all admit that in the early stages of the battle for Iwo Jima, no one could predict the outcome. But they all recall that morale booster and the glimmer of hope that our troops were making forward movement when, on February 23, 1945, the Stars and Stripes were raised atop the most prominent terrain feature on Iwo Jima, Mt. Suribachi. A determined enemy, however, would stand its ground and the war would rage on for another month.

The interviewees all agreed that during the 36-day battle, the color of a man's skin was not an issue. It was "One for all and all for one," they said. Upon returning home, however, they readily acknowledged that very little had changed regarding the issue of discrimination and segregation. When they went to restaurants, movies on military installations, and other public places away from the installations, they still had to endure racial discrimination. As a segregated military moved into the post-war era in the late 1940s in the United States, African American veterans were happy to see President Truman's Executive Order 9981, signed in 1948, mandating the desegregation of the armed forces. Making it a reality would be a hard-fought political battle for the president, but within a decade, it would happen. The Order states in part:

> It is hereby declared to be the policy of the President that there shall be equality of treatment and opportunity for all persons in the armed services without regard to race, color, religion or national origin. This policy shall be put into effect as rapidly as possible, having due regard to the time required to effectuate any necessary changes without impairing efficiency or morale.

All but one of those interviewed for this book had already separated from the military when the order was signed but in their interviews all of them clearly expressed their satisfaction that it had happened.

The Battle of Iwo Jima occurred nearly 65 years ago, yet, it is as clear in these men's minds as it was when they went ashore there in February of 1945. What they and the other United States military fighting men accomplished during that battle is in part responsible for the freedoms our citizens have enjoyed since World War II. In the years since World War II, there have been changes in our society that they never thought would happen in their lifetime. All of them were reared in segregated communities and attended segregated schools. Within ten years after they returned home from Iwo Jima, they would see the United States Supreme Court, in a unanimous decision, outlaw segregation in public school systems when it issued the landmark *Brown vs. Board of Education* decision which would play a major role in the demise of legal segregation in the United States. They saw the Civil Rights Act of 1964 passed, and something that they thought they would never see—the election of the first African American president in the history of the United States. I asked each one of the interviewees the question, "What do you say when people find out that you are an Iwo Jima veteran and call you a hero?" Not one of them considered himself a hero. Each one indicated to me that they were simply doing their job as a citizen and believed that they were simply fulfilling a responsibility of that citizenship. These men, although their service in World War II has been rarely mentioned in American history, were part of what is now widely known as "the Greatest Generation," a term journalist Tom Brokaw uses to refer to those Americans who grew up during the Great Depression and went on to fight in World War II, as well as as those who supported the war effort at home.

Introduction

ON TELEVISION AND AT THE MOVIE theater, viewers were captivated by the exciting sights and sounds that producers, writers, directors and actors employed to bring fictitious or real-life events to the silver screen. They did so in a manner that made images and events seem bigger than life, bigger than people, more vivid than reality, more interesting, more complex, more emotional, more exciting, more defiant, more risky. Watching a movie can be an intense experience and great movies can leave an indelible impression on the viewer. Movie-makers can capture the imagination of movie goers in more ways than one can imagine by twisting the plot, creating stunning car chases, writing scenes with buildings bursting into flames, showing a woman crying and running with a baby in her arms or depicting military men enduring the ravage of war.

"It seemed like a movie," is a phrase commonly used during the interviews by some of the veterans as they described their experiences. These men came face to face with death, devastation and destruction on a tiny, barren, desolate island located 650 nautical miles from Tokyo in one of the bloodiest military campaigns of World War II, and many of them readily admit that it was truly like sitting in a movie theater back home. "In those days, we always went to the movies, and watching the activity from our ship as we waited to go ashore was like looking at a movie from a distance. Only it was not a movie, it was the real thing," said **Roland Durden**. "That first day was almost like the movies I saw made back home in Hollywood and those we would see in the newsreels. I could see the planes dropping their bombs, see the Navy shelling the island with their big guns, see all the landing craft go ashore with troops, and smell the smoke. Only this time, I was really a part of it all," said **Charles Black**.

Even though 900 African Americans participated in the Battle of Iwo Jima, historical accounts of the service of the members of this large segment of American citizens in this widely-publicized and significant event is a little-known fact of American history. Thankfully, many of them are still with us today to talk about their experiences. Eleven of those men chose to share their story to show that honor, integrity, valor and loyalty to country were as colorless then as they are today.

First Sergeant Frederick Gray, USA; Sergeant Eugene Doughty, USMC; First Sergeant Arthur L. Peterson, USA; Corporal Roland Durden, USMC; Technician Fifth Grade Horace Taylor, USA; Corporal Haywood Johnson, USA; Corporal Archibald Mosley, USMC; Corporal Charles Black, USA; Staff Sergeant Sam Green, USA; Technician Fifth Grade Lyman Brent, USA; and First Sergeant Ellis Cunningham, USMC, are the real thing. They were there on the island of Iwo Jima in World War II, and this is their story.

Their lasting impression of the Battle of Iwo Jima and concerns about having to serve in a segregated United States Army and United States Marine Corps are common threads in the accounts of their military service during World War II. These men would not serve on the front lines and assume direct combat roles, but historical accounts of their service support the fact that they effectively served in combat service support roles providing supplies, ammunition, and transportation to support the front line troops and were as much a part of the victory over the enemy at Iwo Jima as any member of the Allied Forces who participated in the conflict.

The Battle of Iwo Jima, which is thought by many to be the beginning of the end of World War II in the Pacific, was one of the fiercest armed conflicts of World War II. The allied victory there severely crippled the ability of the Japanese military to defend its homeland. This book is an account of the extraordinary experiences of some of the African American soldiers and Marines who survived the Battle of Iwo Jima. These men are proud of their service in that iconic battle, and they are excited at the prospect that through this medium there will be an account of their service there.

PART ONE

LIVING IN PREWAR AMERICA AND ANSWERING THE CALL TO DUTY

THE 1940S MARKED CULTURAL and economic change for minorities, women, African Americans, and persons of various ethnic backgrounds. There was a certain dichotomy of feelings among the general population. On one hand, to most people life looked vastly better than it had during the Depression years; hope was in the air. Yet, as the decade continued and the war in Europe raged, a sense of caution became the order of the day.

Popular culture was exploding creatively, intellectually, and politically. People from all walks of life were listening to an ever-increasing list of genres of music from Glenn Miller's big band orchestra to the Andrews Sisters to young non-conformist jazz musicians such as Thelonious Monk. Stars like Hattie McDaniel, Lena Horne, and Paul Robeson added diversity on screen and off. Black sportsmen became popular heroes and paved the way for future generations. These included Joe Louis (boxer), Jesse Owens (runner), and Jackie Robinson (baseball player). Many notable Americans emerged during this era whose achievements still impact our culture today.

Dissatisfied with their plight during the Depression years as farms and jobs in the South began to vanish, many African Americans moved north and west in search of better opportunities for work and education. During the period between World War I and World War II, many African Americans moved to urban areas of the northern and western parts of the United States during the "Great Migration." Many of those leaving the South settled in northern cities where they ran for public offices in an attempt to become a voice to encourage equal opportunities for African Americans. Large

13

African American communities began to emerge in New York, Chicago and other large metropolitan cities outside of the South. African Americans also moved from the economically depressed South to take advantage of the employment opportunities created by World War I and President Roosevelt's New Deal Administration. They did experience somewhat better working conditions and lifestyle but in many cases, segregation and discrimination were still as much of a deterrent to achieving the lifestyle they sought as when they lived in the rural South. Many scholars, artists, scientists, writers, and musicians found that in these metropolitan areas they could express themselves and take advantage of educational opportunities. The Harlem Renaissance, which occurred in New York City in the years prior to World War II, saw the growth of many educational and cultural pursuits in the African American community and was one of the results of the African American intellectual experience in metropolitan areas outside of the South.

There were numerous positive aspects about life in the 1940s, but segregation was not one of them. From the 1880s into the 1960s, a majority of American states enforced segregation through "Jim Crow" laws (so-called after a black character in minstrel shows). From the Northern boundaries to the Southern boundaries of the United States, many states (and cities, too) could impose legal punishments on people for consorting with members of another race. The most common types of laws forbade intermarriage and ordered business owners and public institutions to keep their black and white clientele separated. Daily life in segregated America could be difficult and frustrating, but as the men who lived during that time will tell you, it was just how things were back then.

"We accepted the rules and regulations of that day although we asked why," said **Frederick Gray**. "But, where could we go for help when the United States Supreme Court was in accord with what the system was doing at that time? We knew our place. We knew we could not go in the front door, and we did not go in the front door. We knew that when we went to the movie, we would sit upstairs in the balcony. We knew that; it was a fact. That's the way it was. It was the law of the land. Youngsters of today ask us why we took it. We would tell them that there was nothing we could do about it because that was the way it was back then. They would say, 'Mr. Gray, I just don't think I could have taken that.' I would tell them that that if they had come up in the time that we did, they would have had to. We could do nothing, had nowhere to go, and nobody to sing our song to. We did ask the question why, but we had no recourse and nothing to challenge the issues of the time with."

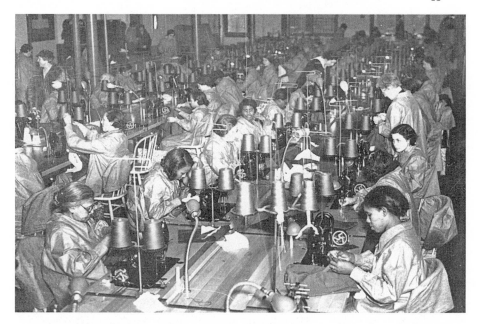

Opportunities for a better lifestyle and relief from racial segregation stimulated a migration of African Americans away from the South in the pre–World War II years. (National Archives)

Held over from the post–Civil War era, de jure and de facto segregation were rampant not only in the South but in other parts of the United States as well. Strong civil rights activity and actions by presidents Roosevelt and Truman in the 1940s, however, began to threaten the existence of segregation. Additionally, prior to World War II large numbers of African Americans began to move from the South to get away from segregationist laws and practices, which denied them the basic freedoms guaranteed by the Constitution. They began to speak out in the press, at the polls, and through civil rights activity, as they gained national and international exposure in education, athletics, and the arts and sciences.

The inclusion of an anti-discrimination clause which established a ten percent quota system to ensure integration in the Selective Training and Service Act of 1940 and the issuance of an Executive Order by President Franklin D. Roosevelt were significant in paving the way for military service for African Americans. It became evident to the War Department in the early 1940s that all available resources of the United States must be ready for war. In that regard, the Selective Training and Service Act of 1940 required that members of minority ethnic groups be called to serve in the military. Among them were young African Americans who would go on to participate in an extraordinary battle that possibly changed the history of the world for all time.

Additionally, on June 25, 1941, President Roosevelt signed Executive Order 8802 which reads in part as follows:

> WHEREAS it is the policy of the United States to encourage full participation in the national defense program by all citizens of the United States, regardless of race, creed, color or national origin, in the firm belief that the democratic way of life within the Nation can be defended successfully only with the help and support of all groups within its borders....

Essentially, Executive Order 8802 prohibited discrimination by any government entity or government contractor doing business with the government, and it ordered the establishment of training programs by federal entities for employees without regard to race, creed, color, or national origin. Additionally, in view of the fact that prominent civil rights activists, including A. Philip Randolph and others, were planning civil rights demonstrations for equality in labor hiring practices, President Roosevelt believed that the order would be a deterrent to strikes in the presence of a global threat of war. Executive Order 8802 was also known as the Fair Employment Act and, as such, it became a catalyst for the service of more African Americans than at any other time in American History, and for the first time in American history, the service of African Americans in the United States Marine Corps. Additionally, many more African American service members began serving in leadership roles and more were entering the officer ranks.

A chronology of events from Morris J. MacGregor, Jr., in his book *Integration of the Armed Forces, 1940–1965,* indicates that one of the major catalysts for integration in the United States armed forces was the proactive civil rights activity of the 1940s. Without question, that activity was a major force that led to the signing of Executive Order 9981, on July 26, 1948, by President Harry Truman, the order which led to the total racial integration of the armed forces. MacGregor reports that on October 30, 1954, the Secretary of Defense announced the abolishment of the last racially segregated unit in the armed forces of the United States. Since the Korean War, military units have been totally integrated, and service members of all ethnic backgrounds have served and are continuing to serve in leadership positions at all levels and are accorded the same opportunities.

The Iwo Jima veterans that you will come to know in this book were young men when the events that led to World War II began. They witnessed

Of those who answered the call to military duty during World War II, 110,000 U.S. troops would participate in the battle of Iwo Jima and nearly 1,000 of them would be African Americans. (National Archives)

and participated in a surge of new opportunities for African Americans in the military and also in America's greater society. Although the barriers faced by African Americans who wished to enter the military were coming down as the United States geared up for war, life for them in and out of the military was still very segregated and would remain so until the end of the war. They served in all branches of the military during World War II and the numbers swelled to more than a million before the war was over. Some of the veterans interviewed for this book do not necessarily see themselves as trailblazers, but many believe they were. They stood in harm's way in support of their country and paved the way to the desegregation of the military and, in a greater sense, the American culture.

CHAPTER 1

Eleven Men Who Would Share an Extraordinary Experience

THE AFRICAN AMERICANS who would participate in the Battle of Iwo Jima were born and reared at a time in American history when segregation was a way of life in the United States. Many of them lived in rural areas in the South and worked on farms owned by white landowners. Thus, when work on the farms did not exist, life became more difficult because that was how most of them had always earned their living.

Many think of the Battle of Iwo Jima as a war that was fought completely by United States Marines. The iconic photograph taken by photographer Joe Rosenthal on February 23, 1945, with five United States Marines and a U.S. Navy Corpsman raising the flag of the United States atop Mount Suribachi has become a symbol of victory in war and the price our military and the people of the world pay when they are engaged in armed conflict. The battle was a joint effort planned and supported by all of the military services. The Marines were the infantry assault troops who faced the main impact of the enemy resistance, but there was heavy participation by the United States Army and Navy as well as the support of the United States Coast Guard. Nine hundred vessels sailed in support of the Allied invasion of Iwo Jima, including 17 aircraft carriers with 1,770 United States Army Air Corps and United States Navy aircraft supporting the Fifth Amphibious Corps.

There were Navy Seabees providing invaluable support building the runways for aircraft and clearing roads to support the forward movement of vehicles supplying the front line troops. Seven of the men featured in this book served with the 476th Amphibian Truck Company, one of the three companies from the United States Army's 43rd Amphibian Truck Battalion. The amphibian truck companies would carry supplies, equipment and personnel ashore and evacuate casualties from the battle area to hospital ships in their DUKWs throughout the invasion. If the unloading point was more than four miles inland, areas would be established where their cargoes would be transferred to trucks and other vehicles used for the rigorous land navigation and the distant locations further inland. After the island was secured, the Army took control of Iwo Jima and became the occupation force. The soldiers interviewed for this book would remain on the island as part of that force, while the Marines would move back to their ships and position themselves for another strike at Japan.

The Soldiers

Frederick Gray is a native of Calvert County, Maryland. "I was born on July the 20th 1925," said Gray. "I was the ninth child; my mother passed away bringing me into the world. When I was born, she asked her best friend, we call her Cousin Mary, to tell her whether she had given birth to a boy or a girl. Cousin Mary told her that she had given birth to a little boy. The doctor told her that she could not save both her and her son. She told the doctor to save her son. Her last words, I am told, were 'Save my boy, save my boy!' That is why I am here today."

Gray remembers that times were tough during the Depression and jobs were scarce for everyone in the United States. The stock market crash of 1929 was a financial disaster for most Americans, and especially for African Americans, many of whom were already living in poverty and in segregated conditions. Even though his father was a skilled worker, getting work was difficult.

"My daddy was a builder down there in Calvert County," he said. "In those days, we used the word 'colored.' We were the only colored builders down there. We built tobacco barns; we built cottages for whites vacationing at the beach, and we built cottages for the YMCA to accommodate young white boys who would come down during the summer. Eventually, we did some construction work down in the Solomon Islands, located in Calvert County, building Navy barracks. The Navy was very segregated, and my father had a hard time getting work as a building contractor at a U.S. Naval facility in Maryland because they did not hire colored people. So, my daddy contacted government officials in Washington, D.C., and told them that he was an accomplished builder in Calvert County, Maryland, and could not get a job building barracks at the Naval facility in the Solomon Islands. He received a phone call after his complaint and was invited to bring in men the next Monday morning to work on the project."

Reared in a large family, everyone did their fair share to support the family—his father insisted on it. "In my family, there were nine of us, three boys and six girls. My daddy remarried, and he had three boys and one girl in his second marriage. We came from a big family. We worked from sunrise to sunset, and my daddy was a man who did not take any foolishness. We worked hard and lived strictly in the country. The primary occupation back in those days was tobacco farming in Calvert County," Gray remembers. "We would walk to school and we carried one or two cents a day in winter. The teacher would cook a pot of beans, and at lunch we would have a cup of hot bean soup. It was a one-room school, and she taught from the first

First Sergeant Frederick Gray, USA. Reared in Calvert County, Maryland, Frederick Gray answered the call to military service in 1941, and five years later returned home from Iwo Jima with the rank of first sergeant. After his discharge in 1946, he worked as a carpenter, police officer and in government service, from which he retired as a construction representative with the National Park Service.

grade to the seventh grade. There was no high school there for coloreds. After they built a high school in 1941 or '42, there was bus transportation from where I lived in St. Leonard to Central High in Prince Frederick."

Horace Taylor was born on August 26, 1924, and grew up in Seneca, South Carolina, in Oconee County. "Seneca was a mill town, and I do not remember it being one of those towns that had really bad segregation problems. It was segregated, but blacks were treated real well around Seneca. We really did not have any racial problems going on in town. Segregation, though, was a fact of life, but you could make it if you knew how to survive. Blacks and whites lived close together in Seneca and that worked out well because everybody was always close to the job. Actually, you could say that we were really neighbors. My family lived in the city and did not live on a farm. We would get up in the morning, get our breakfast, and walk to school. It was about two miles away. We could not go to the white school but walked right by it on our way to our school. There were school busses for the whites, but not for blacks. While I was going to school, we had a department store in Seneca, and I had a part time job there. Before I went to school in the morning, I would stop there and put out displays. After school was out, I would come back. The people who owned that store were very good people; they did not believe in this white and black stuff. I worked there until I went into the service."

Like most of the families in rural America, his family was very involved in church activities. "My stepfather was the chairman of the deacon's board for the Baptist church," he said. "In our house, everybody went to church on Sunday. Going to church was what everybody in my community did on Sunday."

Sam Green is a native of Louisiana. "I was born on August 9, 1925, in Caddo Parrish, Shreveport, Louisiana. I attended school there, but I did not get my diploma until after I had finished my military service," he said. "We had to walk to school. There was no bus transportation for us. The whites had bus transportation, but we had to walk to school. I had two sisters and three brothers, and I was the youngest." Green grew up with segregation and remembers it well. "Signs were posted over water fountains everywhere, labeled white and colored. We had white water and colored water," he said. "I never will forget when I was riding the bus and went to get off the bus and the driver said to me 'Go to the

Technician Fifth Grade Horace Taylor, USA. Taylor was one of three African Americans from his company to be awarded the Silver Star Medal for valor at Iwo Jima. He would return home and be discharged from the Army, but he remained in government service until he retired in 1983.

back, boy.' At the diner, we could be served in the kitchen but not in the dining room. All of that hurt, but there was nothing we could do about it."

Green was raised on a farm. "My dad rented land. We had mules, cows, hogs and all of that. We raised everything that we ate. I remember the times when my dad would go to the store—he only had to buy two or three different items: coffee, sugar, and flour. My daddy was always a self-sufficient man. He never depended on anyone and had his own property that he took care of." Cotton was widely harvested in Louisiana when Green was growing up there and picking it was what many of the people he knew did for a living. "My daddy never did insist on us picking cotton, but we did hoe, plow, and cut hay. I never did like farming and promised myself that when I could, I would choose another means of support, which I did. My dad was fine with that, but he told me that as long as I stayed at home, I would have to work on the farm. I didn't like farm work."

Staff Sergeant Sam Green, USA. Sam Green was working in Caddo Parrish, Louisiana, when he was drafted. As he came to know those in his unit, he intuitively sensed that they were being formed to carry out a special task. The unit would become a valuable component of the ship-to-shore movement on the beaches of Iwo Jima. He returned home to Shreveport, Louisiana, with the rank of staff sergeant, and retired from work as a supervisor with a roofing company there.

Good employment opportunities for African Americans were limited, but Green did find work away from the farm. "When I was 15 years old, I left school and I began working outside of the farm," he said. "On my first job I was making about 15 dollars a week working for a bottling company. That was good money back then. After that, I worked at a packing company and that is where I was working when I was inducted into the military."

Lyman Brent was born on July 24, 1925. He was raised in and attended school in Franklin, Louisiana. "There were five of us, all males, and three of us are still living. Our mother and father are deceased." He lived in the city of Franklin and knew little of the rural life that many of those with whom he would serve had experienced. His father was employed in Franklin by a large sugar cane refinery. "His job was to keep the machinery running. They called the people who did his kind of work engineers during that time." His mother also worked outside the home. "She was a dietician and worked in the school system," he said. Brent went to school under the same conditions as the other African Americans with whom he would serve on Iwo Jima. "I attended school at St. Mary's Parrish Negro Training School in Franklin, Louisiana," he said. "It was all black, and there was no integration at all when I was in school. We walked to school. There were no busses provided for us—people had to walk sometimes five to ten miles to school. Busses were provided for whites but not for us."

He remembers his life as a young man was not that much different than that of any other young African American man living in the rural South. "I didn't play sports or get involved in many activities at school, but I had friends, and a childhood much like any other young boy my age," he said. As it was for most of the South, segregation was also a way of life in his community. "We went to movies and restaurants, but when we did, we went through the back door. There were different entrances to these facilities for blacks and whites." Brent did not finish his education at St. Mary's because he was drafted. The Selective Service Act mandated that all young men 18 years of age be called for an induction examination. "I was 18 and subject to the draft. I was called for the induc-

Technician Fifth Grade Lyman Brent, USA. Lyman Brent was living in Franklin, Louisiana, and was in high school with one year left when he was drafted. He joined the ranks of those going off to war and returned home to complete his education and began a successful working career as a supervisor at Southern University in Baton Rouge, Louisiana.

tion examination one year before I would graduate from high school," he said. "I never had any thought that I would go into the service or whether I would not." As a high school student trying to graduate, military service was not something that he thought about. He did not have a choice in the matter because he was called, he was qualified and he served. He had no idea that he would be one of those who would participate in one of the fiercest battles of World War II.

Haywood Johnson was born in Charlotte, North Carolina, August 23, 1924, into a close-knit family, but moved from there at an early age because of a family tragedy. "I had a brother and four sisters, and I am the only one left," he said. "There was a strong sense of family among us. It did not matter where we all lived, at Christmas and Thanksgiving everybody would be home. At age eight, my mother passed away, and I moved to Washington, D.C., to live with my sister. I never returned to Charlotte to live. I attended junior high and graduated from Cardozo High School in Washington. I am a quiet person, and I participated in activities but was never quick to take the lead. I was not big enough to play football, but I played a little baseball, and my favorite activity in high school was playing in the band.

Corporal Haywood Johnson, USA. Haywood Johnson was reared in Washington, D.C., and had plans for college after high school, but he was drafted. He wanted to serve and welcomed the opportunity to do so. He is proud of his service and feels fortunate to have been able to return home safely to his family and enjoy a successful career in civil service with the federal government.

Moving from the South to the nation's capital, he was surprised to find that life for African Americans there was a reflection of the environment he had left behind. "For blacks, things were as segregated in Washington as they were anywhere. Schools, neighborhoods, and the military were the same way. For the most part, we accepted it. That is the way it was for us then."

Arthur L. Peterson came from a large family and was reared in the nation's capital. "I was born and raised in Washington, D.C., March 1, 1914, at 369 C St. Northwest, downtown near where police headquarters is now.

From there we moved to 420 K St. Northwest. There were nine of us, six boys and three girls. Three of them were born after I was, and everybody is gone but me. On Sunday everybody went to church and the family would have a big dinner, but if we had somebody special coming, we would set up tables in the backyard. I attended school in Washington, D.C., finished grade school at Banneker, and then I went to Cook School and Armstrong. I lived three blocks from school and walked to school. I did not play sports in school. I was involved strictly in academics. I graduated from high school well before the war."

He too, recalls the segregation and discrimination in the 1940s. "At that time, blacks could not go into a restaurant, sit down, and eat. Schools were segregated also, but we could mingle with the whites. Things are different now. Before the war, Negroes did not have a voice. When we went to the movies, we had to go into the side door. Discrimination was a way of life then. We played ball and things like that, but went to different schools."

Charles Black is a native of Washington, D.C. "I was born on August 31, 1925. I was raised in Anacostia in southeast Washington, D.C., as a child and lived there until I went into the service," he said. "I attended elementary school there in southeast Washington and I attended Cardozo High School in Northwest Washington and completed three and a half years of schooling there. When I was in high school, I was in the senior orchestra and the marching band, which happened to be the first marching band at the high school." He did not play

First Sergeant Arthur L. Peterson, USA. Arthur Peterson was born in 1914 in Washington, D.C., and at the age of 30, was considerably older than most of the men in his unit. He would become his company's supply sergeant and be promoted to first sergeant and return home to a career in the insurance business.

any sports in high school but was an avid football fan. He, too, remembers that blacks and whites, as throughout most of the South, did not mix in Washington, D.C. "Segregation did exist in Washington, D.C., when I was growing up here. We had our own schools and at the movie theaters we had to sit upstairs in the balcony. At the five and ten stores, we could not sit at the counter, and some of the department stores would not serve us at all or hesitated to," he recalls.

Black admits that in the 11th grade, he wanted to work rather than go to school. "I did not graduate with my class, but I eventually did receive my high school certificate of graduation. I quit school in the 11th grade, and my parents allowed me to go to work at age 16. I started working for the government at the Department of Defense. I started out as a messenger and file

Corporal Charles Black, USA. Charles Black, a native of Washington, D.C., was drafted into the Army while working in the civil service with the Department of the Army. His veteran status and prior government service provided him the opportunity to reenter and retire from government service after World War II.

clerk for the Department of the Army, as many of us minorities did, in the Pentagon. I remember, while working as a messenger, the blackouts early in the war and being allowed out on the streets when the general population could not be. I would take messages to various government agencies that could not otherwise be distributed to them. I went from there to work in an office in the National Guard Bureau and there were only a few minorities working there. My opportunities for promotion were much better there." Black was also the product of a small but close-knit family. "I had two sisters and one brother. I was the youngest. There are only two of us now, a sister and myself," he said. His mother and father were also government employees. "My father worked in the mail room at the Pentagon, but he did not have the opportunities for promotion that I did," said Black. "And my mother, too, was a civil service worker. She was employed at the government printing office and also had little opportunity for promotion."

The Marines

Ellis Cunningham was born in Williamsburg County, South Carolina, October 26, 1925, and clearly remembers the time when he was ten years old, but he does not remember too much before that. "I remember that time because that is when my father died," he said. "I remember the day after the funeral, my mother and the six of us were sitting there and wondering what we were going to do. My grandparents came and rescued us and from that time on, I remember them mostly as my parents, but they were really my grandparents. They had 11 children, one of which was my mother, and her six children, including me. We got along real fine, and we all grew up together as sisters and brothers. We used to go to town on Saturday evening, and the main mode of transportation was a mule and a wagon. My granddaddy used to say, 'Don't harass that mule because I have to plow.' So the mule did double duty. The mule would plow during the week and take us to town on Saturday. We did not have a lot of spare time because we always had something to do, and houses were not built close together then like they are now. They were a pretty good distance apart, so to mingle with others outside your family required an effort. That's the way life was. The main town in Williamsburg County was Kingstree. There were farms in every direction. Farming was the primary way of life, and that is what I did before coming into the Marines."

Cunningham has vivid memories of his childhood and his relationship with his family. "As a boy growing up on the farm, I was a determined youngster. I would make up my mind as to what I wanted to do and do it at my own pace. My brother and one of my uncles, both about my age, hung together. You would not believe how we would compete with each other to please my grandfather. My brother was good at pleasing him, and my uncle was only as good as he wanted to be; but my brother was very good at hustling to please him. I, on the other hand, was not very good at hustling, but I would get it done on my terms. My granddaddy used to tell me that I was unusual because of that. I would irritate my grandfather a few times by being that way and taking my time to do what he wanted me to do. He would not hesitate to let me know that I irritated him. Compared to my brother and my uncle, when he told them to do something, they would take off quickly to do it. I was just the opposite, but I would get it done. I did not linger on purpose, it just never occurred to me that I needed to run when he did not tell me to run." Cunningham recalls that his relationship with his grandmother was different. "My relationship with my grandmother was very good," he said. "We were buddy-buddy. Whenever punishments were being given out, I would usually be entitled to some of it, but if my grandmother was nearby, I did not have to worry."

Cunningham remembers that life on the farm was hard work and never ending. "We had lots of work to do, especially in the wintertime. Most of the cows were turned loose to go to the field and some were kept near the house because they were milking cows. We had to milk them, feed the hogs, the mule and all this was done before we went to school. Normally, we would get there about the time the teachers did and sometimes before. I did not go to high school before the military, but I went to grammar school and I did well in school.

First Sergeant Ellis Cunningham, USMC. Born in Williamsburg County, South Carolina, Ellis Cunningham had always wanted to serve in the military. He was among the first African Americans to enter the Marine Corps and he retired from the Marines with 26 years of service. After his military service, he would complete another career in public transportation in Charleston, South Carolina.

I remember one particular day when we had a spelling bee, which was normally dominated by the girls in the class, and I defeated one of them in a spelling bee and moved up to number one in the class."

Looking back on it, he sees a stark contrast in the way he obtained his education and the way children reared in urban and city environments did. "I tell people how I went to school, and most people look at me kind of funny because they don't believe that I am telling the truth," he says. "Myself and children who worked on the farm went to register when the school year started, but the only thing we did that day was register. We did not go to class. After we had registered, we went on back home, took off those school clothes and put on our work clothes. We worked in the field doing the harvesting or did whatever needed to be done on the farm until Thanksgiving. The first Monday after Thanksgiving was the first day we went back to school. On the farm we planted corn, peas, tobacco, greens and potatoes according to a system called 'open range.' That meant that to get your share of it, you had to fence in your piece of allotted property, plant it, and harvest it by Thanksgiving. On the day after Thanksgiving, fences had to be taken down and there were no boundaries—anything that was planted was available to anybody. In January and February, the range was made ready for a new crop. If your stuff was still in the field come Thanksgiving, livestock would have a good time eating it, and others had a good time helping themselves to it. There was nothing you could do about it because that was the rule there."

As other African Americans readily admit, segregation, especially in the schools and on school busses, was a way of life for Cunningham and his family during the 1940s. "I hear so much now about rules and regulations on school busses. Yes, I saw school busses, but I didn't ride on any of them; I walked to school and walked back. The school bus would normally pass me in the morning and evening, but there was not anybody my color on it. Blacks and whites did, however, mingle and worked in the fields together. There was no racial tension that I recall, that's just the way it was. I even remember several occasions when whites would come to the aid of blacks even if it involved problems for them with the law."

Eugene Doughty was born on March 3, 1924, in Stamford, Connecticut, but moved to New York when he was only a toddler. "The family lived there for about three and a half years then relocated to New York City in upper Harlem," said Doughty. "There, the family grew to seven, and I was the oldest of the seven children, four boys and three girls. Unfortunately, in 1936, at the age of 12, I lost my mother as she was giving birth to her last child. The showing of love and compassion by friends and relatives who came to the front when I needed them at the passing of my mother did a great deal to develop within me a love and compassion for people. I do believe that the actions of those friends and relatives at a time when my family needed it helped me come to believe that people are basically good," Doughty said. From the time he lost his mother others would characterize him by his kindness and concern for others.

He readily acknowledges that times were hard during the difficult economic years prior to World War II during which he grew into adulthood. "My father was very fortunate, though, to have a license in plumbing. That was very rare among African Americans back then," Doughty recalls. "He practiced his trade during the height of the Depression, and he was able to make a living with the help of neighbors, friends and family members." Doughty realized the value of an education early in life and set his sights on a college education as a youngster and determined that he would pursue a career in education. "I completed elementary, junior high and high school in Harlem, and I participated in several sports and received several honors from the police athletic league, which offered excellent opportunities for children who did not have the opportunity to excel elsewhere," he said. Doughty remembers, as a young man, the impact of the mobilization for war in New York City. "Brooklyn Navy Yard was active when I came out of high school and there was a lot of hustle and bustle in the city. We were at war. Occasionally, one would hear that someone had been drafted. Men and women could often be seen in uniform out and about. It was not unusual to hear someone say or even say yourself, 'Hey, look, they got so and so; he is now in the Army.' It was very obvious that we were at war. There was a lot of propaganda in the movies, many still pictures with war themes were displayed in many places. I went to the movies often, and there were plenty of war movies shown. The newsstands, papers, and magazines always had war themes."

Sergeant Eugene Doughty, USMC. The oldest of seven children, Eugene Doughty was born in Stamford, Connecticut, but reared in Upper Harlem, New York. He was proud to have served in the military, and was offered the opportunity to make the military a career, but opted instead to finish college and pursue career opportunities in education and social work. He retired as a management supervisor with the Sears Corporation.

He could not understand why many African Americans could not participate in the war effort when there were many opportunities for them to do so. "Anybody my age had almost the same feeling. Those of us who really studied the times and the economic issues that the United States would soon have to face wondered why the tremendous resources that the large numbers of educated African Americans and those willing to work who could contribute to rebuilding the economy and the war effort, were ignored. Why are they jobless and not in the mills and offices, working and contributing to the war effort? It became an issue with me, and I was very concerned about that. In Harlem, as it was everywhere, we were dealing with the same issues regarding discriminatory practices for black people in the workforce. I almost refused to go into the service because I was so emotionally disturbed with the discriminatory policies in this country and all that was happening in the South." Doughty's concerns continued when he joined the military and traveled south for training: "I was a New York boy when I went south and had never been out of the city in 18 years and never really felt the kind of discrimination I saw there. I saw right before my eyes the destruction of the character of the black man. Why were there not blacks in the Marines? Why if you went into the Navy were you labeled as a cook, and that is all there was to it? There should have been concerted efforts to seek complete involvement, complete employment both in civilian and military jobs for everybody. In New York City, Lester Grainger, head of the Urban League, and the Reverend Adam Clayton Powell, Jr., pastor of Abyssinian Baptist Church in Harlem, and other labor leaders, made this a very big issue. They insisted that if they did not receive response from the White House or from the U.S. Congress to those questions, there would be a massive demonstration march in Washington, D.C. So preparations were made during those years prior to 1942 to demonstrate. The issues, however, were resolved in 1942 with President Roosevelt's signed Executive Order 8802, which forbade discrimination in hiring in the United States Government. The president's wife, Eleanor, well-respected in the African American community, also pledged her support for the Executive Order. Had that not happened, we would have seen a huge march on Washington, D.C. Fortunately, because of the Executive Order, it did not occur. So, discussions, gatherings and meetings began to deal with the issues. Those events, filled with labor union members and anyone who would come, were held in many of the chief locations around New York City: Abyssinian Baptist Church, other Baptist and Methodist churches, town halls— even down on 59th Street in the white areas. There were many mixed reactions to that, but, overall, New York City really opened up and displayed interest in the programs advocated by the civil activists to employ African Americans."

Roland Durden was born on February 24, 1926, in New York's Harlem Hospital, and lived with his mother. "My mother and father were born in Savannah, Georgia, and they moved to New York because they thought life would be better than it was in Savannah," he said. Durden vividly recalls the Harlem Renaissance and the cultural awakening occurring in Harlem during the Depression and pre–World War II period. In school, he encountered many of the artists, scholars and educators of the time at school and on visits to the theatre. "I went to elementary school in New York and we had a teacher named Mrs. Handy who was the sister of blues musician W.C. Handy. I also went to P.S.

Corporal Roland Durden, USMC. Roland Durden entered the Marine Corps after having learned much about their courageous exploits in the war. He attributes much of the personal discipline and maturity he carried into a successful career with the New York City subway system to his military service and the life and death situations to which he was exposed on Iwo Jima.

139, which was also called Frederick Douglass School. Our French teacher was poet Countee Cullen, who was a big part of the Negro Renaissance there in Harlem. In the class ahead of me was the well-known writer, James Baldwin. I followed James Baldwin into high school at Dewitt Clinton in the Bronx, which was a very good school when I attended back in the early '40s."

Durden remembers the fast-paced urban environment where he went to school. "When I went to school, we had two shifts because the schools were crowded. I went in the P.M. shift. We didn't ride school buses, we took the subway to school," he noted. "That was in high school, but when I was in the lower grades, we lived close to the elementary and the junior high school I attended and I could walk to school from home," he said. "I graduated from high school at the age of 17 because in junior high school, we took advanced classes and at the time, we could take two classes in one. With the additional credits I earned, I was able to graduate a year early."

The fast pace of life in New York City was quite different from the slower pace of life in Savannah, Georgia. He received what he considers sound advice from his mother on how to survive in the big city. "My mother taught me that people are judged by the company they keep. So while in school, I always tried to avoid trouble, I didn't want to get into trouble. If I happened to be in a neighborhood where I saw a problem, I went the other way so that I would not have to be involved in any conflicts in which I did not have to be." On weekends, he remembers Sundays as days of worship in his family and the day in their week when the family would have a special meal. "As a youngster, our family attended Grace Congregational Church on 139th Street. After church we would have a big Sunday meal. I especially remember that when we had chicken on Sundays, we considered that a delicacy."

He was a very curious and active young man and he enjoyed doing many things. "As a child, we played ball, marbles, and I did a lot of roller skating in the streets. When I had money, I would go out. Generally, on Saturday I would go to the movies. I really enjoyed going to the movies. The movies cost five, ten or 15 cents and we could stay in the movies for hours because we could see cartoons, the news, short subjects and then two feature films. The big thing we did during the week was to listen to the radio to the old programs like *The Shadow*. I went to the Apollo quite often, and I really enjoyed seeing the famous composer and band leader, Duke Ellington, but one of my favorite performers was band and orchestra leader Louis Jordan and his famous Tympany Five orchestra. I went downtown when I was able to afford it. I went to the Paramount and to the Roxie Theater. I saw band leader Tommy Dorsey perform with Frank Sinatra, Lionel Hampton and Teddy Wilson. My mother used to take me to Radio City Music Hall for the big shows and things like that."

The discriminatory policies of the time, he feels, severely limited his ability and that of other African Americans to enjoy, grow, and develop to their fullest potential. "When I was in school, we had prejudice," he said. "We couldn't go to certain high schools in New York. We were limited to where we could go. A lot of us were sent to a trade school in Harlem, but there was an academic high school right there in Harlem on Lennox Avenue and 24th Street that we could have attended. There were boundaries which pretty much restricted us to Harlem. We could not live over by Riverside Drive, or above Sugar Hill, or below 110th Street, which was the beginning of Central Park. There were places when they first built up the concourse in the Bronx where we could not go in the front door. There were restaurants and other businesses downtown that would not admit blacks. My outlook for the future was very limited, and I had no idea about what my future could or would look like because of the limited opportunities available to me. Black men were usually hired to do menial jobs. We couldn't even work on 125th Street as salesmen, and women did mostly domestic work. I was able to get work at the YMCA in downtown New York serving tea for two hours in 1941 and 1942 on Mondays, Tuesdays, and Wednesdays. I bought a suit with some of the money I made to wear for my high school graduation."

Durden remembers a significant incident that turned the tide for opportunities for African Americans in New York City. "In 1942 there was a report that a policeman had beaten up a black soldier, and the incident caused a riot," he said. The frustration level in the African American community began to significantly increase. "The mayor at that time, Fiorello La Guardia, called the black leaders, which included Adam Clayton Powell, Jr., and others, to meet with him to talk about the riots and other issues of concern. The black leaders said that if the blacks were allowed to be considered for more jobs in city government (and there were many being created as a result of men going off to war), the issues would probably take care of themselves. After that meeting, employment opportunities began to open up not just for blacks but for all minorities in the city government and, to some degree, private businesses."

The intense activity and dramatic mobilization for war was in full swing after he finished high school. "During that period, just prior to my entry into the Marine Corps, the war was escalating in Europe and the Pacific. The media reported that the enemy was determined to destroy the United States. The president at that time, President Roosevelt, was a real aristocrat and a real leader. Everybody supported him and the war effort. The men went off to war, and the women left their homes to go to work in the factories. Air raid wardens were volunteering to work in the streets. There was a huge national involvement in the war. The movies we saw were very patriotic, but the war heroes featured on film at the movies were all white. Blacks were not shown in the pictures at that time; we were in always in the background and rarely, if ever, seen. A friend of mine, a big guy about six feet tall, was ready to go and fight for his country, but when he joined the Navy he was assigned duties as a cook. That was not an isolated incident, it happened all the time. For the most part, we did not have the option of serving on the front lines. When I joined the Marines in 1944, I wanted to be a Marine as we all had come to know them from the movies, accounts of their actions in battle and how they could make a man out of you." Durden admits that the training was tough and he believed that he was ready for combat when he finished it, but during his time in, he really considered himself to be a laborer.

Archibald Mosley was born on May 25, 1925, in Carbondale, Illinois. "My father worked on the railroad as a boilermaker on a steam engine. We could always tell when he was coming home because we could hear the steam engine as it came into Carbondale. We had to ensure that if there was a chore to be done, it was done before he came home. We knew he was on his way when we heard the whistle blow around 3:30 P.M." Even though he did not live in the South, Mosley quickly acknowledges that separation of the races was a way of life in other American communities outside the South as well. "Back in those days, discrimination and segregation did exist in my community even though we lived in the North," he said. "Our school was named after Chrispus Attucks, the first man to shed blood for the independence of this country, and he was a black man." The whites went to another school, and no blacks attended that school. Mosley was reared in a very successful family, with four sisters and two brothers. His younger brother, who is retired, holds a doctor of philosophy degree in education. His older brother served as a deputy sheriff. His oldest sister was a teacher and another sister was a registered nurse. That tradition of success continued in his own family. "I have four children, and two of them are educators, and my oldest daughter was superintendent of schools. And my next daughter is a dean at a university, and my youngest one is an attorney." In his later life he served as a chief administrator of a school district and earned a doctor of philosophy degree; he also holds a masters degree in theology.

Corporal Archibald Mosley, USMC. Archibald Mosley was in college when he was called to military service, but he knew that he would return to finish his educational pursuits after the war. He completed his education and has enjoyed a career as an ordained minister and school administrator.

His father was an important force in his life. "In his own way, he instilled in me and my siblings the drive to take advantage of every opportunity to excel." Mosley readily admits that he loved his father and truly believes that his personal view of success is a result of his father's influence. "He truly wanted us to live up to our capabilities. He once said to my two brothers and me that he was going to put us all on top of his shoulder and pronounced he was going to do all that he could to help us in life with whatever vocation we chose. He then said that if we did not stand taller than him, he would tell us that we had failed." Mosley has no doubts that his father left him and his siblings with the motivation to be successful in life, and it worked.

"In school, my brothers and I were all good in sports. I was pretty good in basketball, but I was not as good as my older brother. I could match him in track, but I was better than both of them in football. I was a left halfback," he said. He attended a predominantly white university and he and a friend were the first two blacks to make the football team there. He recalls an incident when he and the only other African American player on the school's team were asked to leave the field at the start of an upcoming football game. "After we made the team and took the first trip to play our first opponent of the year, we went onto the field in uniform with the rest of the team. The game did not start on time and we wondered why. We came to realize that the delay occurred because the home team did not want me and the only other black team member on the field." Mosley was very discouraged by the incident and believed that his coaching staff should have insisted that he and the other black player be allowed to participate in the game. He later approached his coach and suggested that if he had not pulled his black players out of the lineup, and had instead insisted that they be allowed to play, his team would have been assured of a win. He was an athlete, but became very despondent toward the sports program at his school after that incident. He was an avid basketball player as well, but the incident on the football field took the enthusiasm out of his desire to participate in the sports program. "After the incident, the basketball season began and I only participated in two games," he said. He then turned his attention to academic pursuits.

His studies in college were interrupted when he was drafted into the military in 1942. His educational background, however, made him a strong candidate for military service. He quickly admits the Marine Corps uniform was the catalyst for him choosing the Marines. "I had my choice of the Army, Navy and the Marine Corps when I was drafted. I chose the Marines because I wanted to wear that dress blue uniform. To me, it was, by far, the best-looking one of all the services, and it remains so to this day."

Chapter 2

Military Training

Dr. Martha Putney writes that "African Americans did not always have the door to the military open to them. Many of the colonies had laws, ordinances, or resolutions excluding them from the local militias. George Washington, commander of the Continental Army, issued a general order in November 1775 barring the recruitment of blacks. The government, under the Constitution, enacted legislation in 1792 banning blacks from duty in the state militias, which for all practical purposes eliminated blacks from service in the Army. The Marine Corps, from its beginning, was prohibited by an act of Congress in 1798 from enlisting blacks. No blacks were enrolled in the Marines until August 1942, more than six months after we entered World War II."

The United States struggled to maintain its neutrality as war raged in Europe and the Pacific. Although the United States did not declare war until December 8, 1941, it became evident to the War Department in the early 1940s that all available resources of the United States must be ready for the potential of war.

Activities abroad gave much credibility to the fact that there was a strong possibility that war might be inevitable for the United States in the years after the Great Depression. In that regard, the Selective Training and Service Act of 1940 was passed. By then, American factories were hiring new workers for war production, realizing that war might indeed become a possibility. However, African Americans benefited less than white workers from rising employment and increased wages. Discrimination in employment and wage policies continued to create disadvantages for African American workers.

There were nearly 18,000 African Americans serving in uniform prior to World War II. When the war began, however, the language in the Selective Service and Training Act of 1941 and Executive Order 8802 removed the barriers that denied them the opportunity to serve and 2.5 African Americans registered for military service. Not all of those African Americans who registered were inducted, but more than 1 million of them served during World War II. African Americans served in all branches of the military—the Army, Navy, Coast Guard, and the Marine Corps. The official policy for African Americans and whites, however, was segregation and no intermingling. The inclusion of African American males in the military expanded opportunities and offered them new hope for employment and service to their country. It was a dream for many of them to serve in the military, and response to the new opportunities to do so was tremendous.

The military services had the task before them to quickly train new recruits into combat-ready fighting men to face a determined enemy. Boot camp, basic training, and recruit training are terms generally used to refer to that period of training that new inductees must complete prior to entering the ranks of military service. Drill sergeants from all branches of the military teach the new recruits the rudiments of military service. They are taught discipline, how to use their weapons, how to drill, and tactics. Basic training also develops physical and mental stamina so that in

Along with other essential combat skills, training in hand-to-hand combat was stressed in basic training during the World War II era. (National Archives)

combat situations they can effectively contribute to the success of their unit's mission.

Recruits are divided into units, sometimes called platoons, squads, companies, flights or sections depending on the military service affiliation. Service in the military assumes that at some point during the military experience, service on the front lines of combat could happen. Training in boot camp is designed to teach the new recruit how to think and react as part of a whole unit rather than as an individual. Common living conditions, uniforms, instruction, physical appearance, and discipline are clear reflections of that philosophy.

After successful completion of boot camp, recruits are assigned to additional training and duties based on the needs of their branch of service or individual preference when possible. The standard training program at boot camp for all recruits stresses unit integrity and combat readiness; however, there is a myriad of other military occupational specialties and duties to which many of the new military members may be assigned. In addition to advanced training for those assigned to combat units, many receive advanced training in combat, combat support, combat service support, and service in garrison units. Most African American recruits leaving boot camp during World War II were assigned to combat support units or to schools for specialized training after boot camp, which would prepare them for support and garrison duties.

Haywood Johnson remembers his call to duty. "Even though opportunities were tight, I did get a federal job, and I was admitted to Johnson C. Smith University in Charlotte, North Carolina; but I never had the opportunity to go to college, and I had to leave that federal job because I was drafted. Actually, I was eager to go into the military. If I could have taken advantage of the opportunity to go to school instead, though, I would have done that. But I feel that I was fortunate, however, to have had the opportunity to return from the military to that federal job I had for the two months prior to my going into the service."

Arthur Peterson did not enter the military immediately after graduating from high school. He was 30 years old when he entered the Army. "When I finished school, I worked for a brief time at a tailor shop in Washington, and then I went out to Indiana to help my sister operate her business after her husband passed away. We worked some very late hours. When it became too much for her, she closed the business. I then took a job as a private chauffer traveling back and forth to Florida with my employer and his family. I left that job and came back to Washington, D.C. When the military opened up to Negroes, I was drafted into the Army."

Lyman Brent was summoned to military service with another year left in high school. "It did not matter what you were doing—when you reached the age of 18, every young man was considered for induction. We had to go register, and if called, we had to go for examination, and if qualified, we had to go. Before I was called, I saw some who had been drafted before me come back home, but I also remember not seeing some who did not make it back at all." He remembers well the day he went for his examination. "We went to Lafayette, Louisiana," he said. "The bus was filled with guys ordered to report for the examination. About 30 days later, October 1, 1943, they called me into active service," he said. "I reported to Camp Beauregard, Louisiana, and remained there for about six weeks. We were basically staged there waiting for others to arrive, join us and be sent to Camp Plauche, near New Orleans, for basic training. We went through infiltration courses where live ammunition was fired over our heads, 25- and 30-mile hikes, negotiated barbed wire fences along with weapons training and classroom courses, and we lived in Quonset huts with sand on the floor."

After his basic training at Camp Plauche along with the other men who would become members of the 476th Amphibian Truck Company and later deploy to the western Pacific, he went to Camp Gordon Johnston, Florida, for specialized training in the operation of the DUKW. "We learned everything about the DUKW and how to maneuver it in all kind of surf with troop and cargo aboard. On Iwo Jima, he would become the driver of a DUKW with an assistant driver and be responsible for safely and efficiently moving troops and equipment from ship-to-shore.

Eugene Doughty completed high school at the High School of Commerce in New York City. "It was a good business school. I then went on to the City College of New York. I really had my eye on going into education, particularly in the area of coaching, and I decided to major in physical and health education," he said. "I was able to complete one year of college before I was called for service in the Marine Corps. I was 17 when Pearl Harbor was hit, and I knew that at some time I was destined to go into the service. When doors for African Americans to serve in the United States Marine Corps opened in 1942, I knew I would eventually have to serve in the military, so I chose the Marines. I did more than was necessary to qualify because a high school education was more than enough to get into the Marines in 1942. To my surprise, I got a personal letter from the Navy Department, of which the Marine Corps is a part, asking me to join the Marine Corps." Doughty had plans to finish college but he firmly believed that as the war escalated, the United States would become more involved and that he would be called to serve. "Since racial segregation was the policy for training troops in all branches of the military at the time, we were trained at a segregated training facility in North Carolina near Camp Lejeune known as Montford Point, and not at Parris Island with white Marines. Some of us went overseas with the Defense Battalions Depot and Ammunition Companies as I did, but many remained at the facility after recruit training as instructors and performed garrison duties there."

Doughty wanted to be a Marine but had no idea that he would be training in a segregated facility when he volunteered for military service. He passed his examinations and became one of the first African Americans to enlist in the United States Marine Corps in 1943. Having been reared in the North, he had heard and read about the harsh treatment of African Americans in the South, and on the day that he was to leave home for training at Montford Point, he remembers having mixed emotions about what was ahead of him as he headed to North Carolina for boot camp. "This was the first time I had left New York City to head south, and I was a bundle of nerves at that time. I was going into a new situation now and that combined with all of the news I had heard about discrimination, was hard for me to accept." he said. He was traveling with about six other African Americans as he began his trip to Marine basic boot camp. Doughty remembers

A Marine drill instructor addresses his recruits. (National Archives)

Among the many landing craft moving ashore during the Iwo Jima campaign, the agility and mobility of the DUKW in the water and on land would provide rapid, valuable support to the invading forces throughout the battle and during the occupation of the island. (National Archives)

being heckled and required to sit in a car on the train full of smoke, soot, and fumes. "By the time we got to Raleigh, North Carolina, we were blackened by the soot, and we were not allowed to leave the car even though it made a stop there." Doughty does remember African American students from Raleigh's Shaw University meeting the troop train and wishing the new recruits well as they went to training to prepare for military service.

Doughty's first impression of the camp where he would complete his recruit training was not at all what he had imagined it would be. "When we arrived at Montford Point, what we saw was something that looked like a settlement as opposed to a military camp," he said. "We saw a camp that was being built as we were training. We did not see any buildings that would house new troops; we saw tents. Montford Point was a former CCC (Civilian Conservation Camp) that became the training facility for African American Marines. When I enlisted, I thought I would be going to Parris Island for training."

His introduction to military discipline came on his first day at boot camp when he had to stand at attention for three hours waiting for a physical examination upon arriving at Montford Point. "I was told by one of the recruits that it is a form of discipline and if you did not do as you were told, you would be taken out in the field and heckled until they believed you were ready to conform." The pace of everything the new recruits did was double time, Doughty recalls. "You would get up in the morning, and they would give you two minutes for this and two minutes for that and chow was always precisely at 6:30 in the morning, and you had to be there."

When he began boot camp, his drill instructors were white, but that changed while he was in training. "About halfway through my boot camp experience, they were phasing out the white drill instructors, and they were replaced by black drill instructors. The black drill instructors were seasoned and appeared to be well trained," he said "They were selected from among the first group of African Americans trained to be Marines in 1942 to be drill instructors." He was impressed with many of the new recruits. "I found that many of our new recruits were well-versed and educated. Among them were older men who had served in other branches of the military as commissioned officers. There were professionals and there were those who had attended some of the finest schools in the country with advanced degrees from colleges and universities."

Ellis Cunningham, from childhood, had always wanted to enter the military. "Not too long after I started noticing the world around me, I began to see soldiers wearing campaign hats," he noted. "I saw quite a few of them, especially after the war started. They would come to church and other gatherings dressed in their Army uniforms, campaign hats, boots, and leggings. These were cavalrymen. At first, that's what I wanted to be when I signed up to go into the military. I loved to ride horses. Even though many did not want to go into the military during the war, I was just the opposite—I wanted to go. I wanted to be in the military." A chain of unforeseen events caused him to enter the Marine Corps, from which he retired as a first sergeant with 26 years of service. He had served in World War II, in the Korean conflict, and in Vietnam. "When I went to sign up for military service, I requested the Army, but for some reason, they stamped Navy on all my paperwork. I was bound for Great Lakes to train to be a sailor," he said. "By chance, I was offered an opportunity to go home for Christmas before reporting to Navy boot camp. As I was leaving home afterwards to continue on to Great Lakes, our group was stopped and 32 of us were needed to go to the Marine Corps, and I was happy I was one of them. I was happy about that because I did not want to go into the Navy."

He remembers vividly the day he reported to training at Montford Point. "At Montford Point, there was a building there used to process in new recruits. It was the first building you saw when you arrived at Montford Point. It was about 3 A.M. when I arrived there. They took us into that building and lined us up. The fellow on duty there, the duty clerk, typed up a card for each one of us with our name, and so on. I watched him type up our information. He was not a speed typist, it took him most of that morning to get the cards typed up. After my group was processed in, we were issued uniforms. The uniforms were used over and over for new recruits coming in. They were washed by the graduating recruits in the class ahead of us, and they may have been dry or wet when they were issued. It didn't make any difference—we were instructed to put them on anyway. We were all dressed in our civilian clothing, and were told to get out of those civilian clothes and put these on now."

He remembers a typical day beginning with "chow" at the mess hall. "Once the platoon was formed and we were assigned to our barracks, early in the morning around five o'clock or earlier, someone would be designated as the 'chow runner.' His job was to run to the chow hall and set the order in which his platoon would eat. The chow runner would then return to the platoon area and inform the rest of the platoon of the eating arrangement. Once he arrived at the mess hall, the mess sergeant would make the assignment for our platoon. He did not have a chance to wash his face or do anything prior to performing that duty, he said. "The chow runner had one of the most important jobs of the day because the seating priority for the platoons could mean shorter waiting times for planned activities or even possibly how long or short the day would be."

Cunningham remembers that the barracks in which the recruits slept were across the street from the shower and toilet facilities. "At any given time, it was not unusual to see recruits running back and forth from the shower facility in underwear or with a towel wrapped around them. For that reason the recruit barracks were off limits to visitors," he said. "Most days included cleaning the barracks, classes on a variety of military subjects, and spending time at the rifle range. "We were taught in a very short period of time everything we needed to know about the military. We drilled a lot and were always involved in some type of physical training and a lot of the emphasis was placed on learning, firing and understanding the M-1 rifle," he said. For Cunningham, the trip to the rifle range was the culminating experience of boot camp. "Once we finished at the rifle range, we had graduated from boot camp. We all went to the tailor shop to pick up our dress uniforms and shed those old uniforms we were initially issued so the new recruits could use them."

Archibald Mosley received his draft notice, took his examinations and left his home in Carbondale, Illinois, bound for Chicago to be inducted into the military. "When my group arrived in Chicago, they gave me a train ticket to the Montford Point Marine training camp in North Carolina. I rode the Pennsylvania Railroad from Chicago to Washington, D.C., where I changed trains to the Atlantic Coast Line. When I boarded the train, I was not allowed to sit where I wanted to sit. I voiced my concern, and one of the porters tried to calm me down by saying to me, 'Just take it easy, you are down here now.' So I went on into the Jim Crow car, but I had a problem with doing so and when I arrived in Jacksonville, North Carolina, it was even worse. I saw a kind of segregation I had never known before."

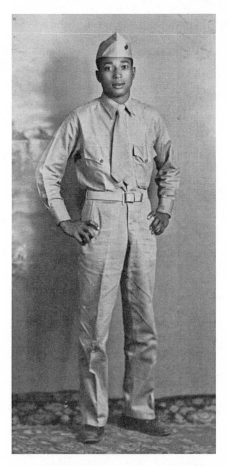

Archibald Mosley, USMC. Corporal Mosley was a weapons instructor at the Montford Point Marine Training Camp, North Carolina, before deploying to Iwo Jima where he would serve as a squad leader with the 36th Marine Depot Company.

Mosley remembers his first days at the camp. "We were living in pasteboard huts, and the white Marines on the other side of the pine trees from us were living in beautiful brick barracks. You can only imagine what our restrooms and showers were like." Since his group were among the first African Americans to train as Marines, all of the instructors at the camp were white. "They really did want blacks to train us," said Mosley. "It was the plan to replace the white drill instructors from the ranks of the new recruits who were beginning their training at Montford Point. Personnel records were checked to select those considered to have the potential to become drill instructors. So when they reviewed my records and found that I had been to college, I was selected to be an instructor," said Mosley.

Prior to his duties as an instructor, Mosley recalls that the training was rough. It was, though, no surprise to him. "When I would go to the movies and see the training that the Marines were going through, I expected the training at Montford Point to be rough," he said. "We were always exercising, 24-hours-a-day, there was no such thing as leisure time. We never walked, we ran to eat, ran to sleep, and ran to get a drink of water." After he completed boot camp, Mosely was assigned duties as a weapons instructor at the rifle range. "There were 16 black weapons instructors," he said. As one of the first African Americans selected to train new recruits at Montford Point, he remained there as an instructor from early 1943 until he left for Iwo Jima in 1944.

The transition from white to African American instructors began as Mosley's class graduated from boot camp. Most of the men who took their training at Montford Point have recollections of the training supervised by African Americans as being more rigorous than that of the training supervised by the white instructors. "That is true," said Mosley. "That is just what happened; we were not intending to be unnecessarily hard. We realized that out of the backgrounds we were coming from, the black man had to be better, and that was our intent."

Frederick Gray received his draft notice in September of 1941. "I took the bus to Baltimore for my examination, and I had to sit in the back of the bus. I was given two weeks to take care of business and after that, I went to the service. I stood on the side of the road and caught the bus again and went to Fort Meade. From there we went to Fort Lee and then we went on down to Camp Plauche, Louisiana, for basic training."

"After basic training we went

Frederick Gray, USA. First Sergeant Frederick Gray deployed to Iwo Jima from Fort Gordon Johnston, Florida, where he would assume duties as a supply assistant to the supply sergeant for the 476th Amphibian Truck Company and would later become the company first sergeant.

to Camp Gordon Johnston, Florida, and began our training in the operation of the DUKW. The camp was located near water with sandy beaches and all the facilities needed to conduct amphibious training with the DUKWs." Gray's company trained there until they were shipped out to Washington State, and became very familiar with how the DUKW would prove to be invaluable in moving troops and equipment to and from shore in amphibious landings. While in training, the 43rd Amphibian Truck Battalion was activated, and the 476th Amphibian Truck Company of that battalion is where Gray would be assigned after basic training. Except for the officers and senior noncommissioned officers in his company, all of the soldiers were African Americans.

Arthur Peterson was older than the average draftee. Most of the men drafted in the early 1940s were in their late teens or early 20s, but he was drafted at the age of 30. He truly believed that because of the rate at which the selective service was drafting men into the military, strong recruitment efforts, and the pace at which the war was escalating, he would be drafted. He readily admits that he would not have chosen to join the military, but if called, he would do his duty to his country and serve. After boot camp he was assigned to the newly-activated 476th Amphibian Truck Company. His age and work experience caught the attention of his senior officers and noncommissioned officers, and he was placed in a high position of responsibility. "I was not in the company more than two months when my officers in charge appointed me to the position of supply sergeant," he said. He was a newly trained soldier with little experience or training as a supply clerk or technician. "I learned how to be a supply sergeant completely on the job," he said. Peterson remained in the position of supply sergeant from that appointment to the time his unit organized in Florida, throughout the movement to the Pacific war zone and throughout the Battle of Iwo Jima. "I was the company supply sergeant. I had a big job on my hands. I had to know what was in every box that I sent out. My assistant and me had everything organized in such a way that that we could instantly locate any item in our inventory. I simply looked at my sheet and told them exactly where anything was," he said.

Horace Taylor was called from his home in Seneca, South Carolina, into the military. "When I received my notice that I was drafted," he said, "I was ordered to report to Columbia, South Carolina, to take my physical and complete paperwork to enter the Army. After a ten-day furlough, I was to report to Fort Bragg, North Carolina. From there, we took a train to Camp Plauche, Louisiana, where we began basic training. We trained for about six weeks. During that time, we learned our weapons, qualified on the rifle range, exercised and became familiar with military customs, traditions and discipline." As it was for many African Americans serving in the military during World War II, Taylor's group began to train to become stevedores and laborers on the docks. "We were training to work in the port companies, so we were being trained to load and unload ships." An interesting turn of events occurred for Taylor and some of his fellow soldiers. "During our training to work in port companies, 13 of us were separated from the rest. We did not know why, but I was one of the 13. We had heard through the grapevine that a new amphibian truck battalion was to be organized. Some of us, including me, were sent to Detroit to learn about a group of new amphibious vehicles that would be assigned to the new battalion. It could travel on land and water. Its tires would deflate while in the water and inflate on solid surfaces."

Haywood Johnson had begun his working career and was considering going to college when he received his draft notice. He had always wanted to join the military and looked forward to the experience. He answered the call with no regrets. "I had many friends and family members who had served and there was something about the uniforms, regimentation and drilling (which I became used to as a band member in high school) that I liked." Johnson would eventually become a driver of an amphibian vehicle, ship-to-shore, during the invasion and he, like the others, would learn how to operate the DUKW at Camp Gordon Johnson in Florida. While in training, he was one of 13 chosen to go to Detroit to learn how to drive and maintain the new amphibian trucks. Like the other interviewees, Johnson was concerned that even though he was being trained to be a soldier to fight for his country, segregation was still alive and well in the Army and the side effects of that frequently caused conflict between the African American and white soldiers. "When we would get paid," he said, "we would go the Post Exchange to buy personal items like shaving cream, razors and so forth, but the African American soldiers would have to wait until the white soldiers had finished before we could go in and usually there would be very little left. The black troops got upset, and on one occasion it almost caused a race riot. When that happened, the policy was changed for all soldiers, black and white, so that service was on a first-come, first-served basis."

Roland Durden wanted to go into the military. "I was a young man, I lived with my mother, and I wanted to stand on my own. I saw the military as an opportunity to serve my country, do my part for the war effort and develop skills that would prepare me for the work force. I went to a very

All military inductees are required to complete a rigorous period of training designed to indoctrinate them into the military, which includes physical and combat training. (National Archives)

good school and learned how to write and read, but it did not teach me those skills that I could use to support myself in the workforce." Most of the draftees did not have the option to choose the branch of the military in which they would serve during the mobilization for World War II. Volunteers, however, were more likely to be placed in the branch of service of their choosing if they qualified for it. Durden wanted to be a Marine. He had heard of the rigorous training and discipline in the Marine Corps, and that is the branch of service in which he chose to serve. "When you are young

Drill instruction is generally recognized as one of the instructional techniques designed to instill discipline and attention to detail in those going through military basic training. (National Archives)

and you want to become a man," he thought, "you choose a tough outfit to help you make it happen."

He recalls that on his first day at Montford Point, he came face to face with the rigorous discipline in Marine boot camp that he had heard about. "New recruits who were wearing all different kinds of civilian hats were approached by drill instructors who would snatch the hats from their heads, throw them to the ground and stomp on them to make the point that that they were not civilians anymore, they were Marines. And when we went to the barbershop, the barbers would ask us how we wanted our hair cut, and we would tell them. They would say 'fine' and then cut it all off."

"We lived in huts," Durden said, "but in most of the previous recruit platoons, everybody lived in tents. It was what I expected. I knew it wasn't going to be easy. I realized that we would have to put all of our civilian life behind and adapt to the military way of doing things. Every day we spent as recruits, the pace at which we did anything was at double time. When we went to lunch or breakfast, we ran. We did not walk unless we were drilling in a formation of troops. A typical training day consisted of activities such as physical training, hand-to-hand combat, learning how to maneuver in live fire situations, drilling, swimming lessons, and training with the rifle. That was our routine every day we were in boot camp."

Durden says that the recruit training experience helped him in his quest to learn responsibility and was a valuable experience. "It helped me develop a strong sense of self discipline, to survive, and I learned how to follow orders. But, I think one of the most valuable lessons my drill instructors and sergeants helped me to realize were leadership skills that I did not know that I had inside of me at the time. Looking back on it, I realize how important those qualities are to being successful in life."

After recruit training, Durden remained at Montford Point for a short period of time. "I was not with the 52nd Defense Battalion very long because a new unit, the 33rd Depot Company, was activated, and I was transferred to it," Durden said. Less than a year after joining the Marine Corps, he would go ashore at Iwo Jima with the 33rd Depot Company.

Sam Green also went to Camp Plauche near New Orleans for basic training, the place where he would meet the men with whom he would serve in the 476th. From his home in Shreveport, he reported to Camp Beauregard at nearby Alexandria, Louisiana, for duty after induction. "That was really a staging area," he said. "That camp is where those from our area were picked who would join up with others from up north and other parts of the country to train and work together as a unit." He really did not know what type of unit it would be, but he was sure that with this particular group of men, he would become a part of some kind of special assignment. "They picked out special people for our company. Ours was not an ordinary company. It was a high caliber group of men that just seemed to stand out of the crowd. I believe that the Army had something in store for us."

"After we had been separated from the others, our group arrived at Camp Plauche and met up with Frederick Gray, Horace Taylor, Haywood Johnson and others from various parts of the country and formed a training unit," said Green. "The men in our company were all African Americans. When we had enough men to complete the unit, we began our basic training experience," he said. "At Plauche, we spent a lot of time at the rifle range. We spent a lot of time learning how to use, clean and carry our weapon. We learned how to dig foxholes, and we did a lot of marching with full field packs on 25–30 mile hikes. We had to complete the infiltration course where live ammunition was fired above our heads as we crawled on the ground through barbed wire fences. We lived in Quonset huts during training. They had no floors, it was all sand. From the first thing in the morning until the last thing at night, they were teaching us how to defend ourselves and survive in combat." After basic training his unit went to the amphibious training base at Camp Gordon Johnston near Tallahassee, Florida, to train at a big amphibious training base and learned how to load and unload ships as well as "how to maintain and handle the guns that would be mounted on our vehicle for the ship to shore movement."

He remembers that Camp Gordon Johnston was segregated. "The blacks and whites could not mix together," he said. The training that he and the others had there would be more specialized and focused on preparing them for the specific task awaiting his company overseas. What they learned there was not quite like the basic infantry training that he had received at Camp Plauche. "We learned about amphibious operations, and how to drive the DUKW on water, how to go out to the ships to load and unload them, and we studied in class more about those kinds of operations and various types of ships and amphibious vehicles. When I saw my first DUKW, it was interesting to me because I never saw a truck that could go out into the water, deflate, and inflate its tires and come up on the beach and keep moving. I had never seen anything like that before." He seemed to be awed by the amphibious capabilities of the DUKW, but as a result of the thorough indoctrination he received in his training, he learned that not knowing how to properly operate the vehicle could be dangerous. "There was a certain way to maneuver the vehicle and back it onto the ship and a certain way to back it off. If it was not done right, it would go under water. I saw two or three of them do that. You really had to know what you were doing when moving one of them on or off the ship."

Charles Black left home to take his basic training at Camp Plauche in Florida on November of 1943. Unusual circumstances, however, caused him to miss basic training altogether. "When I went into the service," he said, "I had problems with my thyroid gland, and when I arrived in New Orleans en route to Camp Plauche for basic training, I was admitted to the hospital and had an operation to correct a thyroid condition. After the operation, I was sent home on a furlough." He was certain that he would be discharged and be declared not fit for duty because of the operation. But that did not happen. "While I was home, I received orders to report to Camp Gordon Johnston, near Tallahassee, Florida, for duty. It was not completely clear to me why I was there. Having recently returned from convalescent leave I did not think that I would remain on active duty. Additionally, I missed basic training because of it. I was sure that having missed basic training and the thyroid condition would disqualify me from service." He fully recovered from his operation, remained on active duty and received the basic training that all the others received in his unit "on the job"—not at Camp Plauche, Louisiana, but at Camp Gordon Johnston in Florida, where he would join the 476th Amphibian Truck Company and become familiar with the DUKW.

When he arrived at his duty station, however, he was not immediately

An officer demonstrates a technique for the use of the bayonet in a combat situation during a training exercise. (National Archives)

assigned to be trained to operate the DUKW. "They assigned me duties as the company clerk and mail courier. I liked that because that was the kind of work I was doing on my government job back home," he said. "I didn't mind all of this, but I wondered how I was to be made a soldier with no training. So here's how they did it. On various days I would go to a class and complete certain parts of my basic training with soldiers from other companies who had missed the parts of basic training that I needed. One day, I would go to the rifle range; another day, I would be sent to the infiltration course; another day, I would take gas mask training and other drills. By completing all of that training, I satisfied the basic training requirement and was qualified to stay in the company." His assignment as a clerk would be short-lived. When his unit deployed to Hawaii, destined for points unknown to them, he was assigned duties as assistant driver on a DUKW and would eventually make the landing on D-Day on Iwo Jima.

Part Two

The 36-Day Battle

Until 1941, the United States had made strong attempts to maintain its neutrality even as countries in Asia and Europe were engaged in armed conflict. Several diplomatic, economic, and World War II policies which sought to establish the United States as a neutral country failed. With huge natural resources and a growing international presence, it would be difficult for the United States to step away from the international stage. With war raging on its western and eastern flanks, many believed that the United States' entry into World War II was inevitable. Germany was gaining ground against Allied Forces in Europe, and Japan was expanding its presence in the Pacific and Asia. After the unprovoked attack on the United States Naval Base at Pearl Harbor, Hawaii, on December 7, 1941, by the Empire of Japan, the United States entered World War II. On the day after the bombing of Pearl Harbor, in his Declaration of War speech to Congress against Japan, President Roosevelt labeled December 7, 1941, as "a date that will live in infamy."

It was clear to the Allies as they planned the war strategy against the Japanese and considered options, that they would need bases from which they could effectively launch ground and air attacks. In the early going immediately after the attack on Pearl Harbor, the disabled American Pacific fleet and the campaign experienced a series of setbacks in the Pacific and Asian theater. As the United States began to rebuild the fleet and make progress on the ground, the momentum changed in its favor. As the war in the Pacific progressed, strategists realized that the most favorable location to gain the advantage they sought against the Japanese would be the island of Iwo Jima. It was within striking distance of the Japanese mainland and there were

President Franklin D. Roosevelt calls for a declaration of war against Japan. (National Archives)

airfields that could be improved to support the landing of the aircraft. The Japanese were fully aware of the threat to their homeland if Iwo Jima fell to the enemy, and began preparing for the defense of the island. They relocated the few residents who lived on the island and transformed it into a series of defensive positions that would take their toll on the invading forces. Everything about the geography of the island was a deterrent to an effective amphibious assault, but it had to be taken to end the war and ensure a victory over Japan.

The water surrounding the island would become a sea of war ships that would provide a barrage of aerial and naval bombardment as well as cover for the assault troops as they moved ashore. Three task-organized Marine infantry divisions would lead the assault, supported by air and naval gunfire. Along with the assault troops, there would be a cadre of support troops to provide those forward troops with everything they needed in their quest to neutralize the enemy's defense. Among them would be nearly 900 African Americans.

CHAPTER 3

Assignment to Iwo Jima

THE JAPANESE HAD DEALT A severe blow to the U.S. Pacific Fleet and they continued to make conquests in the Pacific and Asia. As the U.S. Navy moved quickly to rebuild its Pacific Fleet, General MacArthur was named Supreme Commander of Allied Forces in the Southwest Pacific Area and Admiral Chester Nimitz commanded the U.S. Pacific Fleet. MacArthur's troops sustained setbacks at the Bataan Peninsula, Corregidor, and the U.S. Navy lost the aircraft carrier USS *Yorktown* in the Coral Sea and another was severely damaged and forced to withdraw to Pearl Harbor for repairs. Heavily outnumbered, the invading forces were very successful against the Japanese at the battles of the Coral Sea and Midway, and MacArthur, after ordering a retreat from Bataan, returned there in victory as he vowed he would. Several successful land and sea campaigns followed those victories as the invading forces were making their way closer to Japan, but there was a major obstacle in their way: the island of Iwo Jima. Located only 650 nautical miles south of Tokyo, its close proximity to the Japanese mainland would make Iwo Jima a strong, strategic location for the invading forces. The two airfields on the island where damaged B-29s returning from bombing missions on mainland Japan could make emergency landings, served as bases for the P-51 aircraft.

Twenty-two thousand Japanese troops defended Iwo Jima. Lieutenant General Tadamichi Kuribayashi was the commander of all Japanese troops on the island. He turned the island into a huge fortress with walls and defenses, that for much of the battle would seem to be invincible. Deep underground caves were turned into shelter for the Japanese troops and artillery. Air attacks made by the American planes or projectiles launched by the giant guns of the allied battleships would find it more difficult than anticipated

to inflict the crushing blow to the Japanese defense forces. The most prominent terrain feature, Mount Suribachi, an inactive volcano located on the
southern tip of the island, became a vantage point from which the enemy
could see anything on the island. As the invading troops came ashore, the
Japanese would have excellent fields of fire. They were determined to fight
to the end and General Kuribayashi would not surrender.

On December 7, 1944, U.S. planes began bombing the island. They
attacked almost every day. Some days, American warships would fire on the
island for hours at a time. These bombing raids took place from December
1944 until February 1945. Almost two months of bombing from the air and
shelling from the ships at sea did little damage to the Japanese defense. Safe
in their underground caves, the Japanese soldiers waited through the hours
of explosions that shook the island. Afterward, they would quickly repair
any damage that was done to the gun positions or airfields.

On February 14, 1945, the American invasion force, consisting of nearly
500 ships, sailed for Iwo Jima from Saipan, Guam, and from other Ameri-
can-controlled islands and territories in the Pacific en route to Iwo Jima. In
the days prior to D-Day, February 19, 1945, the Japanese troops on Iwo Jima
saw that American warships had surrounded the island. The big guns of battleships and several smaller ships fired relentlessly at the island in an attempt
to neutralize any enemy resistance ashore, and airplanes from the invasion
fleet's aircraft carriers dropped high explosive bombs and flaming napalm.
U.S. Navy underwater demolition teams planted explosives to destroy underwater barriers which the Japanese had placed along the beaches where
Marines would land. It was difficult to imagine that anyone could survive
such a massive attack. Patiently, deep in the underground caves, the Japanese soldiers simply waited for the earthshaking attacks to end. When they
did, they moved through the maze of tunnels, assumed their firing positions,
which were focused on the beach, and waited for the Allied troops to come
ashore. On D-Day, huge nets were dropped over the sides of the troop transport ships to form giant rope-like ladders to be used by the Marines to climb
down and board landing craft below that would carry them ashore.

African American soldiers of the United States Army's 592nd Port
Company, 471st, 473d, and 476th Amphibian Truck Companies attached
to the Fifth Amphibious Corps for the invasion and African American
Marines of the 8th Ammunition Company and the 36th Depot Company,
too, went ashore in the earliest waves of the invasion on D-Day in support
of combat operations. More African American Marines from 33rd and 34th
Depot companies would join those already ashore as the battle progressed.

As the African American soldiers and Marines who would participate in the battle of Iwo Jima prepared themselves mentally for the many unknowns they were about to face, it was evident that they were headed for a combat zone. They acknowledged that they did not know where they were going when they shipped out for the Pacific, but they felt that they had been well trained to do whatever would be expected of them. Some were trained to drive and maintain the DUKW for ship-to-shore operations; others would handle cargo and equipment. In keeping with the policy of segregation, none would serve in frontline assault units.

Roland Durden remembers traveling by train from North Carolina to Camp Pendleton, California, as his unit deployed. "When we left Camp Pendleton, we sailed to Pearl Harbor, Hawaii. We remained in Hawaii for about four months, and then our company boarded an LST [Landing Ship, Tank], which was really designed to carry vehicles and other equipment, but for this trip our Depot Companies were embarked onboard as well." He did not have a berth or a bunk on the ship. "All the way from Hawaii to Iwo Jima, I slept under a truck on the top deck of the ship. The truck was my roof for that trip," he said. "We did not mingle with the white crew members of the ship or with the white officers in our company, and we had no idea where we were going or what we would be doing," Durden recalls. He does remember the ship's gunnery crew conducting frequent target practice sessions while they were underway. "I remember we made a stop near a sandbar on the way to our final destination, and our ship's gunnery crew began practicing firing the big guns as we swam in the ocean waiting for the ship to get underway."

His company did not go ashore on D-Day, February 19th, with the assault forces. "My unit was scheduled to go ashore on February 23rd, but an enemy mortar hit our ship five times. We had ammunition aboard our ship, and the captain gave the order to pull back out to sea and we did not go ashore until the next day, February 24, 1945. That was my 19th birthday."

Archibald Mosley fondly remembers the trip to the port in Norfolk, Virginia, and remembers being proud to be an inspiration to those who were cheering his unit on and wishing them luck as they began the process of deploying overseas. "We went in a convoy of trucks from Montford Point to Norfolk," he said. "I can still see the convoy. When we went through all of these cities, people would be out there waving and they were so proud of their black Marines. We would wave back, and they would yell wonderful clichés to us and so forth. They made us feel good."

The huge LST (Landing Ship Tank), similar to the one above, was a major source of resupply and support for U.S. forces during World War II. It was capable of delivering troops and vehicles directly to the beach during the Iwo Jima invasion and on D-Day it provided the off-shore platform for the deployment of the DUKWs. (National Archives)

He clearly recalls his unit's departure from Norfolk. "We left aboard ship in the Atlantic Ocean, and the only thing we knew was that were going through the Panama Canal," he said. Mosley remembered studying about the canal in school and was excited at the opportunity to pass through it. His ship's next stop was Hawaii. "We began the task of unloading our ship when we arrived in Hawaii. The boxes were wrapped tightly, and no one knew or really gave any thought to what was in all of those boxes when we loaded them back in the States. But as we unloaded them after reaching Hawaii, we were able to see what was in them. There were boxes of ammunition, hand grenades, and so forth. When we realized what we were carrying, we then began to understand what was happening and we began to see the big picture."

Yet another signal that his unit was about to become involved in the war, was the receipt and distribution of vast amounts of equipment and supplies his unit was handling and the intensive training they went through while in Hawaii. They were given classes that were clearly designed to prepare them for combat. "When we left Hawaii, we spent 49 straight days at sea," he said. Mosley now firmly believed that his unit's involvement in the war in the Pacific was imminent.

Charles Black remembers when his unit left Camp Gordon Johnston, traveling to Fort Lawton, Washington, near Seattle. "We left by train," he said. "At night, when we traveled through white communities, we had to pull down the shades. I really did not know why we had to do that. At first, I could not understand whether they didn't want the light from the train to disturb the residents in the communities through which we were traveling or they didn't want the residents to see the black troops coming through on these trains. We finally concluded that the reason was that they did not want the residents to see us coming through." It was a long train ride from Florida, and the troops slept in their seats and eventually arrived in Washington State. It seemed to simply be a stopping off point as they made their way to their final destination. "We did not stay there more than a week," he said. "After that, we boarded a ship bound for points unknown. Our next stop was Hawaii and while there, I was moved from my job as an office clerk to my new assignment as an assistant driver in one of the DUKWs."

The days during his unit's stay in Hawaii were filled with training. The sandy beaches reminded him of the beaches at Camp Gordon Johnston. He was now beginning to understand why the drivers and assistant drivers had trained off shore and on the sandy beaches at Camp Gordon Johnston, on how to operate the DUKW. "The waters off the coast of Hawaii were extremely rough. The waves were so huge and rough that we had to hold on as we moved from the water or risk being washed away. We were also taught how to handle explosives, hand grenades, and other weapons which we might have to use in combat situations. On the way to our final destination, we coordinated with the Marines and stopped at islands along the way as we island-hopped our way across the Pacific to Iwo Jima."

Frederick Gray, like all the other members of his company, journeyed to New Orleans and took his basic training at nearby Camp Plauche, Louisiana, and then moved on to Camp Gordon Johnston near Tallahassee, Florida, where his company, the 476th Amphibian Truck Company, was organized. When the order came to deploy, he too began the long train ride to Seattle, Washington, and from there, he and his company would begin another journey which would carry them to the beaches of Iwo Jima.

"When we left Camp Gordon Johnston, we traveled by troop train. In those days, the old coal smoke from the locomotive would blow back on us, the train would be jerking, and sleeping was almost impossible and none of us knew where we were going. I would wake up early in the morning as we were traveling west and ask the porter where we were going. I remember asking him several times, 'Where were we going?' and he would reply, 'I can't tell you that.' I would ask many more times, and he would say over and over again, 'I can't tell you.' I finally got the feeling that he really was not going to tell me, so I just settled in for the rest of the long, uncomfortable ride and waited to see where we would end up. When we were just outside Washington State, the porter finally did tell us, and said that we were going to Seattle, Washington."

"We stayed in Washington for a few days and then we boarded a ship bound for the Hawaiian Islands." During his unit's brief stay in Washington, Gray recalls seeing prisoners of war receiving better treatment than the men in his company. "The German prisoners of war were treated better than we were," he said. "The white military policemen who were guarding the prisoners would allow them to get anything they wanted before we could. The enemy had more freedom than we did." The next leg of their journey would end in Hawaii. When his unit arrived there, it linked up with the Marines that his unit would support during the Battle of Iwo Jima and began familiarizing them with the DUKWs which would become their life line from the ship to the shore during that assault.

Ellis Cunningham completed his recruit training at the Marine Corps Montford Point training camp and went home on Christmas leave. When he returned, the Marines were forming the ammunition companies that would support the assault units with the firepower they would need during the Iwo Jima campaign. "The day that I came back from boot leave," he said, "they formed the company that I would go overseas with. I was sent to a different set of barracks at Montford Point that was occupied by the men who would serve with the 8th Ammunition Company. We knew that we would be shipping out to somewhere in the Pacific. Everyone in those companies below the rank of platoon sergeant would be African Americans and those from the rank of platoon sergeant and above were white." In preparation for duties in combat, he became familiar with all types of weapons and ammunition and explosives that could be fired from guns and artillery pieces. "They taught us how to store them and package them for shipping and so on. We even practiced going on and off ships as we prepared for our deployment with dummy ammunition under simulated battlefield

Many European prisoners of war were sent back to the U.S. for incarceration. Some African American troops recalled incidents when the prisoners received better treatment than they did. (National Archives)

conditions." After training, he remembers his company traveled from Camp Lejeune, North Carolina, to California by troop train in August of 1944, where they boarded a ship bound for Hawaii. "We stayed in Hawaii from August until January and we worked and trained with ammunition every day until we left Hawaii," he said.

Horace Taylor completed basic training and remembered being assigned to a group of other soldiers who would eventually become members of the 476th Amphibious Truck Company. As a soldier he never expected to participate in amphibious operations and work closely with Marines or to serve in the Pacific. "When I finished basic training, I was assigned to a port company. There we would work on the ships with the riggers and others connected with amphibious operations," he said. Most of his unit did deploy to the Pacific, but some remained at the amphibious training base at Camp Gordon Johnston, Florida.

"Our deployment overseas began when we boarded a troop train headed for Washington State, and from there we boarded a troop ship," he said. He recalled instances during the train trip that made him realize that segregation was indeed the order of the day. "The troops on the train were all black," he said. "There were certain places that the train would stop to let us exercise and take a break from the long train ride. It would not stop in some of the towns along the way because some locations were not very cordial to blacks." He also remembered seeing preferential treatment being given to prisoners of war during the unit's brief stay in Washington. "When we arrived in Washington, enemy prisoners of war from the European theater were being held on the post where we stopped. They had the freedom of the post. They could go to the PX and had the run of the camp. They were prisoners, but they were white prisoners. They flirted with the women who worked in the canteen. There were skirmishes between the prisoners and our troops while we were there." Taylor's unit made the first stop in its overseas deployment to the Pacific in Hawaii. While in Hawaii, he remembers training with the 4th Marine Division to which his unit would be attached for the battle of Iwo Jima. "When we arrived on Oahu, planning had begun for the invasion," he said. "We were assigned to Marine units to train for joint amphibious assault operations. Planners were trying to determine who would be assigned to what units in the battle. The 4th Marine Division liked the way that our unit performed in training and the efficient way that we handled our vehicles so much that they selected our unit to support them in battle." The 4th and 5th Marine Divisions were the lead assault divisions on D-Day at Iwo Jima. "After the 476th was attached to the 4th Marine Division, they moved to the Island of Oahu. We moved to the island of Maui for advanced training in beach landings and other types of amphibious landings, which included moving various types of guns, equipment and supplies." After the training on Maui, his unit went aboard ship and headed out into the Pacific for points unknown. He does remember his ship stopping at another island before landing on Iwo Jima. "We were in Saipan while the assault forces formed the battle group just before the final leg of our trip to the battle area. We were assigned troops and the equipment we would take ashore while we were there. We were there for about two weeks as troops came in from everywhere. They came in from Guam and other islands all over the Pacific."

Arthur Peterson's work experiences quickly caught the eye of his senior noncommissioned and commissioned officers. "I did not train with the amphibious truck companies," he said. "Immediately after basic training, I was put in supply and became the supply sergeant for the 476th Amphibian Truck Company in charge of all supplies, equipment, records. I learned company supply on the job with no formal training and served as company supply sergeant throughout the Iwo Jima campaign." As the company geared up for deployment, Peterson, like the others in his company, had no idea about where the company would be going, and he knew that his portion of the operation would not involve direct amphibious activity but that he would be there with them and his focus would be to make sure that those involved in combat activity would have the necessary supplies and equipment to do their job.

As his unit shipped out, Peterson was responsible to the commanding officer of his company for the proper deployment of all of the companies' supplies and equipment. He monitored the movement of all of the logistical support materials from Camp Gordon Johnston in Florida to the mustering point in Hawaii. "While we waited in Hawaii," he said, "the five men in my section were busy ensuring that all of the supplies were packaged and ready to go when the order came. To be sure that we were able to do that, we had to order and receive supplies, inspect them for serviceability, and keep accurate inventories." He knew that when the 476th shipped out of Hawaii, everything had to be in place to support the company in the heat of the battle, which he knew would happen somewhere out there in the Pacific. Peterson rose through the ranks quickly during his short stay in the Army. "When we deployed," he said, "I was a buck sergeant, then a staff sergeant and by the time I left Iwo Jima, I was a first sergeant." Peterson was very confident in his ability to do his job. "I don't brag about myself, but I

The task of supplying the front line troops with the necessary equipment, ammunition food and clothing was crucial to success in battle. (National Archives)

knew where everything was and when it was needed my unit could always provide it. Whenever the DUKWs returned to the ship for a supply run, we had it ready for them."

Haywood Johnson had a feeling that he was about to join the war effort when he was transferred to Camp Gordon Johnston after basic training. The type of training his unit received simulated combat conditions similar to waterborne operations under combat conditions. "At Camp Johnston," he said, "we trained heavily in amphibious operations. We pulled round-the-clock duty in preparation for duty we knew we would have in combat. We practiced loading and unloading ships, how to handle weapons, how to drive the DUKW and we were taught how to maintain them." Johnson, too, remembers the long train ride from the east coast to Washington State and watching the conductors aboard the train coming through the cars and pulling the shades down when they passed through southern towns and the preferential treatment that the European prisoners of war received over the

African American troops. "They did not want people to see the train coming through filled with black troops and that was a fact," he said. "And when we got to our destination in Washington State we saw prisoners of war from the European theater going places and doing things that we could not think of doing."

Sam Green clearly remembers when the 476th Amphibian Truck Company boarded their ship bound for a staging and training camp in Hawaii. While in Hawaii, he trained with the Marines his unit would support in the invasion. "We worked closely with the Marines of the Fourth Marine Division. We even trained them on how to operate the DUKW should something happen to us. We learned how to strap their huge artillery pieces into our DUKWs and maneuver in rough seas with men, supplies and equipment aboard." He remembers the day when his company demonstrated the capabilities of the DUKW for the Marines they would support. "We were asked to demonstrate our ability to handle our vehicles under simulated battlefield conditions similar to those that we might see when we went ashore," he said. "We demonstrated our ability to carry men and equipment in the DUKW and maneuver the vehicle on land and in the water. We did so well that our company was selected to support the 4th Marine Division, the lead division in the assault on Iwo Jima. At the time, we still did not know where we were going or when we would get there, but we now knew that we would be attached to them and would be among some of the first assault troops to go ashore."

After his unit's stay in Hawaii, the troops boarded an LST that would take them on the last leg of their long journey to Iwo Jima. "We went from Honolulu aboard the LST that would take us to Iwo Jima with our task force; we still did not know exactly where we were going, but we had an idea we were headed for a combat zone because the ships were moving slowly, stopping along the way and conducting firing maneuvers and dry runs with the DUKWs every day. The trip to the battle area was a lengthy one, and the closer the ship got to it, there were signs that made us realize that we were going to war," he said. "As we got closer to the battle area, we saw aircraft landing on aircraft carriers, heard the bombs and explosives going off, watched wounded men being brought aboard the ships—we knew there was fighting all around us. When all the ships lined up and made final preparations for the assault, it was February 19th, and that is when we went in," Green said.

Lyman Brent left Camp Gordon Johnston along with the rest of his unit and took the long train ride to Washington State, where they would prepare for the journey across the Pacific to Iwo Jima. "All of the troops on the train were black. We did not mix with the whites anywhere," said Brent. "When we got there, we waited for a short time and then we boarded our ship to go overseas. From Washington, we went to Honolulu." He too remembers the demonstration his company presented which impressed the officers of the 4th Marine Division so much that the Division selected them to support them on the movement to shore in the battle area. "We trained with them on Maui, and then we boarded our ship and headed for Iwo Jima."

CHAPTER 4

Going Ashore

THE SUCCESSFUL ISLAND-HOPPING campaigns by the United States forces against the enemy in the Pacific were clearly paving the way for an attempt to make a strike at mainland Japan. A successful invasion of Iwo Jima would significantly enhance the capability of the invasion forces' aircraft to penetrate the Japanese homeland defenses. As the distance to the Japanese mainland decreased, the plan to use Iwo Jima's strategic location near the Japanese mainland to secure the positioning needed by the invading forces to land a crushing blow to the Japanese in the Pacific was becoming a reality.

On October 3, 1944, the Joint Chiefs of Staff issued a directive to Admiral Nimitz to take Iwo Jima. The campaign to do so was code named "Operation Detachment" and its mission was to capture the airfields on Iwo Jima. In view of the importance of the airfields to the Allied strategy to neutralize the Japanese, the mission was clear: take the airfields! That was the job of the entire Fifth Amphibious Corps. It was task-organized to support that mission. Every unit within it had a subordinate mission that would contribute to the Corps' mission.

Temperatures as high as 130 degrees are not uncommon on Iwo Jima. The soil is mostly volcanic ash and not suitable for cultivating crops. In preparing the island for the U.S. invasion, the Japanese troops had to inhale dangerous sulfur fumes, and there was no drinkable ground water. The Japanese defenders, however, had transformed Mt. Suribachi into a fortress. Other than the volcano, the terrain was flat and level. Both the Allies and the Japanese found that this flat surface was well-suited for the runways needed for landing and servicing their aircraft. Prior to the invasion, there were about 200 households on the island. The island's economy relied upon sulfur mining, sugar cane farming, and fishing. Those living on the island had to import

At 2:00 A.M. on February 19, 1945, assault units headed ashore and the Battle for Iwo Jima began. (National Archives)

practically all of their consumer goods. Since the small island had no natural resources, obtaining needed supplies for the Japanese troops stationed on the island was a serious problem for the defenders, especially as the U.S. forces began to isolate the island. When it was evident that the island would be invaded, the few families and civilians that lived there were evacuated, and the defense force began preparing the island for the invasion.

Roland Durden's unit moved from Pearl Harbor, Hawaii, into the battle area aboard a U.S. Navy LST. "My first glimpse of the island of Iwo Jima came as our ship entered the battle area on D-Day. We arrived in the battle area in the early morning, and as the sun rose, we saw the island of Iwo Jima." His unit did not go ashore in the first wave, but remained aboard ship until February 23. While waiting to go ashore, he witnessed one of the fiercest battles of World War II unfold. "Once the battle began, because of the smoke from the heavy bombardment from ships at sea and our aircraft, it was difficult to see anything," he said.

The water surrounding the island on D-Day was filled with an array of ships, troops, equipment, and air power task-organized to support the invasion. "All the troop ships, including my ship, the supply ships, the hospital ships, were all in an inner perimeter. All of the warships, which included the cruisers, battleships, and the destroyers, were all on the outer parameter firing at enemy targets on the island. From time to time, through the thick smoke, I could see planes being shot down. I remember seeing very clearly the flamethrowers and the assault troops maneuvering on the island involved in firefights on the ground. We were only two or three football fields away from the island. I was far enough away that I could not see the individual Marines, but I could see troops moving toward the shore and hear the small arms fire and all the bombing going on," he said.

Eugene Doughty was given a furlough to go home as the ammo and depot companies were being established at Montford Point, and when he returned to his unit, he was reassigned from his garrison duties as a clerk to the 36th Depot Company as a squad leader. He had a strong feeling prior to shipping out that he would soon be heading into combat. "Looking back at all that was happening with the buildup of troop strength, it was evident that the support from the Marine Corps depot and ammunition companies would have the mission to support Marine assault campaigns in the Pacific," he said.

When Doughty's company shipped out, he remembers that his unit went by ship to Hawaii by way of California and Virginia for additional training. "The trip from Hawaii to the area of operations was taxing, because we were destined to rendezvous with an armada of ships and remain with them at sea for about three to four weeks. Not only were there troops on board, but there was a massive amount of equipment on board to include a huge landing craft mounted on top of the LST on which we were traveling. We had various duties to perform on the ship. My squad had the job of passing ammunition up to the ship's big guns from the hole of the ship." When his ship finally arrived at the area of operations, he was in awe. "I was amazed at the amount of activity that was going on. The bombing, strafing and naval bombardment seemed to never end," he said. When he saw this little island, he could not believe the magnitude of the effort that would be required to take it. "We had no idea that the island was only four miles wide, with no trees and no inhabitants. I could never have imagined that it would take all that we would have give up and the lives we would lose to take it."

Archibald Mosley, another member of the 36th Depot Company, remembers his departure from Montford Point. "As we embarked from our ship into landing craft on the morning of D-Day, we knew that we were going ashore, but we could not see the island. Our ships were bombarding it, but all we could see was smoke, the flashing of naval gunfire, and lots of explosions," he said. "As we got closer to the island, we could begin to see its outline and land ahead of us. Curiosity would tempt us to take a look at the island, but with the incoming fire from the enemy, that really was not a good idea. The water in the landing area was filled with landing craft similar to ours. They too were filled with people, equipment, ammunition, and explosives. Enemy fire from the island would frequently score direct hits, and there would be explosions all around us."

"When we finally arrived at the beach, the front ramp would go down, and we would run off the craft as quickly as possible onto the beach." Unloading the landing craft depended entirely on the tide and the water level on the beach. The volcanic ash upon which they had to unload equipment, maneuver, and work, was a huge deterrent to efficient operations.

"During those first three days, because of the large number of troops going ashore, enemy resistance and no opportunity for cover and concealment, so many Marines died in the initial landings that the water was no longer clear. After the first three days, we were able to move far enough onto the beach to dig foxholes. We had problems digging foxholes. As we tried to dig in, the volcanic ash would simply fill the hole up again," said Mosley

Frederick Gray recalls being on a ship for a number of days. "I forget how long we were on the ship after we left Hawaii heading toward the battle area. The water was rough. On our ship, we would have numerous air raids. Sleeping was difficult, and some of the troops slept in their vehicle," he said. "When we got close to Iwo Jima, there were so many ships surrounding the island. There were aircraft carriers with planes flying on and off of them 24 hours a day. There were battleships, hospital ships, and LSTs. The battleships with their long guns pounded the island for days." Throughout the invasion, Gray served as the assistant supply sergeant for the 476th Amphibian Truck Company to provide forward support to the DUKW drivers ashore. He would establish a supply point ashore for the duration of the battle and become the company first sergeant after the battle, but in that moment, he watched the first group of DUKWs depart their LST ship for a trip into history.

Ellis Cunningham did not know where his unit was going when they boarded the ships in Hawaii. "We believed that we were headed to a combat zone somewhere in the Pacific. We left in January of 1945, and it took us about a month to get where we were going. We traveled on an LST. The weather was warm, and we slept above deck on our bed rolls and under a canvas shelter. We made a stop on the island of Saipan, and then our convoy of more than 30 ships went back out into the Pacific. We had submarines and destroyers supporting our movement all the way. Our convoy of ships was transporting supplies and ammunition, but as we got closer to our final destination, another convoy joined us and went ahead of us. Those ships were carrying the assault troops that would lead the attack ashore just two days later."

"On D-Day, I remember seeing the assault troops circling in the water in their landing crafts, and then after awhile they all formed an assault line several waves deep and headed ashore," he said. "They went ashore with ammunition initially, but we followed a few waves later with the ammunition that we knew they would need as they used all they could carry. I remember seeing, shortly after the assault waves formed, airplanes flying across the front of the beach and putting out huge amounts of smoke. While that smoke was hanging there, the first wave went ashore from the small landing craft in which they were being transported. I was told later on that the first two waves met almost no resistance at all. I believe that was the way the Japanese commander had planned it. There were a lot of casualties when the Japanese began firing." When Cunningham's unit went ashore, the troops were not transported in the smaller landing craft. "Our LST went straight up to the beach, dropped its ramp at the bow of the ship, and off we went."

"We had to use bulldozers to get our supplies ashore. The Navy Seabees assisted in getting the ammunition and equipment ashore from our ship. We happened to notice that there were African Americans among them," he remembered. "The bulldozers would drag steel matting up to the ship and the trucks could then achieve the necessary traction to move through the sand and volcanic ash. That made it much easier to get the supplies and ammunition ashore. Once we got ashore, the bulldozers would cut trenches for us to store the ammunition. The Seabees were there; they kept busy all the time and tremendously contributed to the victory on Iwo Jima."

Horace Taylor remembers the day his ship entered the battle area. "We moved into the battle area on our assigned DUKWs. These vehicles were located in a compartment such that when the ramp at the front of the ship would open, we could just roll the vehicle off into the ocean," he said. "On our DUKW, we carried the 105 howitzers and six rounds of ammo for the 105 howitzers. The gun was lashed in the DUKW and the barrel was situated for the trip ashore between the driver and the assistant driver. They had it situated so that if need be, they could fire the howitzer from the DUKW. Each DUKW had a gun crew and the gun."

"The scene on the beach was something I will never forget," said Horace Taylor. (National Archives)

"The battleships were very close to the beach as our ship arrived in the battle area very early on the morning of D-Day. The planes were softening up the area and dropping bombs on Iwo, and the battleships were also shelling the island with their big guns," he said. He remembers that his unit did not go in as scheduled. "We were supposed to go ashore early on that morning, but we were afraid to go ashore after seeing all that was going on. If anyone could have seen the explosion of one of these shells that landed on that island and everything else that was going on, I guarantee you it is something they would never forget."

Taylor prepared himself for his first trip ashore. "I was the driver of my DUKW that morning. My assistant driver and I took our positions and prepared ourselves to take our troops and their equipment ashore. Including the 105 Howitzer crew, there were about eight of us on each DUKW, along with our guns and ammo. We did not go in on the first few waves—the infantry went first. When the time came to move ashore, they told us to 'saddle up.' We were ready to go. Everybody got into their vehicles; we put our life jackets on, helmets, and checked our weapons and ammunition. When they gave us our orders to hit the water, we began our trip ashore. When we got to the beach, it was cluttered with knocked-out trucks, landing craft casualties, and vehicles trying to navigate through the volcanic ash and enemy fire. On the way to the beach, the Japanese saw all of the howitzers and artillery we were bringing ashore in the second wave to support the pinned down infantry troops on the beach and began to fire at us. After making it ashore, we would return to the ship to load and bring ammo and supplies to the gun crews ashore. We would also conduct medical evacuations and other ship-to-shore operations," he said.

Arthur Peterson vividly remembers entering the battle area. "It was a while before we saw the island. There was smoke and noise everywhere. Those who were up topside could see the bombs falling from the airplanes, the explosions on the island from naval gunfire, and all the ships in the surrounding area as the troops prepared to go ashore. Whenever we went below deck, we could not see anything and it was like we were not even there, but only the hull of the ship separated us from the reality that we were." Establishing supply points ashore as soon as possible was extremely important to the advancing infantry troops, and as the supply chief for his company, Peterson was well aware of that. "My supply unit did not go in on the first wave, but it was our job to make sure that all of the supplies necessary to support the Marine infantry troops went in on the DUKWs so that they were readily available when needed. My men did go in on later waves and established supply points to support our infantry troops." Segregation back home was a strong issue, but Peterson clearly noted that he never saw it on the battlefield from the movement ashore and through the battle ashore. "We were together during the fight, and it was one of those things that made you feel good in a way—knowing that we were all in it together and race just was not an issue." It was a while before Peterson went ashore. His men were there in the earliest waves but he remained with the battalion command element and directed the re-supply effort from aboard ship. He did, however, make it to the beach as the effort stabilized ashore. "It was about ten days before I went ashore to ensure that the supply effort was as efficient as it needed to be to support our company ashore. Once ashore, I stayed there for the rest of the battle." He also remembered that the volcanic ash was a major deterrent to movement ashore. "The heavy landing vehicles carrying the Marines had a great deal of difficulty landing the infantry troops ashore. Many of them had to jump off those vehicles into the water and wade ashore. Some of them never made it," he said.

Haywood Johnson also affirmed the versatility of the DUKW and its ability to do what no other vehicle could do. The invading force went ashore in landing crafts that could only go in as far as the beach, and if the waters were rough, many of them would not make it that far. "The DUKW could be depended upon to leave the ship, swim ashore, and inflate its tires and take personnel and cargo anywhere on the beach it needed to go," he said. "It had a crane on it that could lift heavy equipment from inside of it and place it where it needed to be or pick up items on the beach and take them back to the ship. My DUKW was among the first few waves to go ashore with men, ammunition and artillery pieces." His memory of the invasion is as clear as it was on February 19, 1945. "The ships were firing those big guns. The firing barrage was so intense that it seemed like the ships would sink down into the water each time a shell was fired and then resurface again. Planes were flying overhead and conducting bombing missions when we headed ashore with our Marines, artillery, and ammunition. After we got them ashore, we dug our foxholes and stayed the night on the beach, as bullets and all kind of firepower was flying over our heads." After their initial trip ashore in the earliest waves to position the artillery troops and crews, their guns and supplies, Johnson and the other DUKW drivers and assistant drivers assumed a support role for the rest of the battle. "After we had brought the troops and guns ashore, we then began bringing guns, ammunition, supplies, and conducting medical evacuations for the rest of the battle," he said.

Sam Green said that it was not until his unit was at sea and heading to Iwo Jima that they were told where they were going. As his ship entered the waters surrounding the island, he, too, could not believe what he saw. "You could not help but see all of those ships. It seemed like there were hundreds or more of them. Announcements were constantly coming over the loudspeaker telling us that this was it. We were reminded by our commanders that we had received the best training possible for the job we had to do and that now we were on our own. They were trying to tell us that we had to use what we had been taught to protect ourselves, our fellow troops, and get the job done."

"We did lose a few of our DUKWs and a couple of our boys. The rest of us who survived it all were very lucky because every time we made a trip during the battle, going or coming, we, too, were driving directly into enemy fire. I quickly realized the meaning of the phrase 'war is hell,'—believe me it is. Seeing men in the water because their landing craft could not get onto the beach, continuously hearing all kinds of directions and orders coming from the loudspeakers on the ship: 'move out,' 'get that truck out of here,' and so on are sights and sounds I do not like to remember." he said.

Well concealed and with excellent fields of fire inside Mt. Suribachi, the enemy held most of their fire until substantial numbers of the invading troops were ashore and then opened fire. (National Archives)

Lyman Brent remembers the long trip, which took weeks, from Hawaii to the battle area. "I remember the 45-day long trip to Iwo. When we got there, it was early that morning and the island was lit up like a blaze of fire with all the bombardment and explosions. The firing and activity was so heavy that standing up on the deck of the ship was dangerous. That was February 19, 1945, and things were rough; I really did not think that I would get back home. Everything that you hear about the horrors we faced during the landing on Iwo Jima is true. That is the way it was," he said.

"In preparation for going ashore, we loaded our DUKWs with our troops and artillery pieces, ammo and equipment, backed into the water and prepared to follow the assault troops in. When we approached the beach, there was a lot of shooting, landing craft going under water, airplanes flying over. The waves were terrible and the sand was so soft that landing craft could not get to the beach, and the troops were jumping off in the waves trying to make it ashore as the enemy was firing on them. The beach was cluttered with casualties, destroyed or disabled vehicles, and equipment that did not make it to its proper location," said Brent. A life threatening incident in which he was involved could have very easily made him a casualty. "While we were heading ashore, my DUKW stopped in the water before we hit the beach and there were about three or four of us on it. The water surrounding the beach was crowded with ships and landing craft. Suddenly, one of them was approaching my stalled vehicle. It looked as though the ship was going to crash right into us, and everybody jumped off. I was the last one to jump off. Fortunately, the ship did miss our vehicle. I couldn't swim too well, but I did have a life preserver. It, however, malfunctioned. I grabbed one of the others in the water, and someone who had returned to our vehicle held out a long pole and pulled me back into the DUKW. All of this was happening while the enemy was firing on us."

Sam Green remembers that on his first trip ashore, he immediately had to take cover to avoid the steady stream of gunfire that never seemed to end. That was an impossible task on Iwo Jima. "Because of the volcanic ash, we could not dig a foxhole on the beach. As fast as we would dig a hole, it would cave in. There were few trees and almost no opportunity for cover and concealment on that volcanic island. So, the only quick protection against shrapnel and small arms fire we could get was to dig a hole as best we could, fill bags with volcanic ash and use them as a shield," he said. "That is how we spent our first night of the battle." The DUKWs would usually return to their ship before nightfall and begin their missions ashore as the sun rose the next day. It was almost impossible to effectively navigate in the rough waters at night. The uncertain location of the enemy was yet another deterrent to ship-to-shore operations after dark. There were times, however, when remaining ashore could not be avoided. A vehicle breakdown, an enemy attack or weather could make it happen at almost any time. While ashore and serving in support roles rather than on the front lines in direct combat, Green and others from his company do recall some very tense moments while making stops in and out of stationary locations amid artillery and mortar fire. "We all had close calls," he said. "We were constantly running in and out of bomb shelters. Fortunately, I was not hurt, but a lot were and some worse than others. There were no good days during the battle."

CHAPTER 5

Taking the Island

FULLY AWARE OF ALLIED PLANS to invade Iwo Jima and having had the advantage of preparing for it, the Japanese would try to stop the assault forces from taking the island with whatever means available to them. As the Fifth Amphibious Corps made final preparations to go ashore during the early morning hours of February 19, 1945, there was a great deal of activity in the battle area. The island was under continuous fire as the sun rose that morning. Through the noise and smoke of the big guns from the ships off shore and aircraft flying overhead, a silhouette of the island of Iwo Jima emerged. Final preparations were underway by the assault units for movement to contact with the enemy. Additional ammunition was distributed, weapons, equipment and personnel were checked and rechecked for readiness, and troops were positioned in their landing craft. Contact with the enemy was imminent, and at 6:45 A.M., the order to land the landing force was sounded and the invasion of Iwo Jima, code name "Operation Detachment," began.

The DUKWs driven by African American soldiers were among the first waves to land on Iwo Jima on D-Day, supported by a barrage of United States naval and aerial bombardment, and armed resistance by enemy troops. The Marines had landed and 36 days later it would be over and they would be victorious, but there would be a heavy price to pay to take the island. By late morning on D-Day, at least 6,000 troops were ashore. The battle was underway, and the assault troops expected a heavy barrage of artillery, but it did not come immediately. The Japanese had planned to allow the allied forces to move further inland before using the full force of their firepower and as a result, the Marines in the early assault waves encountered only scattered fire as they approached the beach.

Although the pre-invasion bombing campaign was intensive, after-action reports from the battle indicated that the campaign did not do as much damage to the entrenched Japanese positions as the invasion forces had hoped. The maze of deeply buried underground facilities, firing positions, and pillboxes deeply imbedded in Mount Suribachi with excellent fields of fire and other well-concealed strong points would protect the Japanese defenders from the heavy naval and aerial bombardment by the invading forces. It was noted, however, that the impact of that relentless bombing campaign could have had a damaging psychological effect on the hearts and minds of the defenders, and negatively affected their will towards the invading forces. When the Japanese did open up with all of their firepower, a substantial number of troops were on the beach, and the pinned down assault troops sustained heavy casualties, significantly hampering their forward progress. The Japanese would make a strong, defiant stand, and the victory on Iwo Jima for the allied forces would take an unexpected 36 days. The resolve of the Japanese to hold the island, and the high number of casualties the invading forces would sustain, had been underestimated.

A phased movement of units was necessary to eliminate as much congestion as possible on the beach, especially in view of the fact that the invading forces were facing a well-entrenched enemy who could clearly see their every move. There were very few trees on the island and the enemy could sit in pillboxes and caves carved out of the towering Mt. Suribachi and literally pick their target.

Archibald Mosley went in on D-Day and remembers it well. "From the time we landed on the beach, the tempo of activity was high. We were always moving and doing everything we could do to keep the assault troops supplied with ammunition, weapons, food, water, and other supplies necessary to keep them moving forward, and we were also doing everything else we could do to stay alive." He equated the importance of his responsibilities to a statement made by one of world history's well-known warriors, Napoleon, who said "an army marches on its stomach." Like the famous French general, he was inferring that strong logistical support is as important to winning a battle as anything that contributes to it.

During the battle, troops carried their drinking water in canteens, ate C-rations from individual packages that contained bread, coffee, sugar, meat, and vegetables intended to provide nutritional needs for only a few days. The troops subsisted on them for more than a month. Even though C-ration menus were limited, the troops devised ingenious mixtures and methods to combine the contents of their ration with various seasonings to devise meals that many of them would consider a delicacy. The main courses of their

Forward movement in the first days of the invasion seemed to be an impossible task for the assault units in the shadow of Mt. Suribachi. (National Archives)

rations, the meat and vegetables, were packaged in durable, tough, metal cans that would withstand the worst of battle conditions. When troops found the time to eat, opening the cans oftentimes might have seemed an impossible task—their meals were totally encapsulated. Every service member who received rations, however, found in their package what many of the troops called the best invention of World War II, the P-38 can opener, which was used to open the toughest of metal cans.

Planning and providing logistical support for the 110,000 U.S. troops that would participate in the invasion that had been estimated to take about a week, was a challenging task. As the battle raged on for more than a month, supporting the troops ashore became even more of a challenge. There were no established facilities ashore to accommodate the troops for the month-long battle. The island was barren, with no resources which the invading forces could use to support the basic needs of the large number of troops that would come ashore, and the tremendous resistance posed by the island's defenders made it impossible to position hospitals, dining facilities, or anything else to accommodate basic human needs. Their only facilities for supplies, ammunition, intensive medical support, etc. were sitting offshore aboard naval vessels. Any expectation of success in the invasion had to be based on an alert and healthy invasion force. Superior logistical support would prove to be as much a part of the victory on Iwo Jima as anything else.

Roland Durden clearly remembers the day he went ashore. "Our unit initially hit the beach at Iwo Jima on the evening of the 23rd of February. A number of Japanese mortars hit our ship about four or five times. We were carrying ammunition and explosives, and a direct hit could cause it to explode. Realizing that, the ship's captain pulled back out to sea but we returned the next day, which was my birthday, to begin our movement ashore." The ship on which his unit, the 33rd Depot Company, was transported to Iwo Jima, an LST, was equipped with bow doors to facilitate the beaching and offloading of troops, vehicles, and other materials. When they arrived, the battle had been raging for five days. The assault troops were well ahead of them and were making their way to the summit of Mt. Suribachi.

When Durden's unit went ashore on D+5, he saw, first-hand, the horrors of war. "Explosions and enemy fire were everywhere, and it was happening so fast that one very quickly had to react to it," he said. "After seeing the light from the weapon being fired, we would hit the deck as fast as we could and cover ourselves because the shrapnel would surely follow."

Durden was assigned support duties within the depot company but he remembers most vividly having to work in graves registration and being assigned to burial details, which were responsible for taking care of the remains of those killed in action. His job would be a very difficult one. "The first body I saw was the body of a Marine that looked like he had been hit by a .50 caliber bullet. And then," he solemnly said, "we went on to the cemetery and started burying our dead. It had been a nightmare burying young men, seeing them with scars and wounds, and jumping into a hole with the dead to avoid enemy fire; those were the realities of the battle for almost a month." Having no access to information about how the battle was progressing, he could only get a feel for it by considering the casualty count and the sights and sounds of battle. "I could only begin to realize that the fighting was winding down as we began to bury fewer bodies, the bombs were not falling as often as they had been, there were fewer explosions, and there was less gunfire," he said.

"I was the first in my unit to be assigned guard duty. The first night I

Foxholes were the living quarters for U.S. troops during the 36-day battle. (National Archives)

was on the island, I remember there was no light at all, no moonlight, nothing. I felt like a sitting duck hearing all the explosions, gunfire, and bombardment and wondering whether or not I would be taken out during the night. That was a two hour guard duty, but it seemed like a year."

During the battle, the living space for the troops ashore was their foxhole. "I lived in a foxhole for the duration of the battle," he remembers. "The area in which I was assigned to dig my foxhole was solid rock, and I could not dig one there, so I had to join two other black Marines in their foxhole." Although blacks were assigned to garrison and support units and were rarely involved in front line combat activities, Durden did, however, speak of an incident that he remembered when two of them seized the opportunity to provide support to front line troops. "The outfit next to ours was a trucking outfit," he said. "One night their officer asked for two volunteers to drive trucks with supplies up to the front line. None of his troops responded. Two men from my foxhole, black Marines, eagerly responded and risked their lives to drive the truck up to the front lines with the supplies. Durden believed that if any man in his unit would have been called upon to serve on the front lines, they would have done so willingly and held their own as well as any man on the island. With a bit of pride in his voice as he described the actions of the men in his foxhole, he said, "a lot of people do not realize that there were heroes among us, but there were."

Durden believed that after the battle was over, he and his unit would remain on Iwo Jima. An event that would have a catastrophic effect on the outcome of World War II would change that. "The purpose of taking the island of Iwo Jima was to take that island and prepare those airstrips for landings on Iwo Jima so that our planes could refuel and continue their journey to mainland Japan," he said. "We thought we would be doing that along with the Army and the Navy Seabees for the rest of our deployment in the Pacific." But his unit did leave Iwo Jima and shipped out for Hawaii where they remained until the war ended. His unit then relocated to Sasebo, Japan, to assist the Japanese who were beginning the process of rebuilding their country in the aftermath of the devastation it had suffered from the war. "My unit made a relatively quiet, orderly departure from the island aboard a troop ship bound for Hawaii. We remained in Hawaii four months," he said. "While we were there, the atomic bomb was dropped on Japan, the Japanese surrendered and our unit was sent to Sasebo, Japan, to serve as part of the occupation forces. We also spent time in Hiroshima and Nagasaki as part of the occupation forces providing assistance with the cleanup in the aftermath of the dropping of the bomb," he recalls.

Charles Black's unit, on D+1, prepared to go ashore on his assigned DUKW. "I was the assistant driver, and we were among the first few DUKWs to leave our ship," he said. He clearly remembers that all of the vehicles that left the ship ahead of his did not go to the beach. "For some reason those vehicles ahead of us turned and went somewhere else. When that happened, my DUKW then became the number one vehicle from our company to head for the beach. The disappearance of those lead vehicles and ours becoming the first was a concern to me because this was my first combat experience and as I recalled from the movies, the first vehicles to make it ashore were usually the first to be hit. It made me feel better, however, to know that we had among the troops a medical doctor on board," he said. He did, however, have a close call. "A shell hit the water extremely close to the vehicle on the driver's side," he recalls. "We had practiced emergency situations before, but that was my first experience with the real thing." He believed that there was a possibility that his DUKW might have been targeted and another shell could be on the way. He was happy to see his driver react to the incident quickly. "Taking no chances, he quickly began to accelerate the speed of our vehicle toward the beach to avoid direct hits from any mortar or artillery fire to follow. I patted him on the shoulder for what he did, and at the same time tried to remain calm myself."

The characteristics of the volcanic ash provided Black and his driver yet another challenge before they could discharge his cargo and troops. At times, the high tides and surf would not allow the DUKW to lower its wheels and successfully land. "When we did land, the sand was so soft that we had to back off shore into the water," he said. "Among all of the activity ashore we, at times, would have to be towed by another vehicle ashore onto the beach."

He remembers no point during the battle when war seemed to be winding down or coming to an end. For him, that realization happened suddenly. "One day," he said, "we were told that the war had ended, and there was a celebration. Some of us began shooting our carbines into the air." During that celebration, a final reminder of his Iwo Jima experience happened. "I was shooting my carbine in the air; it jammed on me and would not fire." He appreciated it happening then rather than during combat activity during battle he had just endured. "I was surprised that that incident happened, because we cleaned those rifles every day."

The Marines departed Iwo Jima shortly after victory was declared on the island. "My unit did not leave Iwo," he said. "We remained there as part of the occupation forces. We continued doing what we did during the invasion, moving equipment and troops from ship to shore. During the occupation, Black recalls that the atmosphere on the island calmed down significantly. Various types of aircraft were landing on the airstrips, construction on the airstrips moved along, and the troops enjoyed some leisure time. "The foxholes were replaced by tents during the occupation, and we even organized a touch football team. There were still Japanese on the island, but the occupation forces maintained a strong security posture," he said.

Frederick Gray went ashore in one of the earlier waves and his mission was to ensure that supply points were established to provide supplies and equipment from D-Day to the end of the battle for the troops his unit would support. "We had to go ashore with them," said Gray. "We had the 4th Marine Divisions' 105 Howitzers, their ammunition and troops." When he arrived on the beach, like all the other interviewees, he had no idea how difficult it was going to be to move around. "Getting around through the volcanic ash on the beach was almost impossible," he said. "Just trying to get around on foot was difficult enough. I saw that black volcanic ash suck the wheels of one of the DUKWs as the weight of the vehicle created a hole in it. We lost a number of our vehicles because they could not move through it," he said.

Certain isolated experiences will always remind Gray of his Iwo Jima experience. He believes that he saw one of the last attempts by the Japanese to defend the island from the air. "I was in my foxhole when one of the last Japanese planes came over. I heard what I thought was one of our anti-aircraft guns shooting the plane down. The next morning, I went down to see if it had really happened, and there was the shot down plane with the pilot still strapped inside." He also remembers seeing, first hand, casualties suffered by the invading forces throughout the assault. "One of our DUKW drivers drowned as his vehicle went down approaching the beach." In another chilling incident, a young Marine was killed while Gray was involved in a conversation with him. "He asked me where I was from," Gray said. "I told him that I was from Maryland, and that I was a carpenter by trade, He related to me that his family owned a small construction company back home in Arkansas and suggested that the two of us should consider going into business together. Before we could finish our conversation, a Japanese bullet had taken his life."

The unexpected period of time it took to sustain the forward momentum that the invading forces had hoped for was taking its toll on the United States Forces. A nightly radio show hosted by Tokyo Rose attempted to take advantage of a perceived opportunity to demoralize enemy soldiers and turn them against their country. "She would come on the radio at six o'clock every evening and say, 'You cannot go in the front door in your own country. We are your friends, not your enemy.' Her show would often be aimed directly at the black troops and would encourage them to turn against their own country," Gray said. Tokyo Rose was the name given to a female radio announcer who would broadcast radio programs designed to demoralize the troops by playing music and capturing their imagination in such a way that it would distract them from the war efforts in which they were involved. Her voice on the radio was characterized as soft, smooth and sultry as she attempted to encourage the invading troops to lay down their arms, leave their units and remind them of the good life and times they were missing back home.

Even though he did not see the mushroom cloud or hear the effects of the atomic bomb being dropped on mainland Japan, he believes that while stationed on Iwo Jima as part of the occupation forces, he did feel its effects. "I know that is what it was," he said. "The weather turned hot and we did not know what was happening. I remember pulling off my jacket. The waves were swelling and we had no idea what was going on. Then, someone with a shortwave radio informed us that an atomic bomb was dropped on Hiroshima, and another announcement was made just a few short days later that a second bomb was dropped on Nagasaki."

Eugene Doughty remembers that the beachhead at Iwo Jima was more crowded than he could have imagined. "It was littered with ships, and that has to be one reason why we had so much loss of life. The troops could not move quickly and effectively through all the clutter on the beach. Bombardment from our ships at sea and air, high waves and volcanic ash, made the battlefield conditions seemingly impossible." According to Doughty, the African American Marines of the three field depot companies who went ashore were assigned a myriad of tasks such as graves registration, cleaning up the debris on the beach and other noncombat duties while Marines of the only other black unit to go ashore, the ammunition company, were strictly involved in handling and outfitting weapons and ammunition for use by the front line units. Doughty remembers that trying to move around on the beach during the chaos and clutter was an arduous task and the beachmaster, whose job was to supervise all of the activities on the beach, was the busiest man there. "When we landed, my job was to take my squad and try to the find the beachmaster, and that was very difficult to do," he said. "Walking from place to place under combat conditions in the volcanic ash, which would cave in with every step, and fighting off huge land crabs on the beach, was a difficult task. It took almost 45 minutes to make the trip to find him when it should have taken much less than that."

It concerned Doughty that his duties were relegated to clean-up and labor tasks. He wanted to do what he joined the Marine Corps to do, and that was to fight for his country. "I felt that we were taken advantage of. The black Marines were essentially laborers and that did not go well with me. I believed that we, as American citizens, should have had the right to stand beside any man there to take part in opposing the enemy as United States Marines in defense of our country," he said. That would not happen, but there were times when the African American Marines would stand security duty. "After the assault troops had moved beyond one of the airfields, our airplanes had begun landing on the island and my company, along with Marines from the 8th Ammunition Company, would provide security for them, their airplanes and equipment," he said.

He cannot forget the pace of activity ashore and one of his first opportunities to take a break. "On or about D+15," Doughty said, "it was a bright Sunday morning, and we got word from the commanding officer that the hospital ship had just pulled in and was prepared to provide the first hot luncheons for the troops since D-Day. Our unit was invited aboard the ship, and we enjoyed a hot meal and cold beverages. We had a shower and, unlike the C-rations I was eating ashore, a prepared meal." It was one of the high-lights of his Iwo Jima experience. The meal, along with a change of cloth-ing, casual conversation and the absence of direct enemy fire, even for a little while, were greatly appreciated. After a few hours aboard ship, he returned to the battlefield, his squad, and the uncertainties of war.

"When we left the ship, we came back to our area, which was located not too far from Motoyama Airfield #1, which was still being subjected to a lot of enemy shelling and small arms fire." He remembered seeing Navy Seabees diligently working to repair the airfield to land their aircraft. "That airfield had to be constructed at a certain time and nothing was going to stop the Seabees from getting the job done," he said. He had high praise for the Seabees, especially for their construction skills. "Not only did they make those runways operable, they built roads that our vehicles could use to move further inland, they were also able to rig up pipelines so that for the first time since landing on the island 15 days prior, we able to get hot showers. Until that time, we had a ration of water and each man would have to bathe with the water provided to them in their helmet, which amounted to about two canteens of water." Doughty fondly remembers the trip back to the ship, the hot showers, the hot food. It was a huge morale booster for him and it happened on March 3, 1945, his 21st birthday.

"After 32 days on Iwo Jima, the battle had ended for us, and my unit left the island and again went aboard ship, but this time it was to relocate to Hawaii." His unit remained there until the atomic bombs were dropped. "After the Japanese surrendered, my unit shipped out to mainland Japan to serve as part of the occupation force there," he said.

Ellis Cunningham said that when his unit, the 8th Ammunition Company, went ashore, their task would be to set up ammo points to resup-ply the forward troops as they closed in on the enemy. He, too, described the clutter, wrecked vehicles and casualties as a distressing sight. "Once we got away from the beach, the better we could move around because it was not quite as sandy," he said. The urgency of efficient ammunition resupply for the forward troops who were in constant contact with the enemy was extremely important as they moved forward. "We set up ammo points near the airfield, which was further inland. Locating near the airfield would put us away from all the activity going on at the beach and closer to the forward units. For the duration of the battle, we worked from those positions."

He also remembers the day his unit left the island and where they went from there. "I remember that we left the island on the day President

Every trip ashore was filled with uncertainty as the DUKW drivers attempted to get their cargo and personnel ashore in the middle of continuous enemy fire. (National Archives)

Roosevelt died. We boarded a troop ship, and a special meal was prepared to celebrate his service as president." Cunningham believed that his unit was on its way back to the United States when they went aboard ship, but he soon realized that was not what would happen. "We stopped in Hawaii for more training and reloaded the ship, but instead of heading home, we went to mainland Japan to assist in the clean-up after the atomic bomb was dropped."

Horace Taylor saw, in the early stages of the assault, the Japanese effectively use their well-positioned firepower strategically imbedded in Mt. Suribachi to suppress the forward progress of the invading troops. "The Marine infantry was pinned down, and we had the responsibility to get our big guns, the 105 howitzers and their gun crews ashore in our DUKWs," he said. "The infantry could not move. Shortly after the first wave of assault troops made it to the shore, we were called to bring in the artillery on our DUKWs to provide the firepower to remove the enemy threat to the beach so that the infantry could move forward. When each DUKW went ashore, it would be directed to a location that had been designated for the gun we were carrying, and its crew," Taylor said. "There was a crane at each location to take the big artillery piece off of our DUKW and place it into position and after that was done, we would return to the ship for more ammunition to re-supply those units on the beach," he said. "After dropping ammunition off at the ammunition point, we would often pick up the wounded, and carry them to the hospital ship stationed offshore for treatment. We would take the wounded along with the medics, who would hold their IV tubes and care for them. We would leave the beach sometimes in rough water and sometimes under fire, make it out to the hospital ship, pull up alongside it and a crane would pull the entire DUKW up out of the water to the upper deck. Nurses and medics would be there to take the wounded aboard, then the crane would lower the DUKW back into the water so that it could continue its re-supply mission."

He recounted two events that he would never forget. "As our DUKW was departing the ship for one of our trips to shore, I noticed one of our DUKWs spinning around in the water; one of our drivers had lost control of his vehicle. I knew what the problem was," he said. "The rudder pin on the vehicle had come loose, and the driver could not control the vehicle. It was filled with cargo and personnel on its way to the beach. When me and my assistant driver saw what was happening, we pulled our DUKW alongside the disabled vehicle, tied it to ours and towed it back to its ship for repair." In the heat of battle, it is a likely assumption that the quick, heroic actions by him and his assistant driver saved the lives of the men on the disabled vehicle, and the equipment they were carrying to the beach. In an encounter with the enemy, another experience he says is indelibly imprinted in his mind, Taylor and his assistant driver once again exhibited extraordinary presence of mind in a tense situation. They skillfully piloted their DUKW ashore against heavy enemy fire, and made it to the beach without a single casualty. "We made that trip as an enemy pounded us with heavy machine gun fire shortly after we began a trip ashore on D-Day. We did not realize that their nest was directly ahead of us until they began firing," he said. Taylor and his assistant driver were two of three African Americans from his company awarded the third highest recognition for heroism in combat on Iwo Jima, the Silver Star Medal. Another Silver Star was awarded to a DUKW driver from his unit who was killed in action during the assault. "They called me and my assistant driver out in formation and presented us the medal while we were on Iwo Jima. There were no details, and I can't remember anything being said about why we received it, but I do believe that incident was the reason why we were awarded the medal. We were recognized again for receiving the medal at another ceremony when we returned home to Fort Bragg, North Carolina."

The African Americans who drove the DUKWs, according to Taylor, provided a strong link between the troops ashore and their logistical support aboard the ships at sea. He also recalls even having to rescue aviators who had to abandon damaged aircraft returning from bombing raids over Tokyo. "Sometimes B-29s that had been shot up so bad by anti-aircraft guns on mainland Japan after bombing missions, they would fly near Iwo Jima and bail out of their airplane. It could not land or make it back to their bases in Guam and Saipan. When we saw their parachutes, we would man our DUKWs, go out and rescue them and bring them ashore," he said.

Taylor's unit remained on Iwo Jima as part of the occupation force after the battle ended. He remembers that the water surrounding Iwo Jima was so deep that it was difficult to build piers and docks up to the beach to accommodate the huge LSTs and other supply ships supporting the occupation forces. "The DUKWs were used to accommodate the ship-to-shore operations, which included bringing troops or supplies ashore when conditions would not allow the huge supply ships to directly load their cargo at the pier or on the beach," said Taylor.

Arthur Peterson had serious concerns: amid all of the fighting, many of the men in the assault force would not make it ashore. "We could see bullets flying though the air. The smell of gunpowder was everywhere. I didn't think we were going to make it. It seemed like the deafening sound of big guns and bombs exploding would never end. When I did go ashore in the later waves, the ground was littered with so many more casualties than I thought I would see," he said.

He remembers that African Americans were a vital part of the battle. "If it had not been for us," he said, "our situation would have been worse. We were the main line of supply for the artillery units for the lead assault division and we did our job by bringing the ammunition and supplies they needed so that they could keep fighting. When the front line troops would call for supplies and ammunition, my unit would locate their position and dispatch the DUKW with what they needed. Those DUKW drivers were putting their lives on the line dodging enemy small arms fire, rockets, and artillery fire as they maneuvered around the island to make their deliveries and conduct supply operations ashore in the combat zone. Those drivers were a vital link between the troops ashore and the logistical support they needed to survive ashore, but recorded history has given them little credit for their service."

"After the battle my unit, along with other Army units stationed on ships offshore, came aboard the island after the Marines turned control of it over to the Army, and served as the occupation force until Iwo Jima was returned to the Japanese government," said Peterson. "My unit remained on Iwo Jima for about eight months after the battle ended as part of the allied occupation force." Peterson was able to leave the island earlier than many of the others in his company. His age and the fact that he had achieved the rank of first sergeant provided him with enough points to leave the island.

Sam Green, with his company, remained on Iwo Jima along with other Army units assigned occupation duties there after the island was taken. "We remained on the island after the Marines turned over control of it to the Army. For the most part, hostilities had ceased, and we basically performed the kind of duties we would in a garrison situation, such as training and performing ship-to-shore re-supply duties. For me though, my duties had changed because I had been promoted to platoon sergeant and instead of driving the DUKW, I became a troop handler," he said. During his stay on Iwo Jima after the departure of the Marines, he believed that another combat deployment was imminent. "We had been issued boots and cold weather gear because it was cold in mainland Japan. We were getting ready to go into Japan," he thought, "but the Japanese surrendered."

The successful emergency landing of the first battle-damaged United States Army Air Corps B-29 bomber on March 4, 1945, and the arrival of P-51 U.S. Army Air Corps fighters used for fighter escort missions were clear signs that the island was under the control of the invasion forces. On April 4, 1945, the U.S. Army's 147th Infantry Regiment assumed ground control of the island from the Marines. The Battle of Iwo Jima included the largest number of Marines committed to a single combat operation during World War II. The captured airfields at Iwo Jima saved many B-29 bomber crews from having to crash-land their battle-damaged planes in the sea. By the end of the war, 2,400 bombers carrying 27,000 crewmembers had made unscheduled emergency landings on Iwo Jima. The victory achieved by the United States forces during the battle was an extraordinary experience. It was well planned, supported, and coordinated against a highly disciplined enemy force determined to win at all costs.

Colonel Joseph H. Alexander, U.S. Marine Corps (Ret.) writes:

> African American troops played a significant role in the capture of Iwo Jima. Negro drivers served in the Army DUKW units active throughout the landing. Black Marines of the 8th Ammunition Company and the 36th Depot Company landed on D-Day, served as stevedores on those chaotic beaches, and were joined by the 33d and 34th Depot Companies on D+3. These Marines were incorporated into the VAC Shore Party which did Herculean work sustaining the momentum of the American drive northwards. When Japanese counterattacks penetrated to the beach areas, these Marines dropped their cargo, unslung their carbines, and engaged in well-disciplined fire and maneuver, inflicting more casualties than they sustained.

On March 17, 1945, Admiral Chester Nimitz, Commander of the United States Pacific Fleet, announced that Iwo Jima was secure and signaled the beginning of the stand down that would eventually see the Marines begin to leave the island. A determined enemy, however, was still active and casualties on both sides would continue even after Admiral Nimitz's announcement. Battle weary, starving and much smaller in number during the waning days of the battle, the enemy continued to demonstrate their resolve to fight to the end. There would be another 2,000 casualties after the announcement and before the Marines turned the island over to the Army.

Casualty counts reveal that 6,621 Americans died in that battle, 19,189 were wounded and 490 were missing in action. The casualty count for the Japanese defense force included 20,703 combatants who died there while American forces captured 216 prisoners of war during the battle. The highest award for valor that can be awarded to a United States military member in combat, the Medal of Honor, was awarded to 27 United States Marines and five United States Navy personnel for heroism during the Battle of Iwo Jima. More than 25 percent of the Medals of Honor awarded to Marines during World War II were for heroic actions on Iwo Jima.

A Flag of Hope

On February 23, 1945, the 3rd Platoon, E Company, 2nd Battalion, 28th Marines raised the first flag on the top of Mt. Suribachi. It was a small flag and was difficult to see from a distance. Commanders decided that a larger one would be more visible. The moment that flag was planted, Associated Press photographer Joe Rosenthal captured that famous scene of the flag raising. Of the six men in the picture, three (Franklin Sousley, Harlon Block, and Michael Strank) did not survive the battle for Iwo Jima; the three survivors (John Bradley, Rene Gagnon, and Ira Hayes) became celebrities upon their identification in the photograph. The photograph was later used by Felix de Weldon as a model to sculpt the USMC War Memorial, located adjacent to Arlington National Cemetery just outside Washington, D.C.

The battle was still underway when the flag was raised, but it was a morale booster for the invading forces on the island. For many of those who saw it going up from ships at sea and those who learned of it at home, it was a sign of hope and a sign that all of the sacrifices that made it happen were not made in vain. Joe Rosenthal captured that historical moment in history for all time on film. The planting of the American flag brought a

The raising of the Stars and Stripes atop Mt. Suribachi was a strong indication that the U.S. forces were making progress and served as an inspiration to troops on the island and those at home. (National Archives)

great swell of pride and exultation among Iwo Jima's combat-weary troops. Soon, those on the home front would be seeing Joe Rosenthal's photograph on billboards and in theaters and newspapers everywhere.

Roland Durden's unit did not go ashore on Iwo Jima until February 24th—the day after the flag was raised atop Mt. Suribachi. "I did see the flag flying on Mt. Suribachi," he said. "It was a sign that in spite of everything, we were making progress against the enemy." He also readily admitted that although the raising of the flag was an inspiration, the reality of the situation was that the battle was far from being over. But to millions around the world, at the time that iconic event offered a ray of hope that the battle would soon be over.

Durden did believe that the citizens on the home front would now have a reasonable expectation for victory not only on Iwo Jima but in the war in the Pacific as well. But to him, there was much more work to be done. "For those of us that were there, the nightmare continued," he said. He remembered, too, the jubilation and excitement of hearing the news of the Allied victory in Europe. He noted that there must have been the same kind of reaction in many parts of the world when the flag was raised on Iwo Jima. "There is a difference though, when you are face-to-face with the reality of things," he said. "We were still in the middle of a heated battle, it was not over yet. Casualties were still mounting and we were still burying our dead, still taking small arms fire and enduring rocket and mortar attacks. The horrors of war still surrounded us."

Archibald Mosley saw the Stars and Stripes go up on Mt. Suribachi. "When the guns went off as the flag was being raised, we could hear guys shooting and throwing their helmets up in the air. We thought it was all over, but it wasn't," he said. In the heat of battle it was difficult to determine, at least in the early going, how the war was progressing for many of the troops—they simply followed their orders. "We really had no idea of how the battle was progressing; we just continued doing our job until we knew for sure that it was really over. The raising of the flag was an indication that the battle might be winding down and that we had the upper hand, but the enemy was still very active," he said. "To see our flag flying atop Mt. Suribachi did seem to give the battle weary troops a sense of accomplishment and some feeling that we were making headway. We were still in the heat of battle, though, and after the flag was raised, we just went back to work. We did not have access to a situation report. The first real indication that the battle was beginning to change in our favor was when I began to notice fewer requests for the logistical services our unit had been providing," he said.

In a last ditch effort to repel the invaders, an organized attack by the Japanese was staged on United States troops occupying a temporary encampment near one of the airfields. Mosley and other African American Marines from the depot and ammunition companies were providing security for aircraft, supplies, and aviation personnel near the airfield. "We all thought that we would sleep well that night, but that was the night that the Japanese staged a Banzai attack on our location. It was a surprise attack, and it was repelled, but it did claim the lives of some of our troops bivouacked there." Japanese Banzai attacks, also known as suicide attacks, were used by Japanese soldiers en masse as a final effort to defeat their enemy.

Mosley feels that the battle was a harrowing experience for every man who was there. He also has concerns that African Americans and other support personnel did not receive recognition they should have in the historical documentation of the Iwo Jima battle. "The Marines who climbed Mt. Suribachi and raised the flag, along with many others who served on the front lines, went home to ticker tape parades everywhere, and were celebrated with parades and commendations, may not have climbed that mountain or won the war without the efforts of support personnel," he said.

Frederick Gray remembers the day that the flag was raised on Mt. Suribachi. "I saw it from my foxhole on that day," he said. "Fighting was still going on and continued for about another three weeks," he said. He would remain on the island for almost a year after the battle was over, serving as part of the occupation force. "I did travel the entire island, visit and stand on top of Mt. Suribachi after the fighting stopped," he said. He and friends would visit the caves and pillboxes that the Japanese had used during the battle. It was not until he had returned to the United States from Iwo Jima that he realized how close he had stood in harm's way on his visits to Mt. Suribachi. "After I had returned home, well after the war was over, I happened to read in the newspaper that 250 Japanese had been found still in those caves and tunnels of Mt. Suribachi. They did not know that the battle was over," Gray said.

Horace Taylor, too, remembers seeing the flag raised on Mt. Suribachi. "On one of my trips from the ship to the shore, I saw the flag going up, but I really did not know what was happening," he said. As he looked up at the top of Mt. Suribachi and witnessed that historic event, he was happy to see it. "We knew that the Marines were trying to make their way up the mountain, and I knew when I saw that flag that we were making progress." He complimented the Marine infantry in their efforts to take Iwo Jima. "One thing I admired about the Marines is that they fought hard. They did not give up." He too, however, was reminded that the battle was still underway. "I looked up to see the flag waving and while I was doing so, my vehicle took a hit. We were all ready for it to be over."

Sam Green also remembers seeing the flag raised on Iwo Jima and feeling the promise of victory it represented. Without question, he believed that the event was a tremendous morale booster for all of the men there and all of them felt good seeing the flag flying atop Mt. Suribachi. He too noted that every American involved in the battle pulled together as one to make that flag-raising happen and that that fact should be more prominently stated in the history books. Although there were racial issues at home, there were none on Iwo on that day or any other day that he could see while he was there. "We did not think of that," he said. "We got along just fine and did everything together. There may have been isolated racial incidents, but for the most part, it did not seem to be a problem."

PART THREE

BACK IN AMERICA

ON MARCH 26, 1945, THE GRUELING, costly, Battle of Iwo Jima was over. Admiral Chester Nimitz said, "The battle of Iwo Island has been won. The United States Marines by their individual and collective courage have conquered a base which is as necessary to us in our continuing forward movement toward final victory as it was vital to the enemy in staving off ultimate defeat. By their victory, the 3rd, 4th and 5th Marine Divisions and other units of the Fifth Amphibious Corps have made an accounting to their country which only history will be able to value fully. Among the Americans who served on Iwo Island, uncommon valor was a common virtue."

The battle was over and it made an indelible impact on a determined enemy who refused to give up. Though their numbers were significantly smaller than those of the Allies, they did have the advantage of preparing a defense on a desolate island that offered the assault troops little cover and concealment. That advantage was one on which they had planned to heavily rely in order to defend the island. U.S. strategists knew that a determined enemy with time to prepare would make it a difficult task for the invading forces. After-action reports indicate that the enemy's resolve and will to resist may have been underestimated. The death toll for the assault forces would be high for control of that island, so small and so far from the United States mainland. The Japanese were defiant in their defense of it, but the relentless assault by the United States forces would be victorious.

Although the battle for Iwo Jima was over, the war in the Pacific would continue until representatives of the Empire of Japan signed the instrument of surrender on September 2, 1945, aboard the USS *Missouri* on behalf of the Japanese government and the Emperor of Japan. With the exception of those who would remain in Japan with the occupation forces, the troops would be coming home, and a jubilant and grateful country awaited their return.

CHAPTER 6

Coming Home

WHILE MILLIONS OF OUR MEN and women were abroad during World War II, the United States moved away from a period during the Great Depression when a huge number of U.S. citizens were poor and out of work. The declaration of war with Japan after the bombing of Pearl Harbor and Germany's declaration of war on the United States energized an economy that was unlike any that the United States had never seen. Government spending helped to revitalize American industry and organized labor to the point that unemployment was almost unheard of and there were actually labor shortages in some industries. Veterans found a very different quality of life when they returned home. The wartime economy had stimulated new financial opportunities, a rise in home ownership, and the development of new technologies. The returning veterans would also see a work force with more women employed outside of the home than ever before as a result of men going off to war.

The large number of veterans returning to the work force included more African Americans than in any post-war period in United States history. As the mobilization for the war ended, many of them returned to civilian life. The entire country was jubilant and excited about the war's outcome and welcomed our service men and women home with parades and celebrations all over the country. The rationing, blackouts and other restrictions imposed to support the war effort were ending, and the war was over. However, there was very little fanfare or celebration for African American veterans when the war ended. The majority of them were not awarded medals for heroism on the front lines, and many returned to small communities where they were welcomed home by gatherings of friends and family.

Segregation had relegated most of the African Americans who served

The draft created a tremendous shortage of manpower to fill critical positions in the labor market. Many of the job vacancies created by men going off to war would be filled by women. (National Archives)

in the war to duties in the military that would not translate into profitable vocations in civilian life when they returned. The few good jobs that were available came with strong prerequisites which most African Americans had not had an opportunity to develop prior to or during the war. Because of advances in technology, new ways of doing business and the transition from rural to urban living, much of the demand for the type of labor so prominent in the United States prior to the war was giving way to a new, more educated work force. The GI Bill would provide college or vocational education for returning World War II veterans. Many African American GIs took full advantage of the bill as they prepared themselves for the emerging technical and diverse world in which they would live. The bill stimulated the enrollment in colleges, universities, and technical colleges that paved the way for ongoing significant increases in African American college enrollments. The government also offered returning veterans funds while they were looking for work under a program known as the 52–20 clause, which allowed all former servicemen to receive $20 once a week for 52 weeks a year, while they were looking for work. Some of the returning GIs did take advantage of the "52–20" club, as it came to be known, but most of that money was not distributed because most of the veterans either found work or went back to school. There was even a home loan guarantee offered for the veterans. The GI Bill had good intentions, but there was discrimination in buying homes and in gaining admittance to certain schools, especially in the South. For many African American veterans a still very segregated society would not allow them take advantage of all of the opportunities offered by the bill.

Strong civil rights activity, presidential executive orders and an emerging African American middle class were beginning to signal the demise of legal segregation in the United States in the post-war period. African Americans continued to migrate from the rural South to the urban North to improve their economic status. Income levels in African American families were increasing, but they were still far below those of whites. After having answered their country's call but being still relegated to second-class citizenship at home, protests among many former GIs for better employment opportunities sharply increased. Following the lead of civil rights groups of the time such as the Brotherhood of Sleeping Car Porters, the National Association for the Advancement of Colored People (NAACP), the Congress of Racial Equality (CORE) and African American newspapers such as the *Pittsburgh Courier*, African American veterans began to take a stronger stand against segregation and discrimination. Their concerns were heard. In 1947 at the NAACP convention, President Harry Truman and Mrs.

Eleanor Roosevelt took a stand for civil rights and Truman's Executive Order 9981 paved the way for the desegregation of the military while proactive steps taken by civil rights activists were major catalysts for integration in the United States armed forces in the late 1940s. Truman also formed a committee on civil rights after the war. Due to opposition by Southern politicians, recommendations made by the committee were slow to become law until the Civil Rights Act of 1964 was passed during President Lyndon Johnson's administration.

Roland Durden remembers well his return home from the war. "Getting work was difficult when I returned home. The war effort had wound down, all the big industrial plants were closing down; the war was over. The economy was struggling to recover from the closure of businesses, plants, and factories after the war, and there just weren't many jobs available. I delivered groceries down on Madison Avenue after the war, and I was also able to find another job working for a printing outfit delivering printed material." From his entry into the military he maintained that he wanted to have the opportunity to train in a skill that would be useful to him when he returned to civilian life. The priorities of war and the limited opportunities for African Americans serving in World War II would not give him those opportunities.

"The one smart thing that a lot of veterans did was go to college under the GI Bill but I did not do it," said Durden. "My grades in high school were not that great, but I believe that I could have made it through. I just did not take advantage of the opportunity." After struggling to find job opportunities that satisfied him, he began a career with the New York City Department of Transportation in 1949 and retired from there after 37 years of service.

Proud that he was one of the pioneers in the desegregation of the United States Armed Forces and that he was able to witness some very positive breakthroughs for all Americans no matter what race, creed or color, Durden said, "We are Americans, not just African Americans; and we, all Americans, should be allowed to serve and advance in the military and in the greater society according to our abilities."

Archibald Mosley came home when the war ended and used his benefits. "My intention was to go back home and resume my studies and finish college. I knew where I wanted to go, I wanted to get my divinity degree and become a clergyman and a college degree was a prerequisite for me to accomplish that goal. I doubled up on my coursework and accumulated enough coursework to complete the requirements for my college education and Bachelor of Theology degree at the same time." Mosley had high praise for the action on the part of the United States government to enact the GI Bill. "I took full advantage of it. Support from my family was limited and so were my personal resources. Without the GI Bill, I would not have gotten very far."

Mosley never considered himself a hero and never, in all the years since the war, considered the significance of his service as being anything more than a response to a call to duty. He maintains that he and all of the African Americans who participated in the battle of Iwo Jima played a significant part in the victory achieved there although history, for the most part, has kept their involvement in the shadows.

Charles Black, when the war ended, remained on Iwo Jima with the occupation forces and did not leave the island until the year after the battle ended. Looking back on the experience, he vividly recalls the horrors of war. "The smell of death is terrible. I saw a lot of bodies, both Japanese and American. When I think of it, I realize that there were many men left on that foreign soil. I often think that one of those men could have been me," he said.

Because he had accumulated enough points, Black was able to leave the island before many of the occupation troops with whom he was serving. As the hostilities ceased and garrison duties replaced the combat activity that had ravaged the island shortly before he left, he actually became attached to his surroundings. He remembers that some of his fellow servicemen formed a touch football league and that was one of his favorite pastimes. His team was up for the championship and he admits that he pondered the idea of remaining on the island to see the season through. "Our team had just tied for the lead among the teams on the island and I wanted to be there to see if we would have won, but I just could not turn down this chance to go home," he said.

On February 1, 1946, he boarded a troop ship bound for San Francisco to be discharged and returned home. "When I got off the ship, I kissed the ground I had missed and loved. I was returning to the world that I had learned to appreciate, and hoping to God that we would always have peace. I was fortunate to have been able to resume my position in the federal government and retire with 37 years of service. When asked whether or not he considered his extraordinary experience to be special in any way, he simply said, patriotically, like the others interviewed for this book, "I did what my country called upon me to do."

Frederick Gray, like most of the veterans returning home after the war, was discharged. He too remained on the island for 13 months after the battle as part of the occupation forces and was one of the last men in the 476th Amphibian Truck Company to leave the island. Gray, like some of his fellow soldiers, said that age, marital status, time in the service, etc., dictated the number of points a soldier would accrue. "Most of the older fellows in our company left shortly after the Japanese surrendered," he said. "The younger fellows, like me, had to stay on the island until we had earned the necessary points to leave. I was promoted to company first sergeant and became the senior ranking man in the group left behind; I had a large part to play in closing down the company. I left the island in March of 1946 when the 476th was disbanded to return home and was released from active duty. I went home and began working again with my daddy to build houses in Calvert County. I also served as a police officer with the Washington, D.C., Metropolitan Police Department, and retired as a construction representative with the National Park Service."

Eugene Doughty and his officers believed that he had the leadership skills and other qualities to become a career Marine. "I was asked by my commanding officer to remain in the Marine Corps after the war. He thought I was a good Marine and that I had good leadership qualities. I believe that was the reason I was promoted to sergeant," said Doughty. He had other plans, however. "My immediate task," he said, "was to return to school. In that regard, I took complete advantage of the GI Bill and did just that." He did recall that some of the returning veterans were having a difficult time finding employment upon their return. "I had friends and relatives who had nothing to support them in finding a job. They had no vocation to support themselves and a very difficult time getting into college. In that regard, they could not take advantage of the tuition assistance program; they did not have the skills to compete in the job market, and no financial backing to take advantage of the home loan guarantee. Some of them, however, did take participate in the 52–20 club to obtain some financial assistance," said Doughty. "I was fortunate to have had a vocation and a part-time job that helped to support me along with the GI Bill while I was attending school."

Ellis Cunningham, unlike many of those who participated in World War II, remained in the Marine Corps and retired as a first sergeant on March 18, 1970, with 26 years of service in the Marine Corps. Along with his service in World War II, he is a veteran of the Korean War and the Vietnam War as well. As he looks back over the years since he returned home from the war, he believes that participation in the war opened the doors to opportunities for African Americans that had previously been closed to them. "Black Americans proved their value to our country and President Truman saw it as well." He believes that the president's efforts with respect to the Executive Order he signed that led to the desegregation of the armed forces, are a testimony to that.

Horace Taylor remained on Iwo Jima with the occupation forces for seven months after the Iwo Jima victory. Troop strength grew smaller and smaller after the Japanese surrender, but when he could do so, he, like all of the others in his company, took full advantage of the point system to come home. "I left Iwo Jima on Christmas Eve of 1945," said Taylor. "The Silver Star afforded me enough points to leave earlier than many of my buddies. I came home on the World War II aircraft carrier, USS *Bunker Hill*." The *Bunker*

After returning from World War II, Ellis Cunningham would remain in the Marine Corps and retire with 26 years of service at the rank of first sergeant.

Hill, highly decorated for its participation in the Pacific campaign, was a huge vessel capable of carrying many troops and was one of the many ships tasked with bringing our troops home from battlegrounds in the Pacific. "When I left Iwo Jima, I went to Saipan and joined up with many other servicemen coming back at the same time who had been stationed at other locations in the Pacific. The ship was crowded with troops when we returned home," he said. "Then, on a troop train, I returned home to Fort Bragg, North Carolina." Even though he had spent nearly a year living in a foxhole, had participated in one of the bloodiest battles in United States history, and had been awarded one of the highest awards for valor, he clearly remembers returning home to racial segregation. "As we came back home on the train, they did not allow us to eat or stop in Southern towns. They just pulled the window shades down and went full speed ahead and did not stop. Usually, they would stop and allow the troops to get off after traveling for long periods of time and we were allowed to exercise or stretch our legs, but we did not stop in certain areas because things were bad for black soldiers," Taylor said. "That is the way it was, and there was nothing I could do about it. I was just going to move on and do the best I could." When he returned from the war, he went back to his home in Seneca, South Carolina, but moved north shortly thereafter. "After a short visit at home, I moved to Washington, D.C., and I have been here since then. I went to work for the government at the Naval Surface Warfare Center in the District of Columbia, and I retired from there in 1983."

As he reflects on the value of his service and the effect it had on the generation that has followed his, he believes that it has had a positive impact. He does not believe that many who are enjoying the freedoms they have today truly understand the sacrifices that many who came before them endured so that those who are enjoying them now could do so. In retrospect, he believes that in some way, what he and thousands of United States military men did on Iwo Jima in 1945 had something to do with the prosperity and freedom our citizens have enjoyed since World War II.

Arthur Peterson was among the first of those allowed to leave Iwo Jima. His age and rank were significant in determining the points he would receive. "I left the island by ship and went to California where I was discharged from the Army after the war ended in 1945." Even though he was part of a segregated unit, he was proud to have had the opportunity to serve his country. When he returned, he resumed his civilian working career after enduring an extraordinary experience that most Americans can only imagine. He worked as an insurance agent and retired 20 years later. "I felt it was my duty to do my part as an American citizen to help protect our country and I feel that the service of the African Americans during World War II opened the eyes of many people, black and white, and has drawn us closer together." Though he believes that we are not where we need to be with respect to race relations, Peterson believes that the war marked a turning point in race relations in the United States. "Whites saw that we could handle ourselves in combat and stand up in battle as well as any man. I believe that before the war they did not think that we could handle ourselves the way we did in combat."

Haywood Johnson returned home as a corporal and was separated from the Army at Fort Meade, Maryland. He feels fortunate that he was able to return to the job he had before he was drafted into the Army. "In some parts of the country, there were riots and problems because some African

American veterans could not get jobs and they believed that they had earned the right to fair treatment," he said. The Iwo Jima experience had a significant impact on his life. "I developed a higher value for everything in general, and especially life itself, and a strong regard for my country that I am not sure I had before the Iwo Jima experience." He also believes that in some small way he did have a part in paving the way for African Americans that would follow. "After the war, I recall seeing an African American Navy admiral, and I had never seen an admiral before," he said. "We could not have imagined such a thing when I was in the service, and it made me smile."

Sam Green left Iwo Jima in 1946. "We left the island for Saipan on a small ship. Enroute, we had nothing but rough seas that made us all sick. In Saipan we boarded a larger troop ship and returned home. Our first stop was San Francisco. I remember seeing German prisoners, again, who were working in kitchens eating steaks, and we had to eat the same government-issued C-rations we ate on Iwo Jima. Then we all got on a troop train. All of us were together—blacks and whites together—and we came on back to Fort Smith, Arkansas. When we got off the train, the whites were told to stand together in one place and the blacks were told to stand in another location. That really got to me. On Iwo Jima, we laughed together, slept in the same foxholes, and played cards together all the way back home. After that experience, some of the whites came over and talked to me and told me how terrible the whole thing was." Two years later, President Truman signed the Executive Order that led to the desegregation of the armed forces.

Lyman Brent also left the island of Iwo Jima in 1946. "We went by ship to San Pedro, California, and from there to Tyler, Texas, by train to be discharged. While on furlough in New Orleans after my return, I was standing in line at a bus station and a white soldier came up to me and got in front of me and said, 'get in the back.' The result of that was an altercation which was broken up by the military police." Upon the return of our troops, the anomaly of racism continued. When they were on Iwo Jima fighting for a common cause, it was one for all and all for one, without regard for cultural or ethnic differences.

Brent entered the work force when he was discharged and took advantage of the GI Bill and went back to school. "I went to work operating machinery for a short period of time just after I was discharged, and I went back to finish high school and then to Southern University in Baton Rouge, Louisiana, where I studied auto mechanics. I was offered a job in my hometown to teach at a trade school, but I did not take it because I had another offer to work at Southern University taking care of all of the school vehicles and I took that. I eventually retired from Southern University as maintenance assistant superintendent."

The African American men who served in the battle of Iwo Jima are a rare breed. They were born and reared in various parts of the country, and they came from a variety of backgrounds, but their family life and their values are amazingly similar. They were born in a time when segregation was a way of life here in the United States and opportunities to develop to their fullest potential were not an option for them. They had to live within the confines of the rules of the society in which they lived.

CHAPTER 7

Life after Iwo Jima

CHARLES BLACK CAME BACK FROM Iwo Jima after being discharged from the Army in 1946 and returned to the job he had left behind when he was drafted into military service. "I had worked for the government for about 18 months as a messenger for the Department of the Army before I went into military service. My service time and the fact that I had been drafted gave me an advantage when I came back and started looking for employment," he said. "So when I came back and checked with my previous employer, I found that all I had to do was report back to work. I was fortunate—because as the war was winding down there were people out of work and being laid off everywhere. Veterans had preference. Having that military service was a definite benefit for me when I came home. Without military preference, I could very well have been one of those in the employment line struggling to find a job."

"I came out of the military with a new perspective on life. I was younger when I went in and the two years I spent in the Army helped me to refocus on the way I wanted to spend the rest of my life," he said. His priority when he was discharged was to readjust to civilian life and meet that special someone to spend the rest of his life with. "I had a girlfriend before I went into service, but that was not the case when I returned home. So I had to renew my search to find that special someone," he said. "Shortly after I came home from the war I met the lady who would become my wife. After we got married, we had two children, a son and a daughter. The home we are living in now is our third residence and we have been living here since 1959."

As he reflects on his military service, he knew that he more than likely would be drafted. There was no question in his mind as to whether or not he would serve if called. He did believe that it was the duty of everybody to support the war effort. He wanted to be a productive citizen and he knew, too, that more than likely meant service in the military. The country was at war, and he was 18. It was the early 1940s, and all 18 year olds were eligible for the draft. He had not finished high school when he was inducted, but had dropped out of school to enter the world of work. When he finished his military service and reentered the work force, one of his goals was to get his high school diploma. He did just that by successfully completing the high school equivalency exam, and in doing so, opened a door that would serve him well in his civil service career with the Army. "My job was clerical, and I was a clerk mainly in the officer's branch and was part of a team that monitored Army officers' records. We monitored all aspects of their careers including their assignments, schooling, and so on and ensured that everything they did during their Army service was a matter of record. I worked there until I retired in 1982," he said. He remembers, however, that for two years, he worked in the enlisted branch monitoring records and careers there as well. "My duties there involved monitoring records and making recommendations for assignments to Vietnam. We carefully monitored records to ensure that we did not recommend soldiers for repeat tours of duty there."

Having worked in the Department of Defense for his entire working career, he has seen firsthand the barriers that supported the institution of segregation fade away little by little over the 64 years since he left active duty in the Army. But mental images of the way it was when he was on active duty are still with him. "When I now see military men and women together, I no longer see all white or all black units but rather an integrated unit working and serving together like we never saw when I was in the Army." Even in Washington, D.C., where he was born and raised, he remembers the kind of mandated segregation that he does not see now. It was worse, he believes, in other areas of the country than it was in Washington, D.C. It was the nation's capital, but there was no question that segregation existed there as well. "We were able to move around and participate in certain activities but we, like the blacks who lived in the South, oftentimes had to sit in balconies at the theater and were not allowed to go certain places," he said. One of the strongest indications that the barriers of segregation were indeed beginning to fall was the creation of equal opportunity offices. The purpose of these offices was to foster an environment that offers all employees an opportunity to progress in the work force to the limits of their potential. At one point, while working for the Department of the Army in its National Guard bureau, Black was assigned duties in the Guard's equal opportunities office. He had mixed emotions about his duties there. "I did work there, but for me personally, I did not feel comfortable in that job. I would much rather have been in a position to be more effective at making input to the process rather than serving as its administrator."

Black's career in military and civil service reflected a very successful career progression. He dropped out of high school during World War II and took a job as a messenger. He entered the military, and in two years attained the rank of sergeant, returned to civil service and retired with a federal government General Schedule pay scale (GS) rating of 11. The GS includes most professional, technical, administrative, and clerical positions in the federal civil service. He remembers that the journey was not always easy. "There was a point in time when minorities were more or less suppressed in some of the offices I worked. They were kept below a

The war effort produced the beginnings of equal opportunities for all Americans. Government initiatives and civil rights activists demanded it. President Lyndon Johnson signed the Civil Rights Act of 1964 and made it the law. (National Archives)

certain grade level. Most of us were no higher than GS-5 on the General Schedule pay scale. When things began to change as the civil rights movement began to have an effect on discriminatory practices, more of us began to make higher ratings." He vividly remembers when things began to change for minorities. "I can still see myself working in offices where I was the only black person there or one of a very few. Before that, everybody in the room was white." Black feels that once he was able to get into job situations that offered upward mobility, he took full advantage of the opportunity.

The struggle for equality was a hard one. Segregation, he believed, was simply based on a mindset that evolved out of slavery. He had hoped that the service of the African Americans in the military would dispel the concept more quickly than it did. The civil rights activities did not cease with the end of World War II, they continued into the 1950s and 1960s. Although support from the government declined, significant events did occur that laid the groundwork for the total integration of the armed forces: the landmark *Brown vs. Board of Education* decision, the historic March on Washington in 1963, and the Civil Rights Act of 1964. He readily admits that he was not directly involved in the demonstrations, but he remembers it all. "I am not a marcher, but I wholeheartedly supported the activity," he said. "The crowds and marchers do get attention and can be instrumental in getting decision makers to the table, but it is what happens there that is most important. We wanted equality, and the civil rights activists were doing everything they could to make it happen. Separation of the races was wrong, and I think that what they were doing was right on target. Not only was it for the good of our race, it was good for all of us," he said. "We really appreciated and supported the work they did to get to where we are today."

His life after Iwo Jima has been a rewarding one. "I have enjoyed my family and such activities as tutoring in the schools, exercising, and gardening," he said. As a high school dropout, the future was bleak for him but he took every advantage of every opportunity to rise above what was a very difficult start in life. As he thinks back on his experience on Iwo Jima, he is grateful that he lived through it and was able to make it home. "On almost any day, any hour, minute or second a stray bullet or exploding shell could have ended any life in the combat zone. I could not help but think about survival. So many of those who landed on the beach at Iwo did not survive, and many of those who did come back have had health issues and problems related to their service there. I can't help but think that I could have been in that number. To be able to come back from combat and have no lasting effects is indeed a blessing. I am so glad, happy, blessed and thankful that I survived it all and was able to come back home safely."

Ellis Cunningham was the only one of the 11 Iwo Jima veterans interviewed for this book who remained in the military and made it a career. He retired from the Marine Corps with 26 years of service. "I made up my mind before I even returned to the states that I wanted to stay in. While my unit was in Guam, I signed up to stay in even before I returned to the States," he said. "When we reached California, everybody was trying to figure out what they were going to do next, but I knew what I was going to do, I had already reenlisted to stay in. While most of the others were mustering out or trying to get home, I just became part of the crowd and waited for the train ride back to Montford Point, which would be my next duty station."

He had no idea what he would actually do as a Marine; he had been an ammo handler on Iwo Jima. "At Montford Point the bulk of the guys coming back home were being discharged, but I got a two month furlough and went home," Cunningham said. African Americans had never served on active duty in a peace time Marine Corps. Other than the locations where they had been deployed for short periods of time, Montford Point had been home for them when they were stationed in the United States during the war.

Segregation was still the policy in the military after the war was over and except for special deployments all African American Marines were permanently stationed at Montford Point and were not assigned to any other Marine Corps posts or stations. "When we would leave Montford Point and return from temporary duty assignments, they would make work for us to do," he said. "I was happy, though, to see that an anti-aircraft artillery outfit was being formed. It existed in name only, and they did not have the people to assign to it right away. It would be commanded by a white officer, but the enlisted personnel would be black Marines," Cunningham said. "I was one of the Marines assigned to the new unit and when I reported in, the commanding officer asked me what I wanted to do. I told him that I wanted to be the individual that pulled the lanyard that fired the shell from the big 90 millimeter gun. But I never had the opportunity to fire the first shot because a new detachment was being formed at a naval ammunition depot in Oklahoma, and Marines from Montford Point would be sent there to join the unit and I was one of them," he said. "Forty-five of us were sent to the depot to join another group of African Americans already there.

"It was a very large depot, and there was some very sophisticated ammunition stored there. I became part of a guard detail that stood watch over the depot. It was out in the middle of nowhere, and I stayed in Oklahoma for two years." Since returning home from the war, Cunningham had spent nearly all of his time in the Marine Corps standing guard duty, and now he was being transferred back to Montford Point not really sure where he would be assigned. "When I arrived there, I was not immediately put to work; I was sent home on furlough again.

"When I returned to Montford Point from furlough, they needed about the same number of people to do the same thing we did in Oklahoma. We would stand guard duty at another ammunition depot in New Jersey," he said. "We went there at a time when they had a snowstorm that was one of the worst ones there in many, many years," he said. Having been reared in South Carolina and having served in the military in warmer climates, he had never experienced weather like he was introduced to on his first trip north. "The whole area was covered in knee-deep snow. We had vehicles, though, that could get through it." He did not stay in New Jersey very long;

In the Marine Corps from 1942 until 1949 African American troops would serve in segregated units at Montford Point, but that would change in 1949 when the camp was closed after President Truman issued Executive Order 9981 to desegregate the military (National Archives).

the group of 45 men of which he was a part, was replaced by another group and once again he returned to Montford Point. "Some of our group members somehow got into trouble. What they did, I do not know, but our entire group was returned to Montford Point as a result of it. When we got back to Montford Point, I was assigned to the rifle range," he said.

Upon his return to Montford Point this time, Cunningham began to notice other changes in the Marine Corps regarding assignment and opportunities for African Americans. "It became a requirement in 1949 that written examinations would be the basis for promotion to all enlisted ranks throughout the Marine Corps, regardless of color. I was one of the first blacks to take the test when it was given at Montford Point. The white guys sat beside the black guys, and everybody took the same test," he said. "When the results of the test came back, there were only six corporals at Montford Point who made the score to be promoted to sergeant in my group, and I was fortunate to be one of those six people. I had been a corporal since 1944, and now I would make sergeant. I was happy about that." Along with the written examination requirement, Cunningham remembers that another significant barrier to equal opportunity in the Marine Corps begin to disappear. "Before 1949, black Marines could not be put in a position to supervise whites who held a lower rank than they did, but in 1949 that all changed," he said. Before that change, promotion and opportunities to enter other military specialties were limited for African Americans. "Until then, there was nothing else I could do to move up. My only option was to get out of the Marine Corps, and I did not want to do that."

"When I was promoted, I was working at the rifle range at Camp Lejeune where all Marines at the base qualified with firearms, but all of the black Marines were still housed at Montford Point. In 1949, after Montford Point was closed as a training base, I was transferred to Hadnot Point, which is where the base headquarters was located at Camp Lejeune," he said. President Truman's Executive Order to end segregation in the military caused actions to be taken that began a process that saw the beginning of the end for segregation in the military. One of the first efforts on the part of the Marine Corps to adhere to the spirit of the order was the closure of the segregated training camp at Montford Point. Cunningham recalls that there were remnants of segregation that did surface, however, after the segregated training facility at Montford Point was closed as a training facility. "There were certain posts where black Marines were not assigned. Some of the white officers and noncommissioned officers would select guard posts for the black Marines so that they would be out of sight. Montford Point had been turned into a supply base and the guards on duty there were mostly black Marines." He recalls an incident involving a conflict between him and a senior noncommissioned officer, which resulted in his commanding officer assigning him to be the first African American Marine as a sergeant-of-the-guard at the main post at Camp Lejeune. "They transferred me to a different barracks where there were five sergeants; I was the sixth and I was the only black one. That was the first time that had ever happened." he said. "I had been put in a huge guard company which provided guards to all of the base activities except Montford Point. As sergeant of my guard detachment, I had several lower-ranking Marines reporting to me and they were all white.

On June 25, 1950, the North Koreans suddenly attacked South Korea shortly after he had assumed his new assignment. The United States would once again commit troops to an armed conflict overseas and Ellis Cunningham would be one of them. On this deployment he would be assigned to an integrated infantry unit. An enemy bullet disabled him shortly after he went ashore in Korea. "I was only on the ground for eight days and I was hit," he said. "Almost immediately, I was medically evacuated to the naval hospital in Charleston, S.C." While he was recuperating from his wounds, he was promoted to staff sergeant and was awarded the Purple Heart for being wounded in action. After he was discharged from the hospital, he again returned to Camp Lejeune and reported to the rifle range for duty. He had witnessed and been a part of some significant positive changes in race relations in the Marine Corps, but one day while he was working on the range detail, he heard racial slurs directed toward some African American Marines who were working on the range. Although tremendous strides were being made to improve race relations in and out of the military, that incident reminded him that there was still a ways to go.

Cunningham continued to be a pioneer in the integration of the enlisted ranks of the Marine Corps. When he was transferred from Camp Lejeune, his next assignment would be sea duty, where he was promoted to his next rank. When the Continental Congress called for the establishment of the United States Marine Corps on November 10, 1775, the primary duty of the Marine Corps was to serve as "Soldiers of the Sea" on board naval warships. Sea duty has always been considered special duty and those assigned to it were considered to be exemplary Marines. "I was promoted to gunnery sergeant after I was transferred to the aircraft carrier, USS *Coral Sea,* and served as the senior enlisted man for the Marine detachment," he said.

He was again reassigned to Korea after the conflict there ended and upon his return to the United States, he spent several years at Marine Corps Base Camp Pendleton and Twentynine Palms, California. It was when he returned to Camp Lejeune as an instructor at the infantry training regiment that he would be promoted to first sergeant. He believes that his time at the training regiment was one of his best assignments. "I always considered myself to be a gung ho, take charge Marine and I enjoyed working with those young new Marines," he said. "After that I was promoted to first sergeant and received orders to report to an infantry unit in Vietnam. I spent a year there and when I returned to the States in 1970, I retired from the Marine Corps."

Cunningham believes that there has been a great deal of change in the armed forces and in our greater society since he began his military career and returned home from Iwo Jima. "It seems unreal," he said. "I hear military personnel coming back from the conflicts today, and they talk about how many times they have come home and returned for another tour of duty. When we went over to Iwo Jima, there was no such thing as multiple tours of duty and there was no thought of coming home, we stayed until the job was done." As he compares the Marine Corps of today with the Marine Corps in which he served, he is most impressed with the new technology and sophisticated equipment that has been introduced into our military inventory. "I look at the weapons that our forces are using nowadays. They are a tremendous improvement over what we had to use." He, too, remembers the time when there were no African Americans serving in the Marine Corps, and now the number of African American Marines in all ranks from private to lieutenant general is something he thought he would never see.

When he retired from the Marine Corps, Cunningham began another career. He worked for 21 years in the Charleston, S.C., public transportation system and became a major spokesperson for the Transportation Workers Union. In his military and civilian career, he has noted significant sociological changes in our country and believes we are headed in the right direction, but there is more to be done. He believes that many of the ingrained and embedded attitudes that hamper the process of harmonious coexistence must change before we can get there. As he takes note of how far our country has come during his lifetime, he firmly believes that as future generations reflect on the times in which we are living, they will wonder why racism, bigotry and segregation ever existed.

Roland Durden did not have enough points to return home after the battle at Iwo Jima. He remained overseas with his unit to assist in occupation duties on mainland Japan and did not have an opportunity to take part in all the celebrations in honor of the returning veterans. He did, however, have some few friends and family members waiting when he returned. "I did have my mother and an uncle to welcome me home and I was well received by them," he said. The industrial war machine that had offered tremendous employment opportunities during the war had shut down for the most part or was in the process of doing so. "My first income was the money I collected from the 52–20 club. When I returned home, the war had been over for several months. All of the good employment opportunities had been taken by those who were able to get back as soon as the war ended. It took a while, but eventually I did get a job with a magazine printer. It was a very small business and had only one employee. At the time, it was the best I could do."

Competition was keen for the few jobs that were available. Many of the returning African American veterans from the rural South moved north to the large urban areas in search of employment. "At that time, African Americans were referred to as Negroes or colored," said Durden. He believed that the odds were against him finding a good job to support him and take care of his mother, who was not well. "The money I was making with the printer was not nearly enough for us to live on comfortably. When the printing shop went out of business, I took another job delivering groceries to vendors on the street," he said. Two years after he had returned home unable to find suitable employment, things started to change for him. "I applied for a job at the board of transportation to serve as a conductor with the city subway system. My application was reviewed and shortly after that, I was called to take a test and I passed it," he said. His new job made him an icon in the community. He wore a uniform as a conductor and drew a lot of attention from people who saw him wearing it. He wanted to learn a skill when he went into the Marine Corps, but that would not happen for him. However, he did leave Iwo Jima with some lessons for life that would take him on a successful career path that he never expected. He was a bright student in school, and his superiors in the military realized his potential. They assigned him duties and jobs at which he consistently performed well. In a segregated environment, however, the options for the kind of duties that would have helped him develop the skills he sought when he entered the military were limited. Although he was not able to accomplish that, he believes that he did develop qualities and basic values in the military that would eventually make him successful in later life.

Becoming a conductor in charge of a train with the job to check tickets, announce stops, and attend to passengers' needs and safety with the New York subway system was his first opportunity since high school to do something other than manual labor. He was excited to have the chance to begin what he considered a meaningful career, and his new job as a conductor was only the first in a series of promotions that would lead to the satisfying work experience he wanted. "After a while, I took the test to become a motorman with the subway system. I was assigned to drive the 'A' train. Instead of taking fares and announcing stops, I became the person who was driving the train, and I loved the job," he said. Music, the arts, and theater were always among his favorite pastimes. As he piloted his train through the underground tunnels of New York City, he often thought about the song made popular by Duke Ellington and Ella Fitzgerald entitled "Take the A Train" and found himself, on many occasions, singing it between stops on his route. Having always wanted to achieve the level of responsibility that he enjoyed as a motorman, he was extremely satisfied with the job. "At my position I was alone and in control of a ten car train, often with as many as 2,000 passengers. As a young man in my early 20s, I considered that to be a huge responsibility." Another promotion was in store for him. "I also passed the test for train dispatcher and was offered an opportunity to become one. I took the offer. Things were looking up for me, and I had a little more authority. I had to report the condition of trains and determine whether there were any problems with them," he said. "I do believe that my military service and the experience on Iwo Jima helped me, because it, in many ways, helped to introduce me to some of the realities of life and instill within me, without me realizing it, the discipline and qualities to make it."

Durden often thinks about the way it was for African Americans in World War II, and as he looks back on the 64 years since he was discharged, he readily admits that he has seen some striking changes. He, too, commented on the progress the military has made in recent years in race relations. "I read recently that more blacks were being promoted to higher ranks in all services than I could have imagined when I was in the military. I did manage to make it to the rank of corporal, but there were not nearly the amount of blacks in the military serving in the higher ranks that I have seen in recent years," he said. "This generation of military men and women are recruited and serve in very different ways than we did. Recruiting is a big business and the services make it look good to young men and women. Young military people of today have many more career options in today's military than we could have ever hoped to have," he said.

Like all of the 110,000 U.S. troops who served on the battlefield on Iwo Jima, Roland Durden and the other nearly 1,000 African Americans who were there with him on Iwo Jima stood in harm's way, but historical accounts in books, movies, articles, and reports of their participation in that epic battle are scarce. And like Durden, the other African Americans who served there feel the same way. "Although we did not fight on the front lines, our jobs were necessary and had to be done but the reports going home excluded us," he said. "When they dedicated the cemetery where my unit worked and raised the flag, we were taken away and did not participate in the ceremony. Although the Battle of Iwo Jima stands as a symbol of World War II and is recognized as an event that contributed to the lifestyle and freedoms that we enjoy today, accounts of it, for the most part, do not indicate that we were even there." It was many years after his service on Iwo Jima that he received a very special "thank you" for his service. "It happened when I attended a rally at a local college for the then presidential candidate Obama. I was wearing my "Iwo Jima" cap. I believe, for that reason, the

There is little documentation of the service of African Americans on Iwo Jima. "Although we did not fight on the front lines, our jobs were necessary and had to be done, but the reports going home excluded us," said Roland Durden. (National Archives)

campaign workers offered me a special seat near where Mr. Obama was delivering his campaign speech. After his speech, Mr. Obama began to move through the crowd, and when he approached me and saw my hat, he extended his hand. I reached out shook it, and he said, 'Thank you, sir, for your service.' It was a very special thank you that I will always remember."

Eugene Doughty was heartily welcomed by close friends and family from the war. "I was able to return home sooner than some of the others because I had enough points to do so. I had enlisted in 1943 and my time in service allowed for more points than some of the younger troops," he said. "The war had been over less than a year when I did return home, and I was able get a feel for the excitement and appreciation that the home front was feeling for our victory in the war more than many of those who would return later," he said. The famous boxer Sugar Ray Robinson served in World War II, and Doughty believed that many people thought that he had a strong physical resemblance to him. "As I walked the streets of New York in my uniform, I was often mistaken for him," said Doughty.

"Many of the people that I had known before the war had moved to other parts of the city and the parades and celebrations were over, but those who were still there were very happy to see me and quickly helped me realize that I had changed in ways I had not realized," he said. "I was met with comments such as, 'Is it really you, Gene?' 'Gee whiz,' some of them said, 'I have never seen a black Marine—especially one wearing three stripes,'" he said. "Hearing those comments made me feel like a giant. After all, being face-to-face with death on a daily basis, it was good to know that our service was appreciated, and it was good to be home," he said. "The first thing many of them asked me was 'Were you on Iwo Jima?' And realizing that I had served with the largest number of blacks to serve in history, they all wanted to know how we were received and treated when we went down South. Mail was scarce when I was overseas and the family had not heard much from me from the time I left home until I returned from Iwo and it was difficult to keep them informed on what was really going on. I assumed that the people back home did not know much about what we were doing, but from the questions I was getting when I returned, I was surprised that the people back home knew as much about it as they did. They were well aware of the number of lives that were lost and the struggle, and of what had been going on than I thought they could be," he said.

"I was attending college when I entered the Marine Corps but determined to get my degree at as soon as I could," he said. Although he was proud of his service and had made a strong, positive impression on his superiors during his service, the decision to return to college was one he would choose when his enlistment was up. "When I was about to be released, the officers around the camp and those who knew me really tried to get me to stay in," he said. Doughty believed that his superiors felt that he would be an asset to the Marine Corps and an inspiration to young Marines, black and white, as they began their training and service. "The general feeling was that the Marines did not want to lose any talent that had the potential to mold new recruits into good Marines," he said. "They would often say to me, 'You are already a sergeant and you have a good opportunity to achieve much more in the Marine Corps.' At times, I did feel that I would like to have stayed and perhaps, in due time become, an officer. They did everything to encourage me to remain in the Corps, but, again, I really wanted to earn my degree in college and make the contributions to the welfare of six brothers and sisters back home that I felt I needed to," Doughty said.

As he looks back on it, Doughty truly believes that his military service has been extremely valuable to him. "It really prepared me well for adulthood. When I went in, I was just a kid but when I came out, I felt as though I had learned enough to say that I did that," said Doughty. Three of the most important lessons he believes that he learned during his military service and carried into a very successful career outside of the military were commitment, dedication to the task at hand and a respect for others. "Those qualities have enhanced my ability to successfully interact with practically everyone I meet, whoever they are. I could see it in the way people related to me, especially the ones who knew me before I went into the Marine Corps," he said. He truly believed that his compassion for people and the organizational and leadership skills that he developed in the military prepared him well for the world of work as a civilian.

The strong, imposing figure of the man that Doughty was while serving in the military and on Iwo Jima some 64 years ago is still a very big part of his personality. Doughty's demeanor has earned a great deal of respect over the years from many who know him. Although he was only an active duty Marine for three years, Doughty has been and will be a Marine for life.

Doughty remembers his second job out of college as a social caseworker for the New York Department of Social Services with a great deal of sympathy and compassion. "My return to City College of New York was my goal after my discharge, and I wanted to go into health and physical education. For a short time after I had completed my college studies, I actually went into health and physical education, but I eventually moved into the field of social services and spent six years as a social investigator with the city of New York. That position did not pay very well, but I learned so much going into the homes of people and helping them to become productive citizens. It touched me to my heart to see the conditions under which some had to live," said Doughty. He also served as recreation director for the New York Police Department and worked at Sears Roebuck & Co., where he was a manager of one of Sears' retail communication divisions in New York City.

One of the strongest ties he still has to the Marine Corps is his alliance to the Montford Point Marine Association. Doughty has served as national president, for two terms, of the Montford Point Marine Association; he currently serves as its national scholarship program director. The association's stated creed is "To promote and preserve the strong bonds of friendship born from shared adversities and to devote ourselves to the furtherance of these accomplishments to ensure more peaceful times." The organization supports educational assistance programs, veterans programs, and community services. He is held in high regard for all the work that he had done with the association. He remembers a conversation with the association's president, whom he succeeded. "When I was serving as vice president of the Montford Point Marine Association, I remember the president complimenting me on my organizational skills. He said that he was glad that I was his vice president and that he was impressed by my ability to get things done and that he wanted me to serve on his executive committee." Doughty accepted the offer and went on to serve multiple terms as the association's president.

In comparing the military of today with the one in which he served, he sees significant change. "It has grown in many ways, and it continues to maintain a defense posture that is second to none. With regard to the cooperation among the races, one only has to walk the streets, visit the park, or just go anywhere and cultural diversity can be seen everywhere. I have been called upon on numerous occasions by white leaders and asked whether or not I would want to serve on advisory boards," he said. To him those invitations were further evidence that things were changing in the area of race relations. The erosion of strong racial attitudes under which he had to live is evidence to him that race relations were changing for the better. "Just look at the number of generals we have in the military as compared to when I was on active duty during World War II. There were no black officers in the Marine Corps. Its first black officer was commissioned just after the war ended in 1945," he said. "We are not there yet, but we have come a long way from the discrimination and prejudice we have known in the past."

Doughty, too, believes that a true story of what life was all about during the 36 days on Iwo Jima has not been told. "There were blacks and others from different cultural backgrounds serving there, but their service was, for the most part, ignored and they were not shown. We were not necessarily looking for recognition we did not deserve, but we would have appreciated being recognized for our service there." He also feels few accounts of the battle have emerged during the years since Iwo Jima that have succeeded in painting a picture of the destruction and devastation that were experienced during battle. "If anyone could see the real picture of that beachhead with all of the clutter and the enemy overpowering the invasion forces in the early going that have been written about and shown in the movies, they simply would not believe it. The landing was terrifying. We had to crawl and creep, moving only inches at a time. From all accounts of the landing and the battle I have seen or read, not much has ever been shown or written in the detail necessary that can paint a true picture of that side of the battle. For all of us, it was indeed, a frightening experience, and those who were not there cannot possibly know what it was really like."

The strong civil rights activity during the 1940s was the catalyst that opened the door for the integration of the armed forces and a big part of the efforts to desegregate our greater society. "I have to believe that A. Philip

"Taking cover in the volcanic ash, foxholes, and abandoned wreckages from enemy fire was a common occurrence throughout the battle," said Eugene Doughty. (National Archives)

Randolph, Adam Clayton Powell, Thurgood Marshall, the NAACP, and the Congress of Racial Equality led the way that made the difference for the improvement in race relations and equality that we are enjoying today," said Doughty. "Those civil rights activities have made a strong impact on our country in the past 64 years, but who would have ever thought that our generation would ever see a black president."

He entered the segregated military at a time when prejudice and discrimination were firmly entrenched in the American way of life; he is more than grateful and proud to have served his country on Iwo Jima. Doughty said that he joined the Marine Corps to fight and that it was hard not to have the opportunity to do so simply because of the color of his skin. It was hard for him to sit in the background simply because he was an African American and not be able to be directly involved. In spite of that, he was proud to serve and do his part to help win the war. "Even though we were confronted with racism, I would do it all over again. They were celebrated years for me and for our country, and I was a part of it."

Frederick Gray was one the soldiers who remained on the island with the occupation forces and returned home from Iwo Jima after the war had been over for nearly a year. He had served with the Army occupation forces and was one of the last men in his company to leave the island. He remembers returning home one day to a warm welcome from his family and friends and then going back to work with his father as a carpenter the next day. "My father had continued his carpentry and building business all through the war years and when I returned home, I joined him on a project that he was working on in St. Leonard. St. Leonard was on Maryland's western shore and was located near the Chesapeake Bay. We built and remodeled houses, churches, built a school and remodeled the school that my daddy was building when I was born and which I attended as a child," he said.

In 1951, he joined the police force in Washington, D.C. The politics of the Roosevelt and Truman administrations had initiated several efforts and programs that had significantly benefited African Americans. The democrats left office in 1952. He, too, saw civil rights gains as a result of strong civil rights activity such as the integration of the Armed Forces and the *Brown vs. Board of Education* decision. Those gains, however, were not as swift and supported as they were in previous administrations. Domestic violence, civil rights activity, and racism characterized most of the 1950s. It was at the beginning of that decade that Gray assumed a position as a police officer in the nation's capital, a short distance from where he was reared in Maryland. "It was not the opportunity I thought it would be. The force was segregated, and blacks were assigned to work with blacks. I had worked with my father after being discharged from the military and the job with the police department was the first outside job I had taken since the war and it was the first time I realized that segregation was still alive and well back home." Strong civil rights activities of the time resulted in renewed signs of a changing attitude with respect to opening doors for all of its citizens. Gray, too, was one of those who benefited as a result of that new attitude. He left the police department and feels fortunate to have been able to find employment with the federal government. "I was hired as a carpenter with the National Park Service. I was the first black carpenter the Park Service had ever hired. I will never forget the day I went to work there, it was the same day Nikita Khrushchev flew over from Russia to visit our president. The political atmosphere between the Soviet Union and the United States was not very good. Things were very tense in the city when he came. I remember seeing the park police checking the manholes for possible explosives and the tight security around town," he said. The civil rights struggle was at its peak when Gray was building his new career with the federal government, and his success in doing so is a tribute to his initiative and skills. Those qualities that he developed while working as a carpenter with his father and as a young man who moved quickly through the ranks from a private to first sergeant on Iwo Jima followed him through retirement. "After I went to the Park Service, I spent a short period of time working with the Washington, D.C., government to set up a maintenance division, but after that, I returned to the National Park Service and worked there until I retired. During my time at the Park Service, I was the construction representative on several high-powered projects for the federal government. Two of the ones I remember being heavily involved in were the reroofing of Union Station and the John F. Kennedy Center. I was the contracting representative and it was my job to supervise the contracting process."

Upon their return home from World War I and World War II, many African Americans who had served in the defense of their country refused to subject themselves to the humiliation and degradation of segregation and discrimination. Frederick Gray was one of them. "On Iwo Jima, we were all committed to doing our best to protect our country and we did our best to do the jobs we were assigned. Even though we could only work in support-related jobs, we did our best," said Gray. In the military, the way most African Americans were organized, trained and treated was a reflection of the segregated lifestyle in which they had to live prior to entering the military. Although there was a tremendous amount of civil rights activity pushing for equal opportunities for minorities, Gray was convinced that many of those who had the power to make it happen were not listening. "We were not given the jobs that whites were and when we returned from Iwo Jima, we felt badly that we were not treated like our white counterparts and given the same opportunities and credits they were for their service. There was nothing we could do about. That is just the way it was during that time, and there is nothing we could do about it. The policy of segregation was supported from the highest offices in government. What could we do, who could we go to for help?"

African Americans had served in uniform before, but never in the numbers that they did in World War II. On Iwo Jima, there were men from all parts of the country and Gray believes that many of the whites had not worked or had been involved with African Americans to the extent that they were in the military in World War II. "They learned what they did about us from what they had heard or read and came to believe that we could not handle ourselves in combat. I believe that was the basic reason why we were

Hot sulfur showers constructed by the Navy Seabees were rare and were welcomed by the battle-weary troops when they had the opportunity to take advantage of them. (National Archives)

not assigned direct combat assignments," he said. Although segregation was still the official policy there would be more instances in World War II, especially on the small island of Iwo Jima, where African Americans and whites would have to cooperate. Many of the white soldiers and sailors who had never interacted with African Americans would develop very different perspectives and attitudes after serving in combat with them. That attitude, along with the efforts of civil rights activists of the time, provided the push that would begin the process of total integration of the armed forces. "The president signed the order even though there was strong opposition against it by segregationists," Gray said. "They did not want it, but it happened. I didn't think I would live to see what I am seeing in the military today. We have more black generals and top enlisted men than I thought I would ever see. If the old timers could come back and see the number of blacks in the high positions that we are seeing today, they would never believe it," he said.

Gray, too, believes that the service of the African Americans has not been documented very well in news articles and movies of World War II.

His company's DUKW drivers were a large part of the ship-to-shore activity that kept the troops ashore resupplied and ran medical evacuations oftentimes in the face of enemy fire, and performed medical evacuations and rescues at sea. "Some of what has been written and shown in the movies showed some blacks serving on Iwo but not that they played any significant role in the capture of the island or of the service of members of the various branches of the military," Gray said. In recent years, the presence of African Americans among the ranks of the military is beginning to come to light in movies, publications, and documentaries. "Because our service has been excluded for so long, I believe that people who are learning about it for the first time just won't believe it," said Gray. The Iwo Jima invasion was led by the Marines and the victory was indeed based on their determination to take the island, but Gray also feels that there were other service units and members of them that did not receive as much recognition for their participation in the media as they should have. Along with the significant role his unit played in the battle, naval air and the Army Air Corps provided the bombardment that helped neutralize the enemy. Navy corpsman and crews aboard ship, along with United States Coast Guardsmen, were there as well. Navy Seabees built roads to provide the necessary construction expertise needed on the island to facilitate the forward mobility of the invading troops.

The long road to integration in the United States began in earnest in the 1940s and lasted until the Civil Rights Act of 1964 was passed. Gray witnessed it all. "I took annual leave from work to make the trip down Constitution Avenue in Washington, D.C., when Dr. Martin Luther King, Jr., led the historical march on Washington in 1963 and I was there to hear his famous 'I Have a Dream' speech," he said. "The crowd was huge. I actually drove my old 1959 Plymouth in the motorcade and a young, white college student from Iowa joined me as the crowd moved down Constitution Avenue. As I drove along the route toward the monument, he was making the announcement over the loudspeaker that I had attached to my car, 'Join the march on Washington for freedom, jobs, and equality,' to the crowd lining the street. The event touched me so that I could not hold back the tears from my eyes," said Gray. "People were marching five and six deep, holding hands: white, black, young and old, saying and singing the words 'We shall overcome.'" This was a very tender moment for him. He remembered thinking about his time on Iwo Jima and why they were all there, and of his brother who did not survive the war while serving on the battlefield in Italy. It was all for the freedom for himself, countless others, and generations to come, and they would all benefit from this march on Washington. President

Kennedy had met with Dr. King and other leaders of the march and assured them of his support for civil rights legislation. That legislation did happen, but the president would not live to see it. He was assassinated before it was passed.

Sam Green began the final leg of his journey home after he was discharged from the Army at Fort Smith, Arkansas. "We were all headed in different directions. Seven of us were going to Shreveport and rather than taking the bus, four or five of us hired a taxi and took the most direct route. The taxi drivers knew we were anxious to get back, and they were waiting for us at the bus station. We got out of the cab at the bus station at 2:30 in the morning in Shreveport, and then we all went off in different directions. We were home," he said. "My family had a farm and did not live directly in Shreveport. Our family home was about ten miles out of town, so I took another taxi to the farm, but I didn't let him drive directly to the house. I asked him to stop down the road a piece, and I walked the rest of the way. We had a beautiful farm with fruit trees and lots of land. I was glad to be back," he said. "It was early in the morning, and I just walked on up to the porch and knocked on the door. I remember hearing my daddy saying 'who is it?' I replied, 'Staff Sergeant Sam Green, Jr.,' and, boy, all I could hear was feet hitting the floor. When the door opened, everybody threw their arms around me. We had a time that morning; there was endless conversation, crying, and everybody was glad to see me. I don't believe anyone went back to bed that night. It was a time to remember." His family knew that he would be returning soon, but nobody knew exactly when. He had not been able to have much communication with the family while he was on Iwo Jima, and nobody really knew when he would be home. But in those rare instances when he could get a letter through, he chose not to give any information about when he would be back. He wanted to surprise them. Most of the families who lived in his community had at least one member of their family in uniform. His family was no exception. "Among those who welcomed me was my brother-in-law who had also served in the western Pacific in the Navy in the vicinity of Guam and Saipan." Along with his brother-in-law, other family members were there, including his mother, father, sister, and two ladies who, offered a prayer to him for his safe return when he left home to join the military.

The first thing he wanted to do upon his return was to finish high school. "When I left to go to the Army, I did so without my high school diploma. My goal was to get it when I was discharged from the military. One of the first things I did when I returned was to do just that," he said. After completing high school and his military experience, he was ready to start a career for himself. He had been a troop leader on Iwo Jima, and he truly believed that the sense of responsibility and ability to adapt to changing situations he had developed in the military would give him a good start as he began to build that career. His first job out of the military proved that to be true. He was hired by a roofing company and held that job for 36 years until he retired. "I do believe that my ability to stay on that job as long as I did had a lot to do with the skills I developed as a troop leader and the ability to adapt to changing situations." Although working in the factory did not nearly equate to his battlefield experience, he does believe that he developed skills and attitudes that helped him complete a successful career as a civilian. "The determination to get the job done and stay alive was one of most valuable lessons I learned in the military. I made it back home, and I will always believe that what I went through over there prepared me for anything I would have to do in later life. When I went over there, it was my goal to come back alive and I did. I took that attitude as I approached my career in civilian life, and it worked for me again," he said. "I learned in the military how to make decisions, endure hardships, and manage people." He truly believes that he had a good experience in the military, and as he looks back over the years since he left the Army, he has second thoughts about having separated from the military.

Segregation was still an issue for him as it was for other returning African American servicemen when they came home from the war. "In the stores and restaurants, we had white water fountains, colored water fountains, white restrooms, colored restrooms and all of that. There were white break rooms and colored break rooms. Before the war we had to eat in the kitchen and were not allowed to eat in the main dining room, and at the movies, we had to sit upstairs," he said. "I have been fortunate to have lived to see segregation, for the most part, slowly disappear, and integration become a reality in my lifetime. The strong civil rights activity in the form of marches, protests, legal action, and so on put an end to the separation of the races." Green also noticed that the military, along with our greater society, has changed in many ways since Iwo Jima. "When we were in the service during World War II, the races did not mingle. We had black outfits and white outfits. But now, that is not so; there is no such thing as black and white units, as it should have been all along. Some attitudes, though, have a tendency to hang on for generations despite efforts to change them. During World War II we saw very few black officers and senior enlisted men. I do remember when the first group of black pilots, the Tuskegee Airmen,

"Segregation was an issue for African Americans coming home from the war," said Sam Green. "I have been fortunate to have lived to see integration become a reality." (National Archives)

was formed. They were in a segregated group, but the formation of that group was the beginning of initiatives that would see more blacks in technical jobs and in higher positions of responsibility than ever before. My brother was stationed with the Tuskegee Airmen. He was not a pilot, but he was an officer, and for a black man that was rare, but today it is not," he said. "We have come a long way. In this day and time, anybody of any race or color can now enter the military and have a reasonable expectation that they can go as far as their talents and initiatives can carry them. During the war those opportunities were just closed to us because of the color of our skin," he said. Green is happy to see that there have been many improvements in race relations since those steps toward integration in the 1940s. The administration of Franklin D. Roosevelt began the process of reaching out to the African American population with his "New Deal" administration. Seventy-six years later, the United States elected its first African American president. "Who would have ever thought that in our lifetime, we would see a black president?" Green said. He firmly believes that the civil rights and political activity in the 1940s and the service of blacks in World War II and subsequent conflicts have contributed to the tremendous changes we now see in attitudes toward all Americans since World War II.

"Military service is a duty that all American men should perform," said Green. He believes that the strength of the country has, to a great degree, been built on the service of our military men and women. "I hope that our young men and women should serve our country in some way, seek out educational opportunities, and strive to keep the country strong and prosperous not only for the current generation but for generations to come." As he looks back over the years since he left the Army, he has second thoughts about having separated from the military. "I do believe that the Army would have been a good career for me. I had reached the rank of staff sergeant and was a noncommissioned officer. I was even offered the position of first sergeant prior to separating. I had not finished school, and my first priority was to do that. If I had completed school prior to coming in, I do believe that I may have made the Army a career."

Archibald Mosley, upon his return home from the war, remembers that everyone was excited that the war was over and was happy to see him. For many of the returning veterans in small towns around the United States, celebrations were generally limited to gatherings of friends and family, but his return was a bittersweet experience. "My mother took me across the street to a neighbor's home where one of my friends lived who had also gone off to war. We grew up together, played marbles, and ball out in the street," he said. "When we arrived at our neighbor's home, my mother said, 'look, Archie's back, here's Archie.' My friend's mother smiled and looked out toward the train station and said 'oh, my son should be here soon.' He would never come home because he was killed overseas in the war. For me, that was the hardest part of coming home."

Once he began to settle down with the fact that he was home, Mosley, too, determined that the social issues in the community with respect to race relations were the same as they had been when he left. "Black people still had to sit in the back of the theaters, we could not go into the cafes down in the center of town," he said. "That did not help my attitude any at all. I could not understand having to go to war, put my life on the line, come home to this kind of treatment and not have the rights and privileges of a full citizen." He did notice, too, that the traditional family structure was changing. During the war women had taken on many of the tasks and roles in and out of the home that had traditionally been accomplished by men. "I noticed that it had become generally accepted for women to work outside of the home. Before I went into the military women were home-makers and took care of the house and the children while the men went off to work. That began to change somewhat during the war. Women had been supporting the war effort in large numbers and it was not all about filling a void that men had left behind. A lot of it was a desire to just show their patriotism and do their part to win the war," he said.

Mosley would see the years following World War II filled with civil rights activity that would change the face of America in many ways. Within ten years after he was released from the military. The United States Armed Forces would be integrated, a Supreme Court decision would mandate the desegregation of schools and strong civil rights activity would demand equal opportunity in every facet of American life for all of its citizens.

He was discharged from the Marine Corps upon his return home, and once he had been welcomed back and had settled in, he turned his attention to what he would do next. "The next thing I had to do was just what my mother and father expected me to do, and that was to find a job," he said. "At that time in 1946, for a young black man employment opportunities were slim. That is when I decided to take advantage of the GI Bill and go back to school. With that and financial assistance for playing football, I was able to finish my education." His ambition was to become a clergyman, but he was encouraged by his parents to pursue a degree in education as well. "I resumed my studies, which I began before going to the military. The university I was attending did not offer a degree in theology so I transferred to a nearby university which did offer a theology degree and completed the requirements for my degree in theology and then returned to the university in which I had resumed my undergraduate studies after the military to com-plete my bachelor's and master's degrees in education." Mosley pursued both degrees at the urging of his father in order to maximize his opportunities as a marketable jobseeker in more than one profession. When he graduated from college, he did become an ordained minister and educator as well.

Mosley married his wife in 1947 and began raising his family at a time in United States history that saw the beginnings of the civil rights move-ment which would provoke more changes to include minorities into the mainstream of American society than ever before. "The civil rights move-ment really affected the entire world. While en route to Iwo Jima and still a teenager, I remember an encounter with someone of color, but not a U.S. citizen, who indicated to me that they would never consider living in the United States because of the way black Americans were treated there," he said. "I was reminded that even though I was about to enter a war zone to

Shortly before his discharge from the Marine Corps to attend college, Archibald Mosley (second from right) spends time with five of his squad members upon their return from Iwo Jima. (National Archives)

fight for my country, I was still a second class citizen," he said. Living with discrimination and segregation had been a way of life for him, and this chance encounter with someone on the outside looking in made him realize that not all of the rest of the world embraced the concept of separation of the races—some saw it as oppression. He remembers picketing and protesting when he returned home from the war and protesting against segregation back home in the downtown area as the movement began to take hold nationwide. "We protested until the chief of police received a call from some of the town's citizens to stop the protest and to put us in jail if we did not. We did not stop, and the chief began making arrests. My father was able to save me from being arrested. I can truly say that I have never gone to jail, but I would have that day if it had not been for my father."

Mosley remembers well the 1954 *Brown vs. Board of Education* decision, which mandated the desegregation of schools in the United States. By upholding the promise of equality for all, this landmark court decision reaffirmed the promise guaranteed in the Fourteenth Amendment of the Constitution to all of its citizens. It opened the door not only for equality in public education but in our greater society as well. Civil rights activists now had the backing of the highest court in the land as they set out to challenge segregation and discriminatory practices in public places and activities such as restaurants, bus and train stations, parks, hotels, and at voting booths. Changing these practices would be a monumental task, but it would happen. The Civil Rights Act of 1964 would take the strongest stand ever by the United States against racial segregation and discrimination.

"The United States government authenticated the existence of segregation in the public schools with the *Brown vs. Board* decision in 1954, but look at how long it took to be implemented," Mosley said. At the time it was handed down, he was serving as a pastor in Michigan. Much of the inspiration for the civil rights movement evolved from the support and prominence of clergy in the civil rights movement, and Mosley was a part of that. He was very active in the desegregation of public schools in Detroit and Pontiac, Michigan. "Many who denied blacks and other minorities their civil rights in the United States did not accept the idea that segregation needed to be changed. Those who did believe that change was needed took the lead through positive, non-violent action and made it happen." He recalls a personal situation that supports his idea that change does not usually happen unless there is a stimulus to make it happen. His father took action in his community to correct a situation that was an injustice in his mind. "While I was serving as chief administrator of a school in my community with all black students there was another school on the other side of town which had an all white student population and the chief administrator there was white as well." The *Brown vs. Board* Supreme Court decision had mandated that public schools be integrated. The school district in which he was working was compelled to comply because not doing so would cause the school system to lose funds. "The school board proceeded to comply with the integration order by merging the two schools into one. That school would then have only one chief administrator. I was qualified for the position, had three degrees including a master's degree in education, and by all accounts, was proficient as an administrator. The administrator of the other school had one degree, a bachelor's degree. The school board was about to make him the principal of the new school," he said. His father had lived with discrimination and was determined that his children would not have to live with the indignities and issues related to it in their lifetime. "When my father learned of the school board's proposal, he said that this would not happen. He drove to the state capital and took the issue to the state superintendent of education. The next day, the superintendent drove from the state capital to my school district and met with the school board. The school board reversed it's decision and I became the chief administrator of the new school," said Mosley. He believed that the action to deny him the position based on the color of his skin was not consistent with the promise of equality guaranteed by the Fourteenth Amendment of the Constitution and that it was made along racial lines.

As he recalls some of his life experiences, he remembers a personal one on Iwo Jima that has made a lasting impression on him. "I learned a lot of lessons there. One of the things I will never forget and have used many times as a basis for making decisions was a lesson that my company commander taught me. As one of his squad leaders, I had nine men, and on one occasion our whole company was pinned down on the beach by enemy fire from a pillbox just up the slope from us as we tried to make it ashore at Iwo Jima. The company commander assessed the situation and ordered our squad to go up and knock that pillbox out with hand grenades or flamethrowers or anything we could use to disable the enemy." Considering the situation, Mosley believed that if he and his squad crawled to the top of that hill it was likely they would not come back alive and he also believed that his company commander sensed that Mosley's squad believed that. "The company commander came to us and said that if that pillbox was not taken out, our entire company would be. It was war, and the pillbox had to be silenced," Mosley said. Everybody knew that the sacrifice had to be made and he was hoping that his squad would be successful. They all knew that the job had to be done, and the order was made to do so. Mosley said that his squad did silence the pillbox and all of the men in his squad made it back to the company. But the lesson he learned from that experience was that in life sacrifices and decisions, more often than not, will have to be made in order to achieve any objective. All of them may not necessarily have the same outcome, but making decisions and taking calculated risks is the key to success, he thought.

Mosley, too, is concerned that the service on Iwo Jima of African Americans and other minorities has not been recognized. After a conversation with his grandson, however, he now clearly believes that due to the erosion of discriminatory practices and segregation since World War II, future accounts of the service to our country of all Americans will be appropriately recognized in our history. "When my grandson recently viewed a documentary *The Marines of Montford Point: Fighting for Freedom*, which told the story of the segregated service of the first African Americans to serve in the Marine Corps, in which I was interviewed, I asked him to respond to what he saw. His generation is the recipient of the positive benefits of the strong civil rights struggle that my generation contributed to his. His response to my question indicated to me that the struggle is changing attitudes. It was short and to the point. He said, essentially, 'Those days are gone; it is a new day and that will never happen again,'" Mosley said with a sense of pride in his voice. His grandson's definitive response is an indication that the promise of equality offered in the Fourteenth Amendment of the Constitution is taking hold.

Horace Taylor returned home sooner than most of the men in his company because of the points he had accrued as a result of being awarded the Silver Star Medal. "I left to come back to the States on Christmas Eve of 1945, shortly after the bombing of Hiroshima," he said. Although the Battle of Iwo Jima ended in March of 1945, the war in the Pacific raged on until August of 1945. In December of that year, Horace Taylor boarded a ship and returned home. The heroic effort that earned him the Silver Star is little known. He was a war hero, however, and was recognized for heroism in a ceremony on the battlefield at Iwo Jima. He is a modest man and speaks little about what he and his assistant driver did navigating in waters off the coast of Iwo Jima to safely get the men and cargo aboard his DUKW ashore while taking fire from a concealed enemy machine gun nest, or of rescuing the personnel of a disabled DUKW at sea.

Although he was born in Seneca, South Carolina, he did not resettle there to live when he returned from the war. "Shortly after I left the ship upon arriving in California, I went to Fort Bragg, North Carolina, where I was again recognized for being awarded the Silver Star and discharged from the Army," he said. "From there, I went back to Seneca and only spent a few days there to visit the few friends and what family I had there. My mother and some of my family had moved to North

Horace Taylor returned from World War II after being awarded the Silver Star medal. He was discharged from the Army, but remained in government service until he retired in 1983.

Carolina, and I went to visit them also," he said. People were happy to see him when he returned, but he spoke little of his experiences in the war, and few people knew anything of his heroic action for which he was awarded the Silver Star. "Nobody in Seneca asked about what we did over there, and other than my immediate family, I knew very few people in North Carolina. Those I did know had no idea that I had served in the war, and I didn't bring it up," he said.

The end of the war in 1945 brought many soldiers home, but they did not return to the prosperous America that had existed during the war or to the strong agricultural lifestyle in the South with which many of them were so familiar. Along with the winding down of the factories that had fueled the huge war machine, life on the farm was changing. Farming communities that had prospered prior to the war and during the war in support of the war effort were now closing down as developing technology was changing the way in which farmers were doing business. Serious economic issues were facing the American people as the large number of returning veterans were beginning to return from the battlefields overseas. In that regard the small Southern town in which Taylor was raised did not offer the type of career challenges he sought when he returned from overseas. Considering the huge economic downturn as the war was ending—not only in his hometown, but all across the country—he believed that in a larger city his career opportunities would be better.

After his visit with his family, he moved to Washington, D.C., where he would meet and marry his wife, raise a son and a daughter, and retire from work in 1983. He still resides there. His first job out of the military was with the U.S. Treasury Department. His military service, he believes, was a big help in making that happen. "I did not have a hard time finding a job. In fact, I was lucky because I was able to leave the Pacific before the war was over on points, earlier than most of the troops. There were still many troops overseas when I returned. Having been a veteran was a big help for me to find a job," he said. "I was lucky to have been able to return home on points because the big rush for jobs came after I had returned and had found a job. I applied for work at the U.S. Treasury Department there in Washington. I took the civil service examination and was called after about a week or two." He was employed, but employment opportunities were still limited for African Americans. "I was hired as a messenger in the loans and currency division of the Treasury Department. That was about all blacks could do back then even though some of them had college degrees." He believed that he was fortunate to have been able to find employment. All of

All of the veterans interviewed believe that the dream of Dr. Martin Luther King Jr., which he delivered in his famous "I Have a Dream Speech" on August 28, 1963, is coming true. (National Archives)

his work experience immediately after he returned from Iwo Jima was with the Treasury Department. He moved from the loans and currency division to the savings bonds division and then to the Internal Revenue Service.

He did eventually leave the Treasury Department and went to work for the Washington, D.C., National Guard. He felt good about that opportunity because he would have the chance to develop some technical skills. "When I went to work with the Guard, which was located at Camp Simms in southeast Washington, I worked as an anti-aircraft gun mechanic. The Guard, at one time, had the mission to protect the District from an aerial attack during the war and I would be working as one of the mechanics who would repair and maintain the guns assigned to that mission. After taking the position with the Guard, I was sent to Fort Bliss, Texas, for several months to train as a mechanic on anti-aircraft guns," he said. The anti-aircraft guns were eventually replaced by Nike missiles while he was working at Camp Simms, and he once again had to go back to Fort Bliss to retrain as a mechanic on the new missiles. "The entire missile site was closed after awhile, but I was able to get a transfer to the Naval Surface Warfare Center in Washington working with ordinance and explosive devices, and I stayed there until I retired in 1983."

After his service on Iwo Jima, Taylor's employment opportunities kept him very close to the military, although he was not in uniform. He recalls that there have been tremendous changes in the military since he was discharged—some that he believed, like those he served with while in the military, he would never see as a young man in the 1940s. "The military has made a complete turnaround," he said. "There have been many changes, but the number of black officers and senior noncommissioned officers is the greatest change I have seen in the military. When I went in the Army, I did see a few black officers and noncommissioned officers, but the number of them I see today is more than I ever thought I would." He also witnessed firsthand significant changes in race relations and growing opportunities for African Americans in the United States. Living in the nation's capital, he was able to see where much of it began, and he was there for the march on Washington in 1963. "I saw Dr. King and was a part of the crowd the whole day that the march on Washington was going on," he said. "I went along with some of my friends to the mall on the day he delivered his famous 'I Have a Dream' speech." He said that it was a piece of history that he will never forget.

Like other veterans of the Iwo Jima experience, Taylor has seen movies, read articles, books, and other accounts of the battle, and he feels that those accounts do not tell it all. He particularly expressed concern that the service of African Americans is only recently becoming known. "They do not include the service of blacks. We were left out. There were movie cameras and reporters there, but we were not included when the movies were made and the books and articles were written. I remember seeing movie cameras, and there were a lot of press people there but we were edited out of what was being shown and written," he said. Taylor feels that the actions and service of African Americans was disregarded. "That was just the way it was back then—we were overlooked. It's just that simple," he said. As information and other accounts of the service of African Americans on Iwo Jima begins to surface, he, too, believes that it is likely that many will be surprised that they were actually there because their service on Iwo Jima has been generally left out of all accounts of the battle.

Reared in the South, he knew that African Americans were subjected to a double standard. "In my hometown, I do believe that I would not have the opportunity to go as far as my abilities and talents would take me," he said. He believes that his military service, particularly his experiences on

Iwo Jima, contributed a great deal to the "can-do" attitude that he has developed over the years. He is content and happy with his life, accomplishments, and has no regrets. "My military experience helped me to realize that if there was something that I wanted to do, I could do it. As I look back, I do believe that the benefits of the skills and discipline I took away from the military has helped me to do just that," he said.

CHAPTER 8

Personal Memoirs

FOUR OF THE VETERANS INTERVIEWED here chose to share their personal memoirs of their experience on Iwo Jima. Their memoirs are true reflections of their own personalities and are graphic descriptions of an experience that few of us have ever had. Their sentiments, concerns, and memories of the entire sequence of events that took them through the Battle of Iwo Jima compare almost to the letter and are an extension of the interviews and information offered by the other seven veterans interviewed. African Americans represented only a fraction of the more 110,000 Americans involved in the assault, and theirs was a role of support, supply, and service. They did, however, take up arms when necessary and were commended for the job they did during the battle.

Their memoirs are very descriptive and well written. Charles Black, at the age of 18, kept a journal of his experience from the day he deployed until the day he returned to the United States. On the other hand, Roland Durden, Sam Green and Eugene Doughty, all of them now in their mid–80s, sat with the interviewer and recalled without hesitation the minutest details of the battle and their participation in it. The details of the lives and experiences of all of these men are recorded and preserved here through the voices of the men who lived it in such a manner that the readers will be able to visualize the activities during the trips ashore, the landing, and living in foxholes ashore during the ongoing 36-day battle. All of them have decided to share their experience because it is unique in American history. Their experience occurred as a result of actions by the United States government that began the process of removing the barriers that excluded certain groups within its population from government service based on race, color, or national origin.

Although American history records that African Americans previously served in the military in earlier conflicts, it was at the will of the government. World War II was the first time they served as the result of a government action. The men offering their memoirs here were pioneers in that effort by the government, and they made their mark in one of the most historic battles of World War II.

Corporal Charles Black, U.S. Army

This essay is an account of my experience in military service during World War II. My experiences as a U.S. Army veteran of that war will always live in my mind and I will leave those experiences here on paper as a contribution to the history of the World War II experience and the Battle of Iwo Jima.

While in the armed forces, I was assigned to a United States Army Amphibious Truck Company as an assistant driver on an amphibious truck, commonly known as a DUKW or "duck." It is a huge, peculiar-looking vehicle, which is equipped to operate on land and on water. I won't go into detail about it, but you can virtually picture the capabilities of the amphibious truck if I explain it like this: Imagine yourself driving any kind of truck near a beach with the same gears and equipment as any other large truck, and you find a need to navigate a body of water. You'd drive to the edge of the beach, enter the water, and let the air out of your tires by manipulating an inflating and deflating lever on the dashboard. Close some valves to keep out the water, engage a propeller, and then

Charles Black, USA. Corporal Charles Black deployed to Iwo Jima from Fort Gordon Johnston, Florida, where he would assume duties as an assistant driver with the 476th Amphibian Truck Company on the ship-to-shore amphibious vehicle known as the DUKW (pronounced "duck").

drive on out into the water still guiding the vehicle with the steering wheel, but you just use only one gear, preferably second gear. There would be no need to apply brakes; they won't do any good in the water. When coming out of the water, you would just locate a good landing spot and then drive right back up on the beach. After making your way to the highway or a solid surface, simply inflate your tires by manipulating the inflate/deflate lever to normal tire pressure, and continue your journey.

After I was inducted into the Army and began my basic training near New Orleans, Louisiana, at Camp Plauche, and at Camp Gordon Johnston, near Tallahassee, Florida, my unit shipped out to the Pacific by way of Seattle, Washington. We arrived in Hawaii in August 1944. On the island of Oahu we continued our training with our vehicles and equipment, having no idea where we would go from there. While we were there, we were told that we were to give a presentation and demonstration of the capabilities of our vehicles to Army, Navy, and Marine brass (officers). We were required to show them different ways our vehicles could be used, including linking up to ships, unloading supplies and equipment from them, transporting cargo to shore dumps (storage), carrying ammunition, weapons, and howitzers on the truck from ship-to-shore and personnel with their weapons, and evacuating casualties. In other words, show them all the capabilities of the DUKW: everything. We practiced for that demonstration for several weeks and then came the day. There was really a lot of brass there: hundreds of them from captains to admirals. The event took place down at the beach. It was perfect, and everyone seemed to be impressed with our demonstration. We were commended for our skill and ability. The part of the demonstration I participated in was showing how quickly the 105 howitzer, a huge artillery gun, could be brought from ship, unleashed by the team who would operate it and hooked up to the back of the truck and driven to a desired place. It received a special commendation from the officers in attendance.

We all felt that something was in the wind after the demonstration, but we could not imagine what it would be. We soon found out because we were sent to another island in the Hawaiian Islands—Maui—and were assigned to the 4th and 5th Marine Divisions. We were indeed surprised; we knew what to expect because we knew what Marines did and what part they play in a battle. It's a known fact that Marines are the ones who establish a beachhead, take over the island, and withdraw for the Army to take over. We were well aware of the amphibious assaults Marines were known for, the extreme danger involved with them and the likelihood that any unit making an assault with one of their units would face the same kind of danger. I do admit that we had mixed emotions about it.

It was a known fact that we were lined up for an invasion somewhere, but where? No one could imagine. We were assigned to the howitzer units of the Marine divisions, and there we found ourselves working together with fighting men of another race; we wondered how we would get along. We were the only colored troops in this particular camp on Maui and we were flanked on the left by a Marine amphibious tractor company of white Marines and on the right by a battalion of white Navy Seabees. When we first arrived it seemed like everything was tense, and it seemed like the Marines on our left objected to our being there. There were no Post Exchange or theatre facilities set up for us so we had to use theirs. It might have been my imagination, but it seemed we were not wanted in their facilities. I heard that the word came from higher ups that we were to use the same facilities as the Marines. When we were taken to their camp and shown how their amphibian vehicles operated and we showed them how our vehicles worked, the atmosphere soon became friendlier.

The Marines we were to work with were stationed a good distance from us. Each day they would drive down for combined training exercises. These were really a good group of guys. They had recently formed a truck company like ours, and our drivers had to give their drivers different pointers and demonstrations. Then we began going on actual ship-to-shore trial runs. We would load up our trucks with guns, supplies, and Marine personnel and go out on the water practicing driving in formation, landing on beaches, and launching our vehicles from LSTs off shore. We really got along well with each other. I had the impression that they felt a strong dependence on us because it would be our job to get their guns and supplies to shore safely across the pounding waves and through enemy fire as we deployed from the ship.

After this vigorous coordinated training we loaded our trucks for the actual invasion on the LSTs. About the 19th or 20th of January 1945, we left Maui and were shoving off. We still had no idea as to where we were going. I figured we must have had a certain time to be at a certain rendezvous because several times we would stop at isolated islands in the ocean, unload the ships, and invade these islands just like we would do in the real thing. It was fun doing those dry runs, but then the thought began to occur to me that pretty soon it wouldn't be a dry run. One day we would be leaving these ships for the real thing and for some of us, maybe the last time.

After we reached Saipan, we found out that we were to invade the island of Iwo Jima. I was unfamiliar with the island, but I had heard something on the radio about B-29s dropping bombs on an island called Iwo Jima. I don't remember how many days the bombing went on, but it never occurred to me that was where we were headed. We were shown a miniature model of the island and were briefed on the enemy troop strength and where they would likely be located. We were also told how long the battle for the island would take and the likely plan of attack and that the battle was expected to take only five days or less.

We arrived in Saipan on about the 16th of February, 1945. There were many ships in the harbors around Saipan, probably bound for the island of Iwo Jima. After a short stay on Saipan, we began our trek to Iwo Jima. Before reaching Saipan, our journey had been safe and without incident; though we had been alerted that enemy planes were in the area, we never saw them. The ships' gunners practiced shooting every day. We watched them shoot at targets and seeing them respond so quickly when alerted to do so made us feel safer as we moved closer to Iwo Jima.

As we left Saipan, the last island on our journey to Japan, we were warned to expect anything, including enemy and airplanes. Things were getting more and more fixed in my mind as to the seriousness of the situation. I just could not believe that we were headed for combat just about 15 months after entering the Army and just six months after arriving overseas, but it was a fact, and we had to face it. Not knowing how I would fare in this invasion, I felt that if I did not survive I would want some last words written to my mother and my girlfriend and I gave a set to two of my best friends, instructing them to mail them if they survived and I did not.

Fortunately, we did not run into any enemy interference on the way to Iwo Jima. We were to arrive at Iwo Jima on the 19th of February, and we were getting close to that date. As we moved closer to the island, there was a seriousness in the air for what was about to happen that we could all feel. All of us were cleaning our weapons, checking our vehicles and receiving instructions. Every precaution was taken to keep the enemy guessing as to what our plans were. For example, lights aboard ship, as much as possible, were turned off, and smoking on deck was not allowed in an effort to keep from being seen as much as possible by the enemy.

On the night of the 18th of February, I did not expect to sleep any and expected to be kept awake by the sounds of war, but that did not happen. Before I went to sleep that night, however, I had vivid thoughts of what might be in store for us on the next day. It just seemed so unreal to me that I was about to be involved in an invasion. I prayed for guidance as I closed my eyes. When I awakened the next day everything seemed a lot quieter than I expected it to be. So much so, that I wondered if we had arrived at our destination. The word had been passed that we were in the area of operations. It was early morning, and I went up on deck, and it was pitch black dark. I saw big bursts on the water which I knew were from the guns of our ships firing on the island. The island was some distance off and its outline could be seen in the darkness. I could not determine whether or not the enemy was returning fire, and I began to wonder how long it would be before it would all begin.

Soon the darkness turned into the morning light of a dreary, dismal, cloudy day. And suddenly, it began. I thought I was in Hollywood watching a movie, but I was not. This was the real thing. As the saying goes, all hell broke loose. The enemy was returning fire. As the first of the assault troops began their movement to the beach, the others of us watched with different emotions. It was a dramatic moment as the troops began to leave the ship. The first waves of Marines left the ship in all sorts of landing craft. The water was just full of activity. Many men were headed to the island, but God only knew how many would return.

I don't know what happened when the Marines landed, but from radio and written accounts, the enemy was playing a very shrewd waiting game. After the first assault troops landed and were advancing, movement ashore was uninhibited for about the first 300 yards. The enemy remained quietly hidden and allowed our troops to come on shore well into their sites. And then they opened fire. Many men were killed on that first day, and the advancement was slow from that point on. It was not going to be as easy as those who planned the invasion thought it would be.

The Japanese were well entrenched, dug in, and fortified. Though the American bombers had battered the island for at least a month, it seemed that the damage they did was minimal considering the strong resistance the Marines were receiving. The enemies' ability to resist as well as they did was easy to understand when the maze of well-entrenched caves, tunnels, and firing positions were later discovered. The artillery from our naval guns and bombing attacks only damaged the surface of the island and seemed to do little damage to the entrenched enemy, but it all but destroyed the airfields which remained in the open.

I watched the invasion from my ship, always remembering that my turn was coming to leave the ship and head for the shore. I did not know when I would go ashore in my DUKW, but I knew that it could happen at any moment. The day dragged on and our group had not departed the ship. I wondered how our troops were doing against the enemy. I found out later that we were scheduled to go in on the first day, but the water was so rough that we were rescheduled to depart the ship on D+2.

While standing on the deck of my ship and looking out at the island, I began to feel the war getting closer and closer to us because the enemy began to fire from shore at the ships sitting offshore, and we were a good distance from shore. One of the Marines on our ship was killed as a result of that enemy shelling and some others were injured. The horrors of war had touched us before we left the ship.

I was able to see Mt. Suribachi from the deck of the ship. That mountain was a primary target for the Allied ships. It was several hundred feet high, and the enemy was well entrenched in it and had an excellent view of everything around the island for miles. Our ships pounded this mountain day and night. At night, we would shine lights on it and continue the barrage of fire.

As night fell, we still wondered how our forces were doing. I began wondering if we were going to have enemy air raids after dark, and I imagined being awakened in the middle of the night by enemy airplanes bombing our ships. That was a terrible thought. Our ship, besides all of the vehicles it was carrying, was stocked with ammunition and explosives. An aerial attack or hit from the guns at Mt. Suribachi would have been a disaster.

After watching the troops all day go ashore and also watching the ships returning with casualties taken to the hospital ships, I went to bed wondering what the next day would hold for me. The mood of the others on the ship was tense and understandably so. All things considered, I slept reasonably well, but over and over, I wondered how the Marines who had gone ashore on this first day had rested. Without question, I knew I would soon find out. I knew I would go ashore, and I was ready to do so and get it done. The fear of the unknown was getting to me.

At approximately 2 o'clock P.M. on D+2 we were alerted and told to man our vehicles. My heart began to beat very, very fast, for I knew the time had come for us to leave the protection of the ship. We had been watching men in wave after wave for the past day and a half coming from and going to the island and now it was our turn to go in. We were given our instructions and then mounted our DUKWs to await the signal to "turn them over" or start the motor on them. While waiting to start the motors, we started checking our equipment to be sure that everything was ready for the deployment ashore. First, I checked to see if our vehicle was ready for water travel because I did not want any mistakes to happen in the rough water. Then I checked my carbine which I had cleaned so many times to see that it was ready for use. I checked to see that my ammo was fixed in right and that I had enough reserve ammo. Satisfied that my first line of defense was ok, I then looked to see whether or not my life preserver was in good condition and checked several other details. Finding that everything was ready, I sat back to await the start em' up signal and wondered what was to happen once we began our trip to shore. Everything went through my mind. I said a usual prayer, after which I began to say goodbye to some of the sailors I had become acquainted with during our voyage, not knowing whether it was a farewell forever or for just for a while.

On my ship, there were about 24 DUKWs. It so happened that the DUKW I was assigned was number 19. It was the last one loaded onto the ship, and it would be the first one coming off. It was a scary thought, but what could I do? Each vehicle had a crew of two men, the driver and the assistant driver. When we went ashore, we were to carry Marines, supplies, equipment, ammunition and a medical doctor. Our vehicle was equipped with an "A" frame, which was really a winch to be used to unload the 105 howitzer once we got ashore. Our truck company was attached to a Marine howitzer unit. The day we went ashore was dismal. There was drizzling rain and the water was rough.

Then the signal came. "Turn them over." It was loud and clear because there was little chatter among us. Everybody realized that this was it. It was a dramatic moment to hear all those motors start up, priming their motors for the ship-to-shore movement. The sailors assigned to the opening ramp at the front of the ship were at their position awaiting the signal to open it. I knew that when they were opened, it would be time to start rolling and head for whatever our destiny was to be.

The long-awaited signal came. The assigned sailors started the doors to opening, and the ramp came slowly down. I was beginning to get uneasy, especially since our DUKW would be the first to come off the ship. Soon the ramp was down and the light of day literally lit up the opening in the ship created by the lowering of the ramp, and I could look out onto the water and clearly see the many ships in the waters surrounding the island. The time for departure had arrived.

We were instructed to go onto the water and maneuver around the LST until all the DUKWs had departed the ship. Since we had driven directly onto the ship, we had to back off. Slowly, we backed off the ramp and into the water. We began maneuvering around and waiting for the other DUKWs leaving the ship to get into place. While that was happening, I looked to see how far we had to go and kept wondering what awaited us.

As the vehicles were leaving the LST, some of them had problems. Some of them had too much weight on them and sank as a result. Luckily nobody was hurt as they were rescued by other trucks, but some of the artillery pieces that those particular vehicles were to transport ashore were lost. After all of the trucks had come off the LST, we headed for Iwo Jima. The lead DUKW with the Marine officer in charge on board signaled for us to move out. After traveling a short distance, the DUKWs ahead of mine left us (for what reason I do not, to this day, know), and the officer in charge ordered my driver to take the lead. I do not know where they went, but my immediate concern was that my vehicle was now the lead vehicle as we moved ashore and would possibly be the first to encounter enemy fire. I had often heard stories that the enemy would try to knock off anything attempting to land on their soil, and I figured that since we would be the first in line, we would probably be the first to draw fire. Off we went, however, with the others following. Dukws travel slowly on water, and it seemed as though we were walking to shore. We had about a quarter of a mile to go, and it seemed as though we were walking there. I really was not in any hurry to get there, but knowing what was ahead made the ride a difficult one. Everyone had his eyes on the island. Although we managed to talk and laugh, I think it was more a pretense and just an effort to try to ease our nerves. Some of the Marines were veterans of this type of assault and they were a little cooler, but one could not help but wonder whether or not they might be thinking that this might be the last time. It was February 19th, I was 19 years old, and I was riding on truck number 19.

Periodically, I checked my rifle to see whether it was locked or not. I didn't want to get on the island and fire it, and find that it was locked. By the time it would have taken to correct the problem, the enemy could have done anything to me. Slowly, we kept on moving, and the island began to draw closer. Suddenly then there was a big splash that scared all of us. About 10 feet from us a shell exploded. It was evident we had been spotted or something of the sort. We all got quiet, wondering where the next one would hit. Our driver kept going as did all of the other DUKWs. My driver's foot was trembling on the accelerator so I patted him on the back, though I was afraid too. I was trying to calm him and myself down. That was the first time we had been shot at, and we quickly learned what it was like to be shot at and were bullet-tested before we hit the shore. The rest of the trip was without incident. I did not notice any more shells falling, but I kept thinking that this was the beginning.

We were approaching the shore at last. The driver and I began getting the DUKW ready to make the landing, releasing the tires and inflating them so that we make it onto the beach. As we angled the vehicle to make the landing, I began to think that something was about to happen because everything was too quiet. I expected the Japanese guns to focus their attention on us as we attempted to land on the beach. It took us about a half hour to make it to the beach, but it seemed much longer. The trip to shore was over, but what was in store for us was yet to come.

Our first efforts to drive on to the beach failed. We backed off into the water and tried again. While we were trying to beach our craft successfully, I noted the activity on the island. Ships were being unloaded with men, equipment, and supplies to support the war effort ashore. Other ships were being loaded with casualties bound for the hospital ships. As we tried several times to beach our craft, we kept expecting Japanese gunfire to pounce upon us, and we hoped we could make it ashore as quickly as possible. We believed every attempt to land was an opportunity for the enemy to pick us off. We tried lightening our load by letting the Marines get off and run ashore. That didn't work either. Troops on shore tied our vehicle to one already on the shore in an effort to pull us in. Finally, they laid down steel mats so we would not sink in the soft sand. The steel mats worked, and we were able to move onto the island. The beach was cluttered with Marines. I did not know how far the combat troops had gotten, but I figured it could not have been too far due to the amount of men on the beach and how close they were to the water. I did not know very much about what was happening on the front lines even though I was there. It was not until I returned home that I found out that it was one of the bloodiest battles of the Pacific campaign.

As we drove to our designated position on the beach, it was hard to realize that the war was going on, it was so quiet. The reality of it all set in, though, when I saw a Marine with his leg severed being carried on a stretcher to a ship. I began to feel fortunate and honored that our DUKW was the first one from our platoon to land on Iwo Jima without incident.

While we were waiting for the DUKWs with the 105 howitzers to come ashore, I took a look around our immediate area. The ground was volcanic ash, there were no trees, and the island seemed to be incredibly small. Even though we could not see the front line troops, I knew that because of the size of the island, we had to be close to them and that we had to be well within range of enemy guns as well. As I continued to look around, I noticed enemy pillboxes that had been destroyed by Marines as they moved further ashore. They were very well built, positioned, and reinforced with steel and cement. Even where it appeared that they had been hit by bombs, the damage to the well built pillboxes below the surface seemed to be slight. When we received instructions to unload the big guns, everything was still quiet, and we went about that task without incident. The Marine gun crews began manning their guns in the designated positions and getting ready for the order to commence fire.

We expected to return to the ship to pick up another load of ammunition and equipment. We were, however, directed to park our truck, dig in, and remain on the island for the night. My driver and I, along with the Marines, began digging. The volcanic sand was so soft that the more we tried to dig, the more the dirt fell into the hole we were trying to dig. We had almost completed digging our foxhole when all hell broke loose. Gunfire and artillery shells came at us from everywhere. The enemy had waited until nightfall to start this attack. The noise was far worse than any Fourth of July night I had ever experienced and as our guns began firing back, the noise got worse. When the shooting began, my partner and I dropped our shovels and fell into the hole for cover and lay flat on our stomachs.

I shall never forget this first night on the island. Over and over in my mind, I kept wondering whether or not the next shell would be for me. Time and time again, flares would explode and would illuminate our area to the point that it looked as if it were daytime. Whenever the flares appeared, we just knew that the enemy had seen us and would target our position. As the night progressed a lot of things ran through my mind. I started mentally reliving my life, mostly about things I used to do, should have done or would do if ever given the chance. My greatest thought was of God in heaven and of his wondrous love and protection, and hoping that it would be his will that I would be one of the survivors of this mighty spectacle. For some reason my driver had to go to the truck amid all that shooting. He wanted me to go along, but I was reluctant to do so, not only because of the enemy, but because it was night and the armed Marines in our area might mistake us for enemy soldiers that they thought may have infiltrated our area. He made it back safely, guided by my answer to his calls.

I must admit that I did not feel good while my driver was gone. We decided that it might be a good idea to get some sleep. Since there was nothing else we could or would do amid all the activity around us, we decided to get some rest, if we could, because we were sure we might need it. My driver, however, was more successful at getting to sleep than I was. I remember the terrifying noise of a shell hitting very close to our foxhole. He became quiet, and I called him several times before he answered. I was afraid that he might have been hit. I was relieved when he finally answered me. Then, after making sure that my knife and rifle were securely clutched in my hands, I finally dozed off.

We were awakened by the familiar voice of one of the men in our company the next morning calling our names. After the events of the previous night, I could not figure out how he knew where we were. He was there to tell us that we were going back to the ship to prepare for another run. He must have recognized our vehicle and searched the area nearby. It was still dark, but I could tell from the skies that day was about to break. The noise of the guns had subsided tremendously. I was thankful that I had survived that night, and I will remember it for the rest of my life.

As day began to break, I saw some of the effects of the previous night's attack. The first thing I saw was a hole to the right of our foxhole where we had seen four or five Marines digging in before the shooting started. There they were all lying face down as they must have been all during the previous night, dead. Death had come so close to us that night. I also noticed that our DUKW had been disabled by enemy fire, and we went back to the ship. That was a grand and glorious feeling.

After that first day, we established a routine that allowed us to live on the ship and carry supplies and ammunition to the Marines we had taken ashore. Another narrow escape occurred shortly after our first experience on the island. My driver and I were selected to go from the ship to the island at night and ours would be the only DUKW to do so. We were delivering some much needed ammunition to Marines ashore. I do not know why we were selected or who did the selecting, but my driver and I were the ones picked to go out into the pitch black night into the sea, to an unknown destination. We had never made the trip ashore at night before and, not really sure whether or not we would land in enemy or friendly territory, we feared the worst. Thankfully, at the last moment, the mission was aborted. Looking back, I do believe that mission would have been our most challenging one and perhaps our last. My driver and I let out a sigh of relief. As the battle progressed, going from ship to shore became easier. As the front line units advanced and the Japanese were pushed further back, the shooting in our area wasn't as fierce as it was in the beginning.

One of the most pitiful and interesting duties was handling wounded Marines on our DUKW from the shore to the hospital ship which was anchored out in the water. My driver would maneuver the vehicle and as much as I could, I would perform other tasks for them, such as holding plasma jars and lighting cigarettes. Some of them were badly hurt. When we arrived at the hospital ship, I would hook up their specially-made stretchers to a line the ship would drop down to us. The stretchers would then be pulled up to the ship.

After the assault troops had gained enough real estate for our unit to move ashore, we said goodbye to our friends aboard ship and relocated to the island. We had to become very familiar with security procedures in place to avoid enemy infiltration. One of the things we had to do was brush up on challenging procedures in case we were challenged for identification by an allied service member. All military personnel had been instructed on protection against the enemy. An individual would have to learn what to say if they heard the phrase "Halt, who goes there?" We learned codes and responses that would allow us to respond to the challenges. This precaution, we were told, could be the difference between life and death.

While on the island, we continued to live in foxholes but they were larger and had tops on them. In constructing them, we had to dig deep into the ground and prepare the sides so that the sand would not fall into the holes, using any kind of wood we could get our hands on. Then we would construct a roof and cover it with sand. These living quarters were at ground level and we had to crawl into the ground to get into them. We generally lived three or four to a hut. The first hut I lived in was situated just in front of some of our big guns, so it took some time getting used to those big guns blowing their tops and shells whistling over our heads. We thought it was a bad spot because if the enemy tried to silence these guns, their shells could very easily have missed their mark and fallen into our camp. As a matter of fact, one day a fellow soldier and I stood in front of our hut preparing some canned stew to eat by heating it in our steel helmets when a shell landed about four or five feet to our left and exploded. I just knew we were dead because it was so close. Neither one of us got hurt, however, but I was left with a terrible ringing in my ears. When we discovered we were still alive, we scrambled for our huts. Everybody believed that the enemy had targeted us and that the next shell could land right in the middle of our hut, but thankfully nothing more happened that day.

After we took up our positions on the island, everything became routine Army work. The Marines would soon be leaving the island, and it would fall under Army control. After the Marines left the island, the Army remained as the occupation force. Unloading ships and hauling supplies became our main job. All day and all night, it was shore-to-ship, ship-to-shore and to the supply dump. When we weren't working on our trucks, we were doing guard duty or going to the movies. A makeshift theater was set up even though the fighting had not ended. When we went to the movies, we took our rifles. One night, when we were all at the show, we heard a rifle shot nearby, and shortly afterward the theater emptied, thinking that it was an enemy attack. We stood guard duty as well. When we arrived on the island, two of us walked our post together, but eventually the post was reduced to one man. Walking post in the dark alone with nobody to talk to or help you if necessary was a bit scary.

Soon the island was quiet and the island was ours. What had started out with the intention of taking the island in 72 hours, had actually taken more than a month. On February 1, 1946, almost a year after I had arrived, I would leave Iwo Jima. We arrived in San Francisco and when I got off the ship, I kissed the ground I had missed and loved. We flew to New Jersey en route to Fort Meade, Maryland, where, on the 26th of February, 1946, Corporal Charles B. Black became Charles B. Black, civilian. In two years and three months, I had experienced a great deal. I left home at age 18 and was 20 years old when I returned. I came back to the world I had learned to appreciate and love and hoped to God that there would always be a world of peace.

Sergeant Eugene Doughty, U.S. Marine Corps

After graduating from basic training at Montford Point, those of us who had work experience or had certain skills were placed in companies where those skills were needed. Since I had a lot of experience in typing and business operations, they sent me to clerical school. Clerical school lasted perhaps maybe about six or eight weeks, and after I finished clerical school they placed me with the steward's branch as a unit clerk at Montford Point. I, along with two other men, was sent to be screened, and fortunately I was the one who got the position. They were looking for work-experienced men who could handle more than one assignment. In addition to being a clerk, I was assigned the task of locating the troops who would be assigned to the stewards' branch and muster them in. I eventually became a troop handler as well. Sometimes I would be working with three squads at a time. My clerical and troop handling experience was a plus for me because officers and noncommissioned officers seemed to respect my ability to handle different types of assignments.

In December 1944 the Marine Corps established the depot and ammunition companies. The men who served in these companies would provide logistical support for the deployed units. I was told that I would be sent to the 36th Depot Company. When we were notified that we would be shipping out for an unknown destination, which we were sure was in the Pacific, we were joined by the 33rd and 34th Depot Companies and the 8th Ammunition Company. We took the train to Norfolk, Virginia, from Montford Point where there was a troop ship waiting for us. All three depot companies and the ammunition company boarded the ship. Then we set sail without any knowledge as to where we were going. They said we were going to go through the Panama Canal and then into the Pacific Ocean. We were all excited, fully equipped with all the equipment for war. We had knives, machetes, the M-1 semi-automatic rifle, the new rifle that had recently come into the Marine Corps inventory. It would replace the "Springfield," rifle which was first issued to the United States military in 1903 and was used during World War I. We had to qualify on both the new rifle and the M-1. They wanted us to be proficient on both rifles. Going across the Pacific to Hawaii, we exercised regularly, but we had assignments aboard ship to accomplish as well. Each company would take turns performing such tasks as sweeping and mopping the deck, mess duty, and so on. There was plenty of work to do while we were at sea, but we did have time to read and relax. It took us about six or seven days to get through the Canal and get to Hawaii. Going through the Panama Canal and negotiating its locks was quite an experience. Without a doubt, it was one of the major engineering feats at that time. It left us in awe. It just didn't seem possible that something as amazing as the Panama Canal could ever be constructed. While docked at the canal, we were allowed to leave the ship, but we could not leave the port.

Once we arrived in Hawaii, we were sent out to a training camp where Marines were training for operations in the Pacific. We did get the opportunity to learn how to maneuver tanks and other types of amphibious equipment, but all that we would do when we landed on Iwo Jima was handle ammunition and perform manual labor assignments on the battlefield. Some of us were put in security jobs as an additional duty, and I was one of them. It was not easy standing on the sidelines watching it all happen and not having the opportunity to do more. I remember that one of our officers lifted our spirits when he reminded us that we were not involved in this deployment only because laborers were needed. He wanted us to understand that we were also Marines, and we would be expected to rise to the occasion when the time came for us to fight. "You will be expected to do your duty and react appropriately when necessary, and do it well," he said. What he said to us offered some consolation; it made us feel like we were really Marines. All of us were more than ready to fight for our country.

The assault division that our unit would support was the 5th Marine Division. When we got to Honolulu, my company was sent to an advanced training base where I was made a squad leader for the first squad, first platoon. We took a lot of intensive advanced bayonet training, judo and more training in survival skills. The training was so intensive that we concluded that we had to be preparing for combat, and also believed that wherever we were going, we would face strong resistance and there was an expectation that there would be a high casualty count. We were still unsure where we were headed. Some of us looked at various maps of the Pacific and tried to determine which one of the islands we might be headed for. I noticed this pretty large island right off the coast of China that was really not known by a lot of people but had been occupied by the Japanese for several years. That island was Taiwan, and we knew that thousands of Japanese troops were stationed there. Some of us thought we would hit that island, but we learned later that we would to pass it by because its strategic importance was not high enough to risk the resources we would have to expend to take that particular island. So, we bypassed it.

Once we had completed our advanced training for combat, we were given some free time to visit other troop areas and tour the island of Oahu. We actually met a lot of people we had not seen before, including Marines from other depot and ammunition companies. They were very young: 19, 20 and 21 years of age. Ninety percent of them were newly-graduated recruits who had not had the opportunity to go home before they shipped out. The depot and ammunition companies were organized quickly and the need for manpower to fill all the slots in them was immediate. Nearly 50 percent of my company's strength was made up of newly-graduated troops from basic training at Montford Point, and they were eager to learn as much as they could.

When the time came to leave Hawaii we were placed on an LST which would join an armada of other ships to form the invasion force. After boarding the ship to leave Hawaii, we were given work assignments to perform while the ship was underway and again our duties and assignments all involved custodial and labor-related tasks. One of our main tasks involved moving ammunition stored in lower compartments of the ship up to the top deck of the ship to feed the 20 millimeter and 40 millimeter guns. The duties were shared by squads made up of about nine or ten men from the platoons in my company; my squad had the duty about every other day. We performed those duties right on up until the day of the invasion. We had some interesting conversations with the gunner assigned to the big gun to which we were supplying ammunition. He taught us everything about his weapon that there was to know. In a very short period of time we would hear the deafening noise of those big guns time and time again as the battle for Iwo Jima raged on for more than a month.

As we moved on to our objective area, I remember being awakened around midnight about three or four days before the landing by the sounds of loud explosions and naval gunfire. Our convoy had been joined by more ships and had become part of a huge armada of ships. There were ships on our left and right flanks as far as I could see. It was just awesome; as far as we could see, there were ships, just ships. When we left the United States, I really did not know what to expect; it was my first deployment. I do, however, remember some of those on my ship who had participated in other invasions on Saipan and other Pacific campaigns saying that they had never seen such a large number of ships. There were all types of ships. There were even ships we had never seen that had been recently added to the Navy's inventory that would join the amphibious force for this invasion.

Seeing all of this was a sure sign that we had reached the objective area and that the invasion was about to begin. And indeed it was: we were told that morning that we were going to land on an island that was part of the Volcano Islands, an island called Iwo Jima. We were told about the geography and other characteristics of the island and that there were other smaller islands in this group. As we moved closer, Iwo Jima came into view, and we could all see its most prominent terrain feature, Mt. Suribachi. We thought it was a huge mountain, but it was a massive volcano located on one side of the island and it covered the entire side of that island. We were told that the last time that it had an eruption was about 70 years ago. The Japanese had made Mt. Suribachi a fortress and the invading air power was instructed to hit it with as much as it possibly could in an effort to take out the enemy's primary stronghold. We were also told that the U.S. Navy had been dropping bombs into it in an attempt cause a volcanic eruption, but that did not happen. Airplanes had dropped bombs into that crater for more than two months. We also learned that this volcanic formation had inside of it a maze of tunnels, caves and pillboxes constructed by the Japanese, all with an excellent view of the beach.

My 36th Depot Company and the 8th Ammunition were ordered to go ashore as a part of the initial landing force on D-Day. We did not go in the first wave, but we were positioned to go in one of the waves that followed. Our exact position would be decided by the beachmaster who controlled the landing activity on the beach. We loaded our landing craft, boarded it, and went ashore on the afternoon of D-Day, February 19, 1945. The ships were stationed a distance from the island and out of range of small-arms fire, and every effort was being made to get everything ashore as soon as possible to support the assault troops as they moved forward. As we neared the shoreline, there was debris, casualties, and intense activity everywhere. We had a graves registration unit that handled our dead and buried them. There were bodies everywhere and because of strong currents and all of the activity on the beach, it was a tough job retrieving them from the water.

When we landed, there was very little resistance from the enemy. There was some resistance and maybe some small-arms fire here and there, but it became clear that the enemy wanted to allow the first of the assault troops ashore, their sources of supply, artillery, ammunition, and other elements of support, before opening up with their heavy firepower. As we went ashore, there was alot of mud sliding in the volcanic ash, which severely limited the ability of our vehicles to move around in the battle area. Another thing that slowed down the forward movement was the fact that the beach only went about four feet inward, and from there forward, it was all uphill in the volcanic ash which completely covered the ground. We had a terrible problem moving heavy equipment. Also, there were land crabs that were as large as turtles. They came out as bodies accumulated on the beach.

Because of the sloped geological formation of the terrain, we really had to take some hard and firm steps in the sand to make it up that slope in order to reach what you would consider to be the main part of the actual island. Those coming ashore in tanks and motorized vehicles had even more difficulty going ashore. Getting across the beach through that sand was definitely a task, and attempting to do it with the enemy shooting at you made it even worse. At the time we came ashore in the early waves, we were only getting small-arms fire, but even with the small-arms fire, we were sustaining casualties.

Those in the first waves experienced so many difficulties with all the obstacles they had to encounter, that forward movement seemed like it was inch by inch. When the enemy did finally open up with its heavy artillery and mortars, things continued to get worse. The terrain and the well-entrenched, well-concealed enemy made the early going very slow, and many casualties occurred as a result. It was not a pretty picture when we went ashore, but we had a mission to accomplish. The depot and ammunition companies had to ensure that the front line troops had the support, supplies and ammunition they needed to continue to move forward and take the island. And we were determined to make that happen.

When I finally got to the top of the beach, I saw a lot of Marines, Seabees, and others who were in the very first waves either dug in or in the beachmasters' area. They had come ashore with equipment and vehicles and other necessary items to assist the assault troops as they moved forward. I can still hear the beachmaster calling for the troops to hold their position. He was telling everyone, in essence, not to go any further until told to do so because of the incoming enemy fire and the difficulty that the men were having maneuvering and positioning supplies and equipment in the black, volcanic ash. The whole area there was just chaotic. No one knew what to do next. The beachmaster, showing signs of frustration, knew but could not do much considering the terrain conditions, enemy fire coming in and more and more troops and equipment and supplies continuously coming ashore. The many pieces of equipment being brought ashore were not making it to the designated position which had previously been assigned by the beachmaster. Equipment was just all over the beach, and a lot of it had been hit or destroyed by enemy fire.

The assault troops, on the other hand, were traveling a lot lighter, moved a lot faster, and were well beyond us when we hit the beach. The enemy had prepared themselves well for the assault, and the infantry troops in the very first waves sustained a lot of casualties but they were moving ahead. When we finally made it to the beachmaster, we were directed to our position and instructed to set up our equipment. Positions had been planned and designated so that when requests came for certain items or services from the beach, the items could quickly be located and distributed. We reached our position by nightfall and finally bivouacked in the area until morning. Moving to our designated position through the sand was tough enough, but digging in was even more of a task. As soon as we put our shovels in the sand and tried to reach a certain level, it would just slide back into place. With the mobility issue being what it was, it was not difficult to see why we had so many casualties. Then we began the task of receiving and positioning supplies and equipment ashore that would support the assault troops. By the first weekend of the invasion, we had set up on the beach and had routine procedures in place to support the forward troops. We stayed on the beach for a few days. The movement of the assault troops was closely monitored and we had to remain in close proximity with them to ensure that requests for support could be satisfied as quickly as possible. As they moved forward, when it was practical to do so, we followed behind them.

It was only a short distance from the beach of that tiny island to Mt. Suribachi, but with all of the activity it sometimes seemed like every step was a mile. At one point as we moved inland and my squad was positioned about a quarter of a mile from Motoyama Airfield #1. There were three airfields there, but the only one that was operational was Motoyama Airfield #1. The Japanese were in the process of finishing the other two but did not have a chance to do so before the invasion was launched. The Navy Seabees were fiercely working day and night to put the other two airfields in operation. They were working hard and every man was doing what needed to be done to make those airfields operational. Our equipment was far superior to what the Japanese had to work with. The Seabees had rollers, graders, bulldozers and all the equipment needed to improve the airfields and get the job done. Three days from when they started, the Seabees had all three airfields in operation. Their superior equipment, training and positive attitude was a major contribution to the victory on Iwo Jima. They really did a great job and they did it under fire. The Japanese had equipment that seemed ancient compared to what our Seabees were using. The condition of the road leading up to Mt. Suribachi was barely serviceable and was in the same condition as the airfields. The Japanese needed that access to Suribachi, and they were in the process of building a road to the volcano and an access to the top of it when we attacked. The Seabees finished the job of building the road that the Japanese had started. They finished work on the road and did it quickly while the fighting was going on just as they had done when they constructed the runways. Even though the Japanese were dropping small mortar fire on them while they were constructing the roads and runways, the Seabees would work at night with lights and oftentimes work all through the night. The Seabees took some casualties but again, they needed to get those airfields in operation. Access to the top of the volcano was important to the invading force. The threat to our aircraft was necessary to neutralize the enemy threat to air supply coming in from Guam and other locations and also to service our big bombers and other aircraft flying missions over the mainland once the airfields were secured. I happened to see the first landing of a B-29 on the island. It landed on Motoyama Airfield #1, and it was quite exciting to see such a huge airplane land on that small island. The bomber just barely made the landing, but repairs were necessary due to a rough landing. That B-29 needed all the territory the airfield had to offer in order to make that landing. It was a very bumpy landing, but they made it.

There were large ammo dumps, supply points, a bivouac area for the pilots and aircrews, Army units and Seabees positioned very close to the runway, and sentries posted there for security purposes, but the huge amount of activity in the area near the runways required additional security. To meet that requirement, my squad and elements of the ammunition company were assigned security duties. We basically manned two areas: our supply point down on the beachhead and security points for the bivouac area located near Motoyama Airfield #1. As time went by, there was a lull in incoming fire and fighting down at the beach. Apparently the continuous barrage of fire coming from the naval gunfire and the aerial bombardment had knocked out a lot of the long-range Japanese firing capabilities. On or about D+16 of the invasion, things seemed to quiet down a bit. It seemed that the pace of activity had really slowed down, but the fighting never really stopped. Around the airfields there was some strafing by enemy artillery. Even though the intensity of the assault seemed to have slowed a bit, all of our activity was still heavily focused on completing the task at hand and the assault troops were still aggressively moving in to isolate and capture enemy troops.

The airfields were continuously targeted by the Japanese. We believe that the Japanese knew that there were storages of ammunition near the airfield. From their vantage points imbedded in Mt. Suribachi and familiarity with the terrain, there was no reason why they should not have. I feel sure that the enemy had photographs and knew exactly where the storage facilities were. On March 26, 1945, my squad was recalled to the airfield where the munitions and supplies were stored for security duty. At about 5 A.M. that morning we heard small-arms fire, which was not unusual, but when it did not stop, we determined that something out of the ordinary was going on. Naturally, we picked up our weapons and the commanding officer on site ordered that a perimeter be formed around our post. Our men were located right behind the pioneer battalion encampment. And when we were ordered to fire, it was hard to tell who the enemy was and who was not. We, along with the members of the pioneer battalion, were told that there were about 200 Japanese soldiers attacking our position. It was a Banzai attack on the bivouac area, and we were told that several of the flyers in the area died in the attack. We were able to stop the attack. One of the Marines in my squad came into the Marine Corps knowing how to work with weapons and explosives and so on. During the Banzai attack, he was observed by one of the officers disarming a Japanese soldier who was about to discharge a fragmentation grenade capable of doing serious damage and handily taking care of a few enemy soldiers. For his heroism he, along with another one of my squad members, was awarded the Bronze Star, and two other Marines in my squad were awarded the Purple Heart for their actions in that attack. The actions of those men were certainly noteworthy, meritorious and significantly enhanced the image of the black Marine on Iwo Jima. However, in the accounts of the battle of Iwo Jima rarely, if ever, are there any accounts of anything about the heroism, service or accomplishments of blacks during the conflict.

Prior to the end of the battle and leaving the island, I was recommended for promotion to sergeant. We left the island with the 5th Marine Division, to whom we were attached, for Hilo on the island of Hawaii, but we did not stay in Hilo. The black troops were sent from Hilo to another camp which was located among a large number of huge sugar cane factories. The camp that had been constructed for military use and it was quite nice. We were sent there to await our next assignment while the white troops were quartered elsewhere. We had everything we needed, motion pictures, nice quarters and good food and there were opportunities for recreation. The camp was not simply a rest and relaxation stop; we also received a lot of training, especially in chemical warfare. There was no question about it—we knew we were going for another combat deployment. We actually believed that we would be going to mainland Japan, as part of an invasion force with our parent unit, the 5th Marine Division. The amount of training we received gave us some kind of idea as to what the fighting for our next invasion would be like. We were sure that we were training for another landing because the war was not over yet and, because of the type of training we were receiving, it was apparent to me that chemical weapons might be heavily used the next time. The invasion never happened, we were in Hawaii when the atomic bomb was dropped on mainland Japan and the war was over.

We did go to a huge Japanese naval base at Sasebo along with the entire invasion force as part of the occupation troops to help with the cleanup in the aftermath of the dropping of the atomic bomb. We were quartered in the barracks used by the Japanese troops during the war. We had to get used to our new living conditions because they were not as comfortable as the ones we left in Hawaii. When we got to Sasebo, we saw that the training we were getting in chemical warfare was right on target because we found strong evidence that the Japanese might have been planning to use that capability if and when the mainland was attacked. Part of our job there was to assist in dismantling that capability when we arrived in Sasebo. The situation in Japan was very delicate when we were there and the order was issued that there was to be no going into town or unnecessary contact

Sergeant Eugene Doughty, USMC.

with the people. We stayed about three months in Sasebo and then went to Guam.

On the island of Guam, I begin the process of mustering out and going home. I had enough points to go. I ran into some buddies stationed there whom I had known at Montford Point while I was going through boot camp. Those Marines had a lot of racial problems on Guam, quite unlike our situation on Iwo Jima. When I left Guam, I went to Treasure Island, which is located just outside of San Francisco, on a troop ship and began the process of mustering out of the Marine Corps. We had our medical exam there, did a lot of paper work, and after about 48 hours, went to San Diego to board a troop train back to Montford Point. The trip took about seven days; it was a long trip but everybody was more than happy to be going home. We made several stops along the way to exercise, but we were not allowed to go into any towns. They fed us on the train, and the cars were sleeper cars, similar to the Pullman train cars. We thought we were going to have a problem while going through one part of Texas. Some of the people heckled us and shied away from us when they saw black troops aboard. Here we were, coming back from fighting for our country and now having to tolerate that kind of treatment. To this day, I cannot understand why they would turn their backs on us when at any moment during the battle we could have lost our lives protecting our country.

When the company arrived at Montford Point, those of us leaving the Corps were discharged. We were there for about a week. We went through the motions of getting our discharge papers and meeting with the officer in charge. He shook our hands and wished us well individually. There were a lot of us there, and we felt good that he took the time to do that. My commanding officer approached me at one point during the discharge process and said that there will come a time when I would have the opportunity to serve as an officer. My goal was to go on and finish what I had started before I joined the Marines. At the time, I wanted to finish my work for the Bachelor of Arts degree at the City College of New York. I took advantage of the GI Bill and did that.

Corporal Roland Durden, United States Marine Corps

As a teenager, I was very much influenced, like a lot of young men my age, by the movies and recruiting efforts to join the military and participate in the war effort. I went to the movies and saw all of our military men depicted as heroes. The enemy—the Japanese, Germans, and Italians—on the other hand, were depicted in a derogatory manner. The movies did a very good job in their efforts to turn our country against the enemy and incite the general population for war. Everybody, both at home and on the battlefield, was ready to do what was necessary to defeat them. I was an only child and had grown up in the ghetto. I wanted more than that. Life was tough there, and I didn't have that ghetto mentality. I wanted to contribute to the war effort and do more. I believed that going into the military could be a way for me to do that. I was most impressed by the Marines and I wanted to be one.

I remember Sunday, December 7, 1941, when the Japanese made the surprise attack on Pearl Harbor. I was in high school at the time, and I was working part time at the YMCA located near 63rd Street near Central Park. That is where I heard President Roosevelt's speech to the nation directly after the attack. I was a great admirer of President Roosevelt and his speech motivated and helped me even more in my decision to join the military. I knew that going to war could mean that I might not make it back home, but that didn't bother me because I was truly committed to doing my part in the defense of our country and was looking forward to getting training and life skills that would help me in my working career. I knew that eventually I would probably be drafted, but I volunteered for the military because I wanted to go. So when I was old enough, I went down to a building just north of Grand Central Station where the recruiting station was and I joined the Marines.

Shortly after I joined up, I was sent to the segregated Marine Corps training camp known as Montford Point, located in Jacksonville, North Carolina, where I would train to become a Marine. The drill instructors quickly made me and all of the others realize that we were not civilians anymore and that we were now Marines. Discipline and attention to orders would be the order of the day throughout training in preparation for service in the Marine Corps wherever we would be sent to serve.

The Marines had a strong reputation for discipline and esprit de corps. When I joined in 1944, service for blacks was still new to the Marine Corps. The first blacks to serve had only entered two years prior to my arrival at the Montford Point training camp. Some of those first Marines to be trained there went on to graduate and serve as drill instructors for those who would follow them. By the time I got to training, all of the drill instructors were black. They were very tough on us. One thing about those black drill instructors is true for sure: they did everything possible to ensure that when we finished boot camp, we were Marines. Our training at Montford Point was just as rigorous as it was for those white Marines who trained at Parris Island, and when we graduated from boot camp, we were as ready as they were to be Marines.

Even though we had recruits who came from civilian life with college degrees and various professions at Montford Point, the official policy of separating the races limited what we could do as Marines. We did not get all of the opportunities to train in all of the military occupational specialties that were available to our white counterparts. The only assignments available to us were those in service and support specialties such as food service, clerical, personnel and labor-related duties. There were defense battalions established, and some of the Montford Point trained Marines were deployed to the Pacific, but they never saw action there. I spent a short time in one of the defense battalions but was later transferred to the 33rd Marine Depot Company. Had I stayed with the defense battalion, I probably would have been sent to a Pacific island other than Iwo Jima because the defense battalions were not involved in the battle at Iwo Jima. The 33rd Depot Company went ashore on Iwo Jima on my 19th birthday, February 24, 1945, and I was with them. I joined the war effort to serve my country and develop some skills and qualities that I believed would help me become a productive citizen. I did serve and I am proud of my service on Iwo Jima and in the Marine Corps, but it would not be until later in life that I would have the opportunity to develop the personal goals I set for myself. The issue of segregation during World War II would not allow me to do that in the military.

When I joined the 33rd Depot Company, I had no idea what my duties in the company would be. The 33rd consisted of three platoons and we began organizing for what I would soon realize was a deployment overseas. I was only there for about a month before we shipped out. Although it was only a short period of time, we trained every day as we had in boot camp. We received more marksmanship training at the rifle range, more judo instruction, crawled on the ground while live ammunition was being fired over our heads, and received more training in water survival skills. It was similar to the training we received in boot camp, but it was more intensive, and we received much more of it. Even though we had finished boot camp, the emphasis on discipline and regimentation continued. We did a lot of marching in those pine woods surrounding the camp there at Montford Point.

When my company finally did move out, we left North Carolina on a troop train with mostly black troops aboard and headed west. En route we picked up two carloads of German prisoners captured in the European theatre who were on their way to POW camps. They got on the train outside of New Orleans. We traveled to Texas with them. On our way we would stop every so often for water and coal. At one particular stop, the Red Cross nurses brought coffee and doughnuts for the troops. We heard our captain say to the nurses, "Serve the Germans first." We also heard one of the nurses reply to him, "No, we will serve our boys first."

Our unit finally arrived in California where we got off the train at Marine Corps Base, Camp Pendleton. From there we boarded a ship at San Diego that would take us to Hawaii. I believe that the ship on which we sailed out of California was a captured German ship that was being operated by the U.S. Army. The ship was too small and not really built to carry the number of troops we had in our unit, and the living conditions on it were not very good. The water we drank tasted like the water tanks had been painted inside, and I recall that we ate a lot of bratwurst, knackwurst, sauerkraut and hot dogs.

When we arrived in Hawaii, our unit was assigned to a camp that was located between Pearl Harbor and Honolulu. I do not remember much about our stay there or even where we would be going. I do remember, though, that we continued our combat training, and I know now that our camp was a staging area for the Pacific campaign and we would probably move out any day. We did not stay there very long. I think that we were there about four months, and I did have the opportunity to see a little of the island. I truly believe that we were really waiting for the war strategists to finish the task organization for the amphibious force and complete the planning process for the invasion.

After our stay in Hawaii, we were assigned to an LST to complete the trip to Iwo Jima. On the ship I slept on the top deck under a truck all the way from Hawaii to Iwo. At some point all of us had tasks or chores to do. I remember working in the kitchen. We stopped at Eniwetok Island after leaving Hawaii and joined up with an armada of ships in Guam for the last leg of the trip to Iwo Jima. In high school I had read about the island of Eniwetok, and I thought the island would be much larger than what I saw. It wasn't, and in reality it seemed to be no larger than a sandbar that looked like it was only inches above the waterline. I actually enjoyed the time at sea. We were assigned some duties aboard the ship but mainly the heavy emphasis was on making sure that we were ready for an armed conflict that we knew was sure to come. The ship's gunnery crew practiced firing its guns and we checked and rechecked our gear to make sure that we would be ready when we got to the battle area. Sometimes, when the ship stopped or conducted gunnery exercises, we would have the opportunity to leave the ship for swimming before we got into hostile waters.

When we arrived in the battle area, on February 19, 1945, our ship stayed quite a distance off shore among a lot of ships that filled the waters around Iwo Jima. We were in a perimeter of ships which included battleships, destroyers, and other ships that were pounding the island with firepower. I remember seeing a plane crash, explosions, flamethrowers, and troops engaging in firefights on the beach. Our ship was loaded with ammunition and we could not get too close to shore until the beachmaster cleared us to do so. A well-placed enemy round could have taken us out for sure. In our stationary position we could not clearly see all of the action, only figures moving around on the island, smoke, and explosions. We would become very familiar with it, though, when we went ashore.

Our ship was stationary for the most part until the beach was cleared. It headed for the beach on February 23, 1945, but when we did pull in close to the beach, Japanese mortars fired on us several times. The ship's captain decided that the mortar fire was too great of a risk with all the ammunition aboard and decided to move our LST back out to sea until the enemy threat was no longer a problem. On the next morning, February 24, 1945, my birthday, our ship went back to the beach and my unit went ashore. Our LST had the capability to move right up to the beach, open its bow, lower its ramp and unload its cargo. When that happened, we walked across the ramp and went ashore. The infantry troops were a distance away from us by that time, and that is where the enemy was focusing most of its attention when we did pull in. The first thing I noticed on the beach was the volcanic ash, which really looked like sand, that just seemed to cover the island. We continued on to our designated location just up the hill from the beach to the 5th Marine Division cemetery. That is where I would spend most of my time on Iwo Jima. I had no idea what I would be doing ashore, and I did not find out until my unit left the LST. It would be my job to bury those killed in action.

Burying our dead was a very difficult job. Occasionally, we would notice that the condition of some of the men we were burying was so bad that we were shaken just by looking at them. On one occasion, I recall seeing in one of the burial and identification tents a young Marine with surgical scars and wounds from his head to his groin, and it would be our job to bury him. He had surgical scars from head to toe. There were many emotional moments like that and on some occasions, when we had incoming fire, we had to jump down into the graves with the men we were burying. We had no choice because we had no cover. There was no place to go. A caterpillar would dig the graves, and I was assigned to a detail that would bury our fallen troops. One night, I recall seeing at one end of the burial site a huge caterpillar. Its engine was silent, but the operator was sitting patiently while the three chaplains, Catholic, Protestant, and Hebrew, were committing the dead to their final resting place. "Ashes to ashes, dust to dust," we would hear them say. My company, the 33rd and the 34th Depot Company, were the units assigned the duty to bury the dead on Iwo Jima. We would stand among the bodies as the chaplains said the prayers. There were 20 in each grave, two rows of ten, and we were directed to ensure that their heads were to face the cemetery flag, which was the United States flag. No training can prepare anyone to see bodies piled on top of one another. No training can prepare anyone to see human brains, torsos split open with intestines hanging out, or legs separated from bodies and burned beyond recognition. And, of course, no training teaches a teenager just out of high school to handle the dead, to smell death, and see the same flies that had been on those bodies crawling on our mess kits as we tried to eat our K-rations. We sat among the dead while we were eating. When the three chaplains finished praying over the bodies, a few shovels full of the volcanic ash were placed over the bodies, and the caterpillar operator started the engine of his vehicle and proceeded to cover the grave. We were continuously reminded to treat the men with respect and dignity as we did our job. Occasionally, I would perform other support activities, but burying our dead was my primary job. The 33rd and 34th Depot Companies worked together on the burial details, and the 36th Depot Company worked with the 8th Ammunition Company to keep the forward troops supplied with fire support. From the rear of the front lines, we did not see much of the action. We could, however, hear it all and when there was incoming fire, we could feel the effects of it. There were isolated moments, I recall, when some of us did get close to the action. The battle lasted about a month, but we were actually on the island for about four months.

I was the first of our group to stand guard duty after we went ashore, and each time I stood watch, it seemed like I was on duty for an eternity. There was no moon, there was no light at all, and I could not see anything. Feeling a bit uneasy, I kept telling myself that this, too, shall end, but it would take a little over a month to do so—the battle was just beginning. After that long night, there was another time, while we were working near an ammunition site—a fire erupted as a result of a Japanese mortar attack. I tried to protect myself from the fire and explosions I knew would follow. I learned very quickly that when the sound of the explosion is heard and the light from the explosion is seen, it's time to get down on the ground because the next thing that would follow would be debris and shrapnel. If the impact of the direct hit does not get you, the flying debris that will follow the explosion probably will. I did that for the rest of my time on the island whenever I heard an explosion. The possibility of a stray round, explosion or just an accident was always present.

On another occasion, when I was sent out by my sergeant on a mission, I encountered another explosion. As I left the area to complete the assignment, an explosion from a big gun emplacement went off right near me. Remembering the earlier experience I had, I hit the deck. The gun was dug in just below ground and covered with netting. I had no idea that it was there. The explosion was so sudden that I did not even have time to react or be frightened by it. When I looked around after the explosion, I saw the guns. Even to this day, I marvel at how quickly it all happened and that I am here to tell about it. I assumed that our area was reasonably secure. My unit was located in the rear, and I had no idea that there would be such a gun position so close to us. I had no warning that I would stumble upon that gun position. I remember yet another incident when a Marine accidentally kicked a grenade which exploded and caused serious injury to his legs and lower extremities. And there were non-combat issues that we had to deal with as well. One night, we heard something that sounded like digging underground while we were our foxhole. We were always looking out for infiltration or tactics by the enemy to catch us off guard. We thought that the enemy was up to something, but the next day we received a memo that it was actually volcanic activity—another threat that none of us had given any thought to. We were happy that nothing came of it. Thinking back on it all, I guess I wonder sometimes how we got through it, but after awhile I guess we just became conditioned to expect anything. Situations like that were everyday occurrences all over the island. It was, in fact, a battlefield until the day we left. I guess it's just something we came to live with.

The 5th Marine Division cemetery where we worked was located near the Motyama Airfield #1. One of the main reasons for us invading that island was to secure the landing fields there. As the battle progressed, we could see that happening. We could see planes were starting to come in more and more toward the end of the battle. Sometimes I could see the P-51 aircraft coming in from a run over mainland Japan landing on the runway. The P-51s escorted the B-29 bombers on their missions over mainland Japan. The B-29s were really too big to land there and usually did so under emergency conditions. I remember seeing one do so.

I do believe that we were fighting a determined enemy. Working in the rear areas, I had almost no direct contact with them. I do know that our naval gunfire and aircraft pounded the island regularly, and we seemed to have had all the advantage in numbers of troops and firepower as we made the assault. They could not go anywhere. Doing the kind of work I was doing, I am not sure that I was in a position to predict at any given moment who was winning or the enemy's war fighting skills and resolve to win, but I can say I do know that we buried a lot of our own people.

We did not have mess halls or mess tents at all on the island. It was a battlefield. We were issued canned and packaged K- and C-rations which consisted of hard candy, preserved food in cans, and cigarettes and we consumed them wherever we happened to be at the time. The process of resupplying us with chow from the ships was well planned, and issued regularly from various supply points on a daily basis. Not until near the end of the battle did we have any type of cooked meals. Considering the conditions under which we had to work, we did the best we could to enjoy those rations and they served their purpose; they provided the nourishment we needed to keep us going. We bathed and shaved with water we would put in our helmets when and where we could. We did not have much of an opportunity to change clothing; we pretty much wore the same clothes around the clock. About the only items of clothing we would take off with any regularity were our boots and underwear, but our outerwear was with us for just about all of the time were on the island. I don't remember having the opportunity to shower at all while I was on the island. Living in a foxhole in a battle area was not at all like living at home, in a barracks, or even aboard ship; but after a day of doing the kind of work we were doing, our mind and body got used to it, and we sort of settled into it and even learned how to get a good night's sleep in our foxhole. There were three of us in mine. I did not dig my own foxhole because for some reason the ground where I had tried to dig was as hard as a rock, and I could not get my shovel through it, so I joined two others in theirs. Our foxhole was not really much of anything but a hole in the ground. We may have had a piece of canvas pulled over the top of it but that was all.

When we could, we would have religious services. We had a white chaplain from New England who indicated that he had heard comments about black troops that were not consistent with what he experienced when he was with us. I remember him giving us service on Sunday, and on one occasion hearing him disregard those comments and say to us, "When I am with you guys, I know different. With you guys I really feel like I have been in church." Our chaplains were a great source of support for us. When the announcement was made shortly after Iwo Jima was secured that President Roosevelt had died, I will always remember our chaplain reciting over the public address system a part of a poem that concluded with the words "Sail on, oh ship of state. Sail on, oh union strong and great." We had lost a great leader, and I think that the chaplain was telling us that the president would want us to keep going on and continue in the quest to help make the United States and the world safe for democracy.

After Iwo Jima was secured in late March of 1945, victory in Europe was achieved, and the Japanese would surrender a few months after that in September of 1945. Following the victory declared in Europe, we heard a lot of rifles firing rounds in the air and we didn't know what was happening. Where we were working at the cemetery, we did not always have access to the information resources to keep us up on what was going on. We did find out later that the excitement was all about an announcement over the public address system that victory in Europe had been declared.

There were few opportunities for leisure time while we were on Iwo, but I do remember that when they did put up a loudspeaker system, we were treated to news reports and music by artists from home such as the very popular jazz pianist Eddie Haywood, who made popular the song "Begin the Beguine," and Billie Holiday, who would oftentimes be backed up by Eddie Haywood. The collection of music was very limited, and we heard a lot of the same music over and over but it sounded good and it was from home.

Whenever we could get a radio, we could always hear Tokyo Rose playing music from home and trying to break our spirits. We did have mail call and I think I remember getting two or three letters from my mother; with all that was going on, we rarely got mail. I believe that some of the mail going out was censored. With the enemy tracking everything that we did, it was necessary.

From my point of view, it was difficult to tell when the battle was over. My duties had become routine, and my specific job with the burial detail seemed to be a never-ending one. Eventually though, near the end I did see signs that the battle had become less intense. When they brought the music in and began playing it over the public address system and a small Post Exchange was set up where we could buy small items, it occurred to me that things were winding down. Our units' departure from the island was nothing like our arrival. It was quiet and peaceful. Our sergeant simply told us to put on our backpacks, grab our gear and head for the ship. It was over.

When my unit left Iwo, we went to Hawaii briefly and then on to Sasebo, Japan, to help with the cleanup in the wake of the dropping of the atomic bomb on Hiroshima and Nagasaki along with the other units we deployed with from Montford Point. We had spent more than a month on Iwo Jima, but when we arrived on the mainland of Japan and saw the devastation that the bombing campaign against Japan had wrought, it became very real to me. I saw ships lying on their sides in the harbor as we were climbing down the rope ladder from our ship into the landing craft below that would take us to the shore. Those ships and all that I saw were at one time bigger than life before the war, but now had become casualties of war. Sasebo was a very important naval base for the Japanese during the war and now was a mass of wreckage and destruction. All of what I was seeing just overwhelmed me and made me feel that under certain circumstances, any of us could be victims of what I was seeing. The devastation I saw of the large Japanese naval force in Sasebo, the Japanese mainland after the dropping of the atomic bomb, and the battle on Iwo had provided me with some new perspectives on life. I was raised in the big city of New York among millions of people, and I could not help but compare all of the ruin and devastation, in my mind, to what one of our metropolitan cities back home would look like if such a thing would have happened there. As a young man who had just turned 19 years old, I was learning some lessons in life on Iwo Jima and Sasebo about the value of life, and living it in peace and harmony that would stay with me for the rest of my life.

Staff Sergeant Sam Green, U.S. Army

As our country was getting ready for World War II, most young men my age were being called to serve and I knew that eventually I would be called to serve too. When I reached the age of 18, on August 9, 1943, I registered and on October 2 of that same year, and as I knew would happen, I was drafted. I heard stories about draft dodgers, but where I lived, we had very little of that. There were some who were called to duty that just did not report, register, respond to the call to service or deserted after being called. I was ready to go and I considered it my duty as a citizen to do so. I was discharged from the military and rewarded for that service with some outstanding veteran's benefits. The benefit that has been most valuable to me, I truly believe, is the comprehensive medical care I have received during all of those years since my discharge. I have no regrets about my military service to this very day. I knew that if I went in and had to serve in a combat zone, I might return home wounded and there was the possibility that I might not return at all, but not even that would keep me from doing what I considered to be my duty. All across the country, not just in my local area, it seemed that there was a strong effort on the part of everyone to contribute to the war effort. That strong sense of patriotism, and the many jobs that opened up during the mobilization for war, offered employment opportunities for many who had lost jobs during the depression. People were working in factories, on the farms, and at different jobs in preparation for the war. The troops overseas could not have won the war without the support of the home front and they sure had that.

We were fully aware that segregation even in the military was the policy for the service and training of blacks. Our basic training was as much about learning how to be infantry soldiers as it was for the white soldiers who were going through basic training in other training camps. From day one through graduation from basic, we were taught to defend ourselves and to defeat the enemy. They taught us how to survive on the battlefield. Surviving and defeating the enemy was the basis of everything we were taught in basic training, from the time we woke up in the morning until we went to bed at night. We also learned how to function as a team, how to take orders and how to give orders, and how to protect our fellow soldiers.

After basic, the group I trained with did not go to an infantry unit; we went to Camp Gordon Johnston in Florida where we joined the 476th Amphibian Truck Company and learned how to move troops, supplies, and equipment from ship-to-shore in the DUKW. During the battle of Iwo Jima, we would carry the 105 howitzers ashore that would support the 4th Marine Division. We were taught how to drive our vehicles off the LSTs into the water and navigate the seas to get the cargo and troops to shore. Although we were not front line infantry troops, we had been trained to be during basic training in case we did encounter situations in which we had to become combat soldiers. Many members of support and service units on the battlefield did find themselves face-to-face with the enemy and had to fight right along with the infantry troops. We all had to be prepared to engage in combat if necessary.

After basic at Camp Plauche, Louisiana, and advanced training on the operation of the DUKWs at Camp Gordon Johnston, we shipped out, but we really did not know where were going. We believed that we were headed for either the European or Pacific Theater. Everything was top secret. When we left Florida and headed west, we got the idea that we were probably going to the Pacific, but we still did not know where. When we arrived on the West Coast in Washington State, we determined that we would probably see combat in the Pacific. From there, we went to Hawaii to train with the Marines we would support in amphibious operations.

We still did not know that we would be going to Iwo Jima. When we did leave Hawaii on the way to the battle area, we received briefings on what to expect and even then, we still did not know where we were going. We thought we would be going to Okinawa, but we also knew that Iwo Jima was on the route. We thought that we would bypass the tiny island or make a quick landing there, take it in a matter of days and then move on to the bigger island of Okinawa. Our company departed Hawaii on an LST with our DUKWs, the unit we would support in the in the assault of Iwo Jima, the 4th Marine Division. The assault troops would go ahead of us in the landing, and we would immediately follow them with the heavy artillery, troops, ammunition, and supplies.

We had a few dry runs to practice the kind of activities we would be required to do wherever we landed on some of the small islands we encountered en route to the battle area. After the dry runs, we would get back to the ship and move on to our objective. We did not take a direct route to the battle area. I believe that we stopped most of the time to allow the buildup of the task force to be phased in and coordinated so that the complete task force, which was made up of ships and troops coming from various locations, could be assembled. As we stopped at those points along the way, we were joined by more troops and ships. The task force that would make the assault on Iwo Jima was being formed. We always believed that we were headed into a combat zone, that we would be in combat with Japan, and that we would hit some island in the Pacific. We found out for sure when it was announced on the ship's public address system as we moved into the battle area and saw the island of Iwo Jima. "Now this is it. Now hear this," the voice said. The message was a long lecture stressing all of the things we had been taught and had practiced in the training exercises in preparation for what we were about to experience; it stressed that this was now the real thing and that we must use that training and those skills to stay alive and accomplish the mission.

When we arrived just offshore of Iwo Jima, there were ships of all types. Battleships, carriers, hospital ships, and troop ships as far as you could see. It seemed as if the island was completely surrounded. Naval gunfire was constantly hitting the island and the airplanes were unloading bombs on it. All we could hear were explosions and all we could see were clouds of smoke surrounding the island. It was an amazing sight to stand on the deck of that ship and see all that was going on. It seemed to me that with all that firepower hitting the island, it should have just disappeared into the sea. The Japanese fought back for as long as they could. Among one of their best defenses was a huge gun that they had mounted on an elevator inside of Mt. Suribachi. During the battle, it would be raised out through an opening at the top of Mt. Suribachi on an elevator and had the capability to fire at long-range targets stationed offshore. When it was sighted by the battleships offshore, all of the firepower the assault forces could muster from air, land, and sea would zero in on the big gun and start firing at it; the enemy would then lower the big gun back down into the volcano. When the assault forces ceased fire, the big gun would be raised, again, and start firing at targets off shore; then it would be targeted again.

It was a chilling experience to see all that was going on, but we believed that we had been well trained to do what we had to do, and I truly believed that I would make it through all of it. When I left home, I remember that many people wished me well and many prayers were offered for my safe return, and I do believe that those prayers had a big part to play in my safe return. Sadly, though, there were many who made that landing that did not make it back.

During the landing I did not drive a DUKW. As a staff sergeant, I had the responsibility of controlling the activities of a platoon of DUKWs during the assault. I went ashore with them and had the responsibility of making sure that they were equipped to do what they needed to do to make the landing and that they made it to their designated locations ashore, unloaded their cargo and equipment, and returned to the LST to prepare for another trip ashore.

Our DUKWs were basically stationed on the ship when we were not accomplishing resupply missions to the beach. There were times though when we did not make it back to the ship because heavy enemy fire would not allow us to do so, or the cover of darkness posed some serious safety hazards with all of the activity in the waters surrounding the island. In the early phases of the landing, the Japanese allowed a big part of the landing force to come ashore before they began their barrage of heavy gunfire; our movements to and from shore were not affected nearly as much as they were when the enemy opened up with the heavy firepower. When we could, though, we would make our trip ashore and get back to the ship as quickly as possible for another resupply mission to the troops ashore. After the Marine assault troops secured the island and turned control of it over to the Army, and the Marines moved out, the entire unit ceased operation from the ship and all of its personnel, equipment, and supplies did move ashore. By that time most of the enemy resistance had ceased.

When we had to stay on the island instead of going back, which was our normal routine, because of darkness or heavy enemy activity during the assault, we would, like the assault troops, dig a foxhole and stay ashore until we could make it back to the ship and continue our ship-to-shore missions. There was no required plan for a foxhole. We just tried to build something that we thought would cover and protect us from enemy fire. Trying to build a foxhole in all of the volcanic ash was a job. It seemed that the more ash we took out of a hole, the more would slide back into it. Most of us put sandbags filled with volcanic ash in the hole, put a wooden cover on top of the sandbags, put more sandbags on top of the wood for more cover and sometimes put canvas on top of that to keep out moisture. With most of the island covered with volcanic ash, filling all the sandbags we could was no problem. Those sandbags saved many lives. They stopped a lot of bullets and shrapnel. Along with serving as protection for foxholes, our sentry posts were enclosed with sandbags. We felt pretty well protected when we got behind those sandbags. We called it sand, but it was actually volcanic ash which offered more protection than sand because it was really small pieces of rock. We would prepare the size of the foxhole to accommodate the number of people to share it. Most of us in the amphibian truck companies were somewhat more fortunate than those who were stationed ashore during the assault. We spent most of our nights on the ship. Believe me, though, it was not like living in a hotel; but it was shelter, and we were removed from the direct line of fire and all of the chaos ashore.

There was no doubt that the enemy intended to win that battle. Even when they were forced out of Mt. Suribachi and out of their tunnels and into the ocean by the Marines with the flamethrowers, they fought with all they had. From the pillboxes in Suribachi they had a clear view of the advancing assault troops and had been very effective in slowing down their advance in the initial days of the battle. When they came out, prisoners were taken. Even though the Japanese soldiers fought with determination to defeat us, when we did get an opportunity to see them as prisoners of war, they seemed quiet, obedient, and as far as I could see, they were treated well. The fact that they held on as long as they did against a strong, well-equipped and larger force indicates to me that they we were well disciplined and that they had a well-trained army. They did not give up, they held on right to the end, but they were outnumbered and over-powered by our forces. Once they were captured, they were quickly removed from the island.

There were no dining facilities or mess tents ashore. We ate two different types of meals—K-rations and C-rations—that came to us already cooked and prepackaged. After having eaten hot, home-cooked meals all my life, this was quite a change, but believe it or not, some of that food was actually very good. We would get bacon and a lot of good stuff in the C-rations, they tasted better and seemed to be better prepared than K-rations, I thought. The ration packages contained can foods, crackers, candy bars, cigarettes, and the food was dehydrated stuff that would not spoil. There were no cooking facilities during the assault, we just took what was in the boxed meals out, opened the cans, or unwrapped it and ate it. The only prepared food I saw during the entire time we were in the Pacific was when we would go back to the ship after completing missions ashore, and after the battle was over when dining tents were set up to feed us and other occupation troops permanently stationed there. Bathing facilities and clean clothing were luxuries that we had to do without during the battle. Nobody complained though, staying alive and defeating the enemy was our first priority. Occasionally, we had the opportunity to take showers in a hot sulfur pit on the island. The sulfur pits contained hot water, and we would fill tanks with the water and do everything we could to get in to get a shower before the water cooled down. Usually, when we needed to bathe, shave, or brush our teeth, we poured water that was rationed to us in our helmets, and used it to do so.

Bad weather is one thing that really could have made things even more difficult for us. We were fortunate because that was not really a problem on Iwo Jima. We did not have any cold weather, but every now and then a heavy mist just covered the island. We all believed that we would eventually hit Japan's mainland because the war was over in Europe and we thought that the war effort would now be concentrated on defeating the Japanese. It was much colder on the mainland than it was on Iwo Jima. We heard that they would have snow storms there, and in preparation for that cold weather we were being issued cold weather clothes and equipment. We just knew that we were getting prepared for a landing there on the mainland. One man in our company was a carpenter, and he was assigned the duty of building crates and boxes to store the cold weather equipment for use in the colder weather that we would face when we landed there. Fortunately, we never had to use that cold weather gear because the dropping of the atomic bomb caused the Japanese to surrender before an assault on the mainland would happen.

It was only after the battle was over and the island was declared secure and the Marines turned over control to the Army that we begin to enjoy some leisure time and get some sleep on a regular basis. We never relaxed our security though. The whole time we were there, even through the occupation period, we had guards posted everywhere. Mail from home, especially during the battle, was not regular at all. Every now and then, we would get a letter or so, but it was nothing that we could count on. There was someone assigned the duty of getting letters to us when it was possible and when I got mine, I felt like a 16-year-old boy. It was so good to hear from home, but we did not get too much mail. Whenever you hear the words "War is hell," believe me that is a fact. There are no Sundays or parties when you are at war.

The invading troops were beginning to wear down a determined enemy. We believed that the flames fired through the tunnels and caves of Mt. Suribachi and their lack of supplies were affecting the enemy's will to resist. We had been able to cut off their routes of supply with our superior numbers; all we had to do was surround them. When the Marines pulled out, our unit's mission supported the occupation forces on the island along with the cargo support from the LSTs. When the tides would allow them to, the LSTs would beach themselves and open the big doors on their bows, put out their ramps and unload their cargo. There were times, though, that we would have to go out to them because water conditions would not allow them to beach. During the occupation, the LSTs brought in tons of supplies, and the men from our company unloaded a lot of those ships.

During the occupation, after the airfields had been taken, the P-51 Mustang airplanes were stationed on Iwo Jima. The long-range B-29s stationed on Guam and Saipan were still flying bombing missions over mainland Japan. Every hour of the day, every minute of the day, those B-29s were flying overhead headed to Tokyo on bombing missions. The P-51s stationed on Iwo would meet and fly escort for them to keep the Japanese fighters from attacking them. But even with that, some of the B-29s would come back from their missions with wing damage, holes all the way through the fuselage, and their landing gear damaged so badly that they could not operate them and attempt to make a landing on Iwo. If they could not land, then crew members that could do so, would bail out into the water. There were about nine crew members to each of the bombers, and we would stand there and watch to see how many would bail out safely. A lot of times, they would have their buddies in their arms when they jumped out. When we saw them parachuting out of the damaged plane and hitting the water, we would man our DUKWs, go out and rescue them, and bring them to shore. I still remember seeing them moving around in the water. We knew they were alive and in big trouble. We saved many of those pilots and their crew members. I can't help but wonder whether any of them ever remembered us pulling them out of the sea and saving their lives off the coast of Iwo Jima.

While we were in control of the island after the Marines left, we did have some resistance from some of the Japanese soldiers who had hidden in the caves and tunnels they built in preparation for the invasion. For them the war was not over. Even though we had to deal with occasional acts of resistance, it was nothing like it was during the battle. But because of that resistance, we maintained a strong security force during the occupation. Years after the war was over, I read in the newspaper that they found Japanese soldiers who had been living in some of the tunnels all that time. A friend of mine from my company and me would climb to the top of Mt. Suribachi and search through the wreckage of airplanes and pillboxes for battle souvenirs, not knowing that Japanese soldiers were still in the caves and tunnels of that volcano. I never will forget that as we went through the tail end of an old airplane that had been shot down our body weight caused the aircraft to shift as if it was about to turn over. There was a lot of debris, destroyed weapons, and clutter left behind all over the island by both the defenders of the island and the assault troops.

In September 1945, the Japanese surrendered and the war was over. As I look back on the whole experience, the thing that I remember most was seeing all of those ships, all of that firepower, and those airplanes surrounding and shooting at that one little island and the way that those mortars and flamethrowers would be shooting fire into the caves and tunnels. I just don't see how the island stayed afloat. Having to see all of the activity, clutter, the bodies and the wounded on the beach and all over the island is something, too, I will never forget. Men were yelling, crying, firing weapons, and even though many of the wounded were being medically evacuated with serious wounds, they were insisting on going back into action. The beachmaster was working hard through it all to ensure that the landing went according to plan, and as the landing craft came ashore, he would try to steer them away from landing points that had been targeted by the enemy forces. You just cannot see all of that and not feel bad about it. All of us who survived the battle knew that we could have been among the casualty count. The day when I boarded that ship to come home, I looked back at that little island as we moved further and further away and it faded away into the distance. I knew that it would be an experience that I would never forget.

During the war, and on the way back home, there were no issues with segregation that I can remember. All of us black and white did everything together on the on the way back. When we returned to Fort Smith, Arkansas, most of us would be separated from the service. The sergeant greeted us saying, "All right, give me your attention. All you white soldiers, assemble over here, and all you boys, you black boys, assemble over here." Then we went to the barracks. The morning we received our discharge papers, the white soldiers went one way and we went ours, but while we were over there on Iwo Jima, we were all comrades in arms, and the color of our skin was not an issue.

APPENDIX I

A Chronology of African American Service during World War II

September 1941 The U.S. Military Iranian Mission, which would eventually evolve into the Persian Gulf Command by December 1943, began helping the British by building supply facilities in the Persian Gulf area as well as helping them supply Russia through Iran. African American troops with the 352nd Engineering General Service Regiment arrived in March 1943. Unit members helped build the roads used to transport needed supplies to the Soviet Union.

2 September 1941 Captain Benjamin O. Davis, Jr., was the first African American to officially complete a solo flight as an officer of the U.S. Army Air Corps.

October 1941 Secretary of the Navy Frank Knox reiterated the Navy's official policy of enlisting African Americans primarily for service in the nonwhite Steward's Branch.

1 December 1941 Fiorello LaGuardia, director of the U.S. Office of Civilian Defense, formally ordered the formation of the Civil Air Patrol (CAP). In 1942, Willa B. Brown became the first African American woman to be commissioned as a CAP lieutenant.

7 December 1941 Japan attacked the U.S. naval base at Pearl Harbor. During the assault, U.S. Navy messman Doris (Dorie) Miller helped move his mortally wounded commander to shelter, then manned a machine gun on the USS *Arizona* and shot down about six of the Japanese aircraft. This was a particularly notable accomplishment, since combat positions were not open to black sailors and Miller had no formal training on this kind of weapon. After a lengthy press campaign, the Navy awarded Miller the Navy Cross, which Admiral Chester W. Nimitz presented in a ceremony held on 27 May 1942. Miller was one of the more than 600 crewmen killed in November 1943 when the Japanese torpedoed the USS *Liscombe Bay*. In recognition of Miller's valor, the Navy commissioned the destroyer escort USS *Miller* on 30 June 1973.

1941–45 Many black leaders used a dual response to World War II. Known as the

183

"Double V" campaign, they urged African Americans to support the war effort as a way to fight racism abroad, while still criticizing and trying to eliminate segregation and discrimination in the United States. Once again, black Americans hoped their military contributions and patriotism would help break down racial barriers and restrictions. With their increased importance as voters, however, African American demands for equal treatment had more impact than ever before. Many African Americans refused to totally back the war unless they received better treatment. Consequently the slow move away from segregation in the armed forces began before the war ended.

1941–45 Over 2.5 million African Americans registered for military service during World War II, but only 1 million actually served. Black servicemen were stationed in such diverse spots as Casablanca, Italy, the Aleutians, Northern Ireland, Liberia, New Guinea, the China-Burma-India (CBI) theater, Guam, Iwo Jima, Guadalcanal, Bougainville, Saipan, Okinawa, Peleliu, Australia, France, and England.

1942 The U.S. Army activated the 730th, the first black military police battalion.

1942 The U.S. Army activated the 93rd Infantry at Fort Huachuca, Arizona, the first black division formed during World War II. Also this year, the Army combined the 9th and 10th Calvary Regiments (two of the all-black units formed after the Civil War) into the new 2nd Cavalry Division.

1942 Black newspapers that ran articles strongly criticizing segregation and discrimination in the armed forces had trouble obtaining newsprint until they softened their stance. The U.S. Justice Department also threatened to charge 20 editors with sedition.

1942 By this time, at least 1,800 blacks sat on draft boards in the United States. In addition, African Americans served throughout the Selective Service itself. Major (later Lieutenant Colonel) Campbell C. Johnson was the executive assistant to the Selective Service administrator, while black civil servants held administrative and clerical positions in various Selective Service offices.

1942 The Army Nurses Corps selected Lieutenant (later Captain) Della H. Raney to be its first black Chief Nurse, while she was serving at Tuskegee Airfield, Alabama. There were about 500 African American Army nurses in World War II who served in segregated units in the United States and overseas.

9 January 1942 President Roosevelt ordered the U.S. Navy and USMC to enlist African Americans into their regular military units.

February 1942 President Roosevelt approved plans for the construction of a military road through Canada to Alaska. Although a pioneer road, the Alaska (or ALCAN) Highway contributed to the nation's mobilization and defense by linking the continental United States to its northernmost territory, an area threatened by Japan's expansion throughout the Pacific region. Three black regiments—the 93rd, 95th, and 97th Engineer General Service Regiments—helped to build this highway, which was officially opened to U.S. Army truck traffic on 20 November 1942.

March 1942 The Army drafted John Roosevelt Robinson, an outstanding athlete who had lettered in four sports while attending UCLA. After completing basic training at Fort Riley, Kansas, Robinson and several other black soldiers applied for admission to Officers Candidate School (OCS), but they were initially rejected. Robinson was eventually admitted to OCS through the intervention of heavyweight boxing champion Joe Louis.

March 1942 The U.S. Coast Guard recruited its first 150 black volunteers, who underwent basic training at Manhattan Beach, New York. Over 5,000 African Americans served as coast guardsmen in World War II, about 965 of whom were petty or warrant officers. One of the more unique duties to which black coast guardsmen were assigned was the horse patrol unit which kept watch on the beaches in New Jersey.

7 March 1942 Captain Benjamin O. Davis, Jr., and four second lieutenants became the first five graduates of the Tuskegee Flying School. They were also the first members of the 99th Pursuit Squadron, which had been activated with a planned total of 33 pilots and 27 planes. Later known as the 99th Fighter Squadron, the unit grew to 43 men by the end of 1942. These black pilots flew over 500 missions and 3,700 sorties during one year of combat in Italy before the squadron was combined with the 332nd Fighter Group.

April 1942 Black troops with two separate battalions—the 91st and 96th—arrived in Australia to help with the construction of badly needed airfields. The U.S. Army Engineering Corps' separate battalions were used mainly to support other engineer units.

1 April 1942 One of the black tank units deployed to Europe in World War II—the 761st Tank Battalion—was activated at Camp Claiborne, Louisiana, with six white officers, 30 black officers, and 676 enlisted men. Also known as the "Black Panther" Tank Battalion, the unit landed at Omaha Beach on 10 October 1944 and was attached to the 26th Infantry Division, XII Corps, which was part of General George S. Patton's Third Army. One of the more notable members of this well-known unit was Staff Sergeant Ruben Rivers, who was one of seven African Americans to be belatedly awarded the Medal of Honor. By the end of the war, unit members had won 11 Silver Stars, 69 Bronze Stars, and numerous other awards.

2 April 1942 The 24th Infantry Regiment, which had become part of the 93rd Infantry Division, left Fort Benning for San Francisco, where the unit trained briefly before embarking for the Pacific theater. After arriving in-theater on 4 May, the unit was assigned to garrison duty for a logistical base at Efate in the New Hebrides. The Army moved the 24th to Guadalcanal after the fighting ended, where once again unit members were relegated to a support role. Only the 3rd Battalion received credit for participating in the northern Solomons campaign, because it was located far enough forward to come under Japanese bombardment.

7 April 1942 Although the Navy opened its general service branch to blacks, this policy change was not really that progressive because African American sailors were still restricted to shore installations and harbor craft. They were not yet allowed to serve on seagoing combat ships except as stewards or laborers.

May 1942 The Coast Guard began accepting African Americans to serve in other capacities besides messman.

15 May 1942 President Roosevelt signed the act which created the Women's Auxiliary Army Corps (WAAC), later reorganized as the Women's Army Corps (WAC). Over 150,000 WACs served in World War II. The voluntary organization enlisted both black and white female recruits. Charity Adams (Earley) was the first black woman to be commissioned. She and other young African American women like her had backgrounds similar to the corps' white recruits: 80 percent were college educated with experience in office work or teaching, and most had family members in the military.

June 1942 The U.S. Navy began accepting black inductees from the Selective Service Board for the first time. About 167,000 blacks served in the Navy in World War II; 123,000 of these men served overseas. Almost 12,500 African Americans served in the Seabees, as the Navy's construction battalions were known. The Seabees also received assault training supplemental to their primary duty.

June 1942 African Americans began training at the Great Lakes Naval Training Station, where the all-black Camp Robert Smalls compound was named for a black Civil War naval hero. Doreston Carman, Jr., was the first black to report for training in a general rating.

1 June 1942 The U.S. Marine Corps began admitting African American recruits for the first time in 167 years. Howard P. Perry was the first black recruit to report to Montford Point on 26 August. The USMC trained almost 20,000 African Americans during World War II at this segregated facility near Camp LeJeune, North Carolina. Of the 19,168 blacks who served in the Marine Corps during the war, 12,738 served overseas, primarily in defense battalions and combat support companies or as stewards.

18 June 1942 As part of its efforts to increase the number of doctors in service, the Navy offered commissions to medical students, who began their tours of duty once they graduated. Bernard W. Robinson, an African American medical student at Harvard University, was the first black to be awarded a reserve commission as an ensign through this program. Although the Bureau of Naval Personnel subsequently noted that the award had been a "slip," Robinson eventually served as a doctor in the U.S. Naval Reserve. He did not actually report for duty until after the "Golden Thirteen" were commissioned in March 1944.

20 July 1942 The first 40 black women recruits began attending the first WAAC officer candidate training at Fort Des Moines, Iowa. Of these, 36 graduated in October 1942. During the six weeks of training, the African American WAAC officer candidates served in a separate unit that ate and trained with the other 400 white women in the class, but whose living and recreational facilities were segregated.

30 July 1942 President Roosevelt signed the legislation creating the Women Accepted for Voluntary Emergency Service (WAVES), the women's auxiliary of the U.S. Navy. The Secretary of the Navy initially excluded black women from the organization because so few black men went to sea that there was no need for African American women to replace them ashore. After it was opened to African American recruits on 19 October 1944, less than 100 black women served with the WAVES during World War II.

26 August 1942 The Marine Corps established only two black combat units during World War II—the 51st and 52nd Defense Battalions. The first unit began training on this date at Montford Point. Initially designated the 51st Composite Defense Battalion, the unit was under the command of Colonel Samuel A. Woods, Jr. The 19,168 African Americans who served in the Marine Corps during World War II represented only 2 percent of the USMC's entire manpower. About 75 percent of these men were sent overseas, but very few of them saw combat. However, almost 8,000 black USMC stevedores and ammunition handlers served in the Pacific theater, where they usually performed their assigned duties under enemy fire on the beachheads of the South Pacific.

15 October 1942 The U.S. Army reactivated the all-black 92nd Infantry Division at Fort McClellan, Alabama for duty during World War II. About 12,000 enlisted men and officers (200 white and 600 black) served in this division in the war.

20 October 1942 At least four blacks captained Merchant Marine "liberty ships" during World War II. The best known was Hugh Mulzac, who was the first black captain of an American Merchant Marine ship. Although he was the first black sailor to earn a shipmaster's license (1920), this was his first position of command because racism had denied him earlier opportunities to serve as captain. While in charge of the mixed-crew liberty ship SS *Booker T. Washington*, Mulzac and his men saw action several times while on convoy duty in the Atlantic. The ship made 22 round-trip voyages in the 5 years (1942–47) it was in operation, and carried 18,000 troops to the European and Pacific theaters. Unlike the armed forces, the Merchant Marine was integrated from the start of World War II. Of the government-built "liberty ships," 14 were christened for outstanding African Americans, four for deceased black sailors, and four for Negro colleges. The *Booker T. Washington* was turned back over to the Maritime Commission in 1947.

23 November 1942 Congress established the Women's Reserve of the U.S. Coast Guard, commonly referred to as the SPARS (an acronym for the Coast Guard motto: Semper Paratus, Always Ready). Black women were initially excluded from serving in the SPARS.

December 1942 The Advisory Committee on Negro Troop Policies, chaired by Assistant Secretary of War John J. McCloy, recommended that a black parachute battalion be established. Consequently, on 25 February 1943, Chief of Staff George C. Marshall had the Army constitute the 555th Parachute Infantry Company.

1942–43 Because of the relatively high number of African American soldiers assigned to it, the U.S. Army Chemical Warfare Service activated 75 black units during this period. These included 12 chemical maintenance companies (aviation), seven chemical depot companies (aviation), one chemical company (air operations), 20 chemical decontamination companies, three chemical processing companies, two chemical service companies, and 30 chemical smoke generator companies. Of these 75 units, 41 were eventually assigned to overseas duty. Most of them were service units, except for the smoke generator companies, whose members saw frontline action for which they had not been trained. As they attained more experience on the battlefield, however, these all-black units compiled very good combat records.

1943 The U.S. Navy began admitting blacks according to their numbers (10 percent) in the total population. The first African American recruit for the Navy's general service was William Baldwin.

1943 The 1st Marine Depot was the first black USMC unit to be sent overseas in World War II.

1943 The U.S. Coast Guard commissioned former warrant officer Clarence Samuels as its first African American officer. Samuels was also the first black to command a lightship and a Coast Guard cutter (the *Sweetgum*).

1943 The first black medical group sent overseas to Liberia included nine doctors and 30 nurses.

1943 Gordon A. Parks, Sr., was the first African American to work for the U.S. Office of War Information as a photojournalist and war correspondent. He later worked for *Life* magazine. Best known for his photography and as the director of the movie *Shaft* (and five other films), Parks is a prolific author, poet, screenwriter and ballet composer.

1943 John Roosevelt Robinson graduated from Officer's Candidate School and was commissioned as a second lieutenant in the U.S. Army.

1943 The Army's Services of Supply (SOS) units were renamed the Army Service Forces (ASF).

5 January 1943 Judge William H. Hastie resigned his position as Civilian Aide to the Secretary of War because of continuing discrimination and segregation in the armed forces. He was later appointed in 1946 to serve as the first African American governor of the Virgin Islands.

13 February 1943 The Women's Marine Corps was created. It was the only World War II–era women's auxiliary that did not admit any African Americans.

22 February 1943 African American stewards assigned to the U.S. Coast Guard cutter *Campbell* manned a battle station when the ship rammed and sank a German submarine. Medals awarded to the entire crew included a Bronze Star for the captain of the black gun crew.

8 March 1943 African American Private George Watson helped to save several soldiers when their troop ship had to be abandoned after being hit on this date by enemy bombers near New Guinea. Weakened by his efforts to assist those who could not swim, Watson drowned when he was dragged down by the suction of the sinking ship. Although no African American servicemen were awarded the Congressional Medal of Honor in World War II, this error was corrected on 13 January 1997 when seven black veterans (only one was still living) received their long overdue awards. One of those men so honored was Private Watson.

1 April 1943 The final battalion making up the 5th Tank Group—the 784th Tank Battalion—was activated.

24 April 1943 The 99th Pursuit Squadron arrived in French Morocco for training under experienced combat pilots, but they received little help from the white aviators. The squadron had also been sent overseas without much of the required navigational training given to white pilots, because installations without segregated facilities refused to allow black pilots to land. Despite such obstacles, this first group of "Tuskegee Airmen" trained themselves and were prepared to fly their first combat mission in the Mediterranean by 2 June 1943.

May 1943 Captain Benjamin O. Davis, Jr., was promoted to major then to lieutenant colonel in the course of one day. Davis commanded both the 99th Pursuit Squadron and the 332nd Fighter Group.

May 1943 The USMC's last white drill instructor at Montford Point, First Sergeant Robert W. Colwell, was replaced by Sergeant Gilbert "Hashmark" Johnson (who had earned his nickname for his many years of service in the Army's all-black 25th Infantry Regiment). Earlier this year, the Marine Corps had started appointing its first black noncommissioned officers. By the end of April 1943, most of the white drill instructors had been transferred elsewhere.

27 May 1943 The federal government barred all war contractors from discriminating on the basis of race.

June 1943 The all-black 477th Bombardment Group was activated. Included in the group were the 616th, 617th, 618th, and 619th Bombardment Squadrons. The war ended before the group made it overseas.

June 1943 Ohio Congresswoman Frances Payne Bolton successfully introduced an amendment to bar racial discrimination from the Nurses Training bill then under debate. Consequently, more than 2,000 African American women enrolled in the Cadet Nurses Corps.

June 1943 Lieutenant Commander Carlton Skinner's proposal that the U.S. Coast Guard establish an entirely integrated force eventually led to the commissioning of the first integrated ship in the armed forces, the U.S. Coast Guard cutter _Seacloud_. Skinner commanded a 200-man crew that included four African American officers and 100 black enlisted men. Decommissioned in November 1944, this ship's crew helped break down military segregation at sea.

20 June 1943 Despite the existence of Executive Order 8802 and the efforts of the Fair Employment Practices Commission, African Americans still encountered a lot of white hostility to their presence in war plants. On this date, a serious race riot erupted in Detroit, Michigan. Sparked by a fistfight between a white man and a black man, the violence was actually caused by increasing white resentment about the growing numbers of Southern blacks migrating into the city to fill war industry jobs. A total of 25 African Americans and nine whites were killed. The violence was not quelled until President Roosevelt dispatched federal troops to the area.

2 July 1943 Lieutenant Charles B. Hall shot down the first German plane officially credited to the 99th Pursuit Squadron. This outstanding Army Air Corps unit participated in campaigns in North Africa, the Mediterranean, Italy, and Germany. One of the squadron's most notable feats was its destruction of five enemy aircraft in less than four minutes. For this and numerous other accomplishments, the unit earned three Distinguished Unit Citations during World War II.

25 July 1943 Launched in Quincy, Massachusetts, on this date, the USS _Harmon_ was the U.S. Navy's first fighting ship named for an African American. Leonard Roy

Harmon was killed in action while trying to protect a shipmate. The Navy posthumously awarded Harmon the Navy Cross for his heroism during fighting with the Japanese.

21 August 1943 Harriet M. West became the first black woman major in the WACs. She served as the chief of planning for WAC Headquarters' Bureau Control Division in Washington, D.C.

September 1943 The U.S. Army formally rejected the creation of a volunteer integrated division which several black newspaper editors had proposed shortly after the Japanese attack on Pearl Harbor.

15 September 1943 The 761st "Black Panther" Tank Battalion moved to Fort Hood, Texas, for advanced armored training. At that time the unit switched from light to medium tanks. It was here that one of the unit's black officers—Lieutenant John Roosevelt Robinson—ran afoul of the Army's lingering local "Jim Crow" policies.

19 December 1943 Army Ground Forces Headquarters authorized the activation of the 555th Parachute Infantry Company as an all-black volunteer unit with African American officers and enlisted men. Walter Morris was the first black enlisted paratrooper. Officially activated on 30 December 1943 at Fort Benning, Georgia, the unit moved after several weeks of training to Camp Machall, North Carolina, on 25 November 1944. At that time, the unit was reorganized as Company A, 555th Parachute Infantry Battalion. The newly activated battalion was more commonly known as the "Triple Nickels."

1943–1945 Black airmen with the 1345th Air Transport Command in Dacca, India, helped move supplies and fuel the planes that flew "The Hump," the famous air route from India to China that kept Generalissimo Chiang Kai-shek's Kumintang forces supplied during World War II. Thousands of African Americans in the service units helped Allied forces overcome incredible obstacles in the China-Burma-India (CBI) theater. One of their more notable accomplishments was their work on the construction of the "Stilwell Road." This route ran from Ledo, India, through Burma and connected at Kunming with the Burma Road in China. When it was completed, the Stilwell Road reopened the overland supply line between India and China. It was in use for nine months after the first convoy left Ledo on 12 January 1945.

1944 By this time, the percentage of African Americans employed in war production had increased from less than three percent in March 1942 to over eight percent by 1944.

1944 Charles F. Anderson was the first black Marine to be promoted to Sergeant Major. That same year, James E. Johnson became the USMC's first black warrant officer.

1944 Problems with racial tension and violent outbreaks due to rigid segregation were so serious by this time that the War Department had to prohibit racial discrimination in recreational and transportation facilities on all U.S. Army posts to help ease the situation. Although conditions for African American servicemen improved somewhat, the lack of uniform local enforcement and continuing black resentment about the Army's other discriminatory policies remained a problem throughout the war.

1944 American film director Frank Capra produced _The Negro Soldier_, the first U.S. Army training film to favorably depict African American servicemen. Assisting with the film were Brigadier General Benjamin O. Davis, Sr., who served as a consultant, black screenwriter and filmmaker Carlton Moss, director Stuart Heisler, and a large group of black soldiers. The film was designed to improve race relations by introducing white and black servicemen to the history of black Americans' considerable and often heroic military contributions. The film had a powerful impact not only on the soldiers who saw it, but also on civilian audiences when it was released to the public after the war. Many contemporary observers and later scholars have argued that the film helped to accelerate the desegregation of the armed forces as well as other areas of American society. The United Auto Workers used the film to prepare union members for an integrated work force.

1944 The proportion of black soldiers in the U.S. Army reached a high point of 8.74 percent. Despite some changes in the Army's racial policy, the continuation of segregated units exacted a high price in terms of African American morale and efficiency.

1944 By this time, the War Department's critical need for troops overseas helped to ease opposition to the dispatch of black servicemen to the European or Pacific theaters. The number of African Americans serving in-theater jumped from 97,725 in 1941 to 504,000 in 1943. However, 425,000 black troops remained in the United States. The military claimed that allied foreign nations objected to the presence of black troops, but it was usually American commanders overseas who opposed their assignment.

1944 The U.S. Army's racial policies became an important issue during this year's presidential campaign. Black leaders continued to criticize the Army's restricted use of black troops in combat, while Roosevelt's Republican political opponents used the issue to challenge the president's reelection.

February 1944 The USMC's first all-black combat unit, the 51st Defense Battalion, was sent to the Pacific theater, where it was assigned to guard duty in the Ellice and Marshall Islands. The battalion was never used in combat.

23 February 1944 The U.S. Navy's Bureau of Naval Personnel established a Special Unit in August 1943 that unexpectedly helped this branch of the U.S. armed forces to begin moving toward full integration. By this date, the Special Unit had persuaded the Navy to man two sea-going vessels with all-black enlisted personnel, though both ships still had only white officers.

March 1944 The U.S. Navy commissioned 13 African Americans (12 ensigns and one warrant officer) as its first black officers. These men later dubbed themselves the "Golden 13" (a designation subsequently adopted by the Navy), because of their pioneering efforts to integrate the Navy. The Navy commissioned about 60 African Americans during World War II.

11 March 1944 Bowing to increasing pressure that African American troops be allowed to fight, the War Department instructed the Army to transfer control of the 1st Battalion, 24th Infantry Regiment to the operational control of the 148th Infantry Regiment. Company B came under attack the same day that it moved forward to reinforce other Army units in contact with Japanese forces on Bougainville, making it the first black American infantry unit to engage in combat during the war. Two of the company's men—Private First Class Leonard Brooks and Private Annias Jolly—were the first members of the 24th Infantry Regiment (as well as the first black infantrymen) killed by enemy fire in World War II.

17 March 1944 The U.S. Army Air Corps' all-black 332nd Fighter Group (which included the 100th, 301st and 302nd Fighter Squadrons) first saw combat. Activated at Tuskegee Airfield on 26 May 1942, Colonel Benjamin O. Davis, Jr., assumed command of the group at Selfridge Field, Michigan, in October 1943. The 99th Fighter Squadron joined the 332nd in July 1944. The famed "Tuskegee Airmen" flew 1,578 missions and 15,533 sorties, during which they destroyed 261 enemy aircraft and damaged another 148 planes. The Germans called the group the Black Birdmen (or *Schwartze Vogelmann*), while many white U.S. bomber crews referred to their escorts as the "Redtail Angels." The group lost 66 men who were killed in action between 1941 and 1945. The 332nd received a Presidential Unit Citation on 24 March 1945 for "outstanding courage, aggressiveness, and combat technique" while escorting heavy bombers over Germany.

20 March 1944 Commissioned at Boston Navy Yard, the USS *Mason*, a destroyer escort, was the first naval warship with a predominantly black crew and at least one black officer. Referred to by some as "Eleanor's Folly" (a reference to First Lady Eleanor Roosevelt, who pushed for the desegregation of the armed forces), many white leaders expected this "experiment" to fail. However, the *Mason* turned out to be a remarkable World War II success story. This was due to the superior leadership of Lieutenant Commander William M. Blackford, who skippered the *Mason*, as well as to the determination, ability, and commitment of the destroyer's black crew. Although the ship was sold for scrap in 1947, the *Mason's* proud history has been preserved at the Boston National Historical Park.

28 March 1944 The 25th Combat Team, which was part of the 93rd Division, also fought against the Japanese on Bougainville. The team was composed of the 25th Infantry Regiment; the 593rd and 596th Field Artillery Battalions; Company A, 318th Combat Engineers Battalion; Company A and one platoon of Company D, 318th Medical Battalion; and detachments from the 93rd Signal Company, the 793rd Ordnance Company, and the 93rd Military Police Platoon. The 93rd Division's first four men were killed on 4 April 1944 as they returned from a supply mission. Enemy forces also ambushed the untried soldiers of the unit's Company K in an early engagement, killing one officer and nine enlisted men. Another 20 enlisted men were wounded, primarily by friendly fire, as the remainder of the company withdrew in disarray. Unfortunately, although Company K and the rest of the 25th helped to defeat the Japanese as the campaign progressed, an unfounded rumor spread that the 93rd Division had broken under fire. Despite the fact that white troops experienced the same problems, the false report endured. Even efforts by General Douglas MacArthur to squelch this misinformation were unsuccessful.

May 1944 The 366th Infantry Regiment first arrived in Italy and was used to guard airbases. It became the 92nd Infantry Division's fourth regiment on 30 November

1944, although it was not deployed as a regiment. Instead, battalion and company elements were attached to other divisional units.

10 May 1944 The 2nd Cavalry Division, to which the 9th and 10th Cavalry Regiments had been reassigned, was inactivated immediately after it arrived in the Mediterranean. The official reason for this action was "to hold together an Army of 89 divisions," and to avoid the World War I problem of activating divisions that "became hardly more than paper organizations." The division's combat-trained African American troops were reassigned to support units in North Africa. In contrast, white soldiers affected by such reorganizations usually went to other combat units.

6 June 1944 The D-Day landings on the beaches of Normandy, France, began. The 320th Negro Anti-Aircraft Barrage Balloon Battalion assisted with this assault against the Germans, and were the only African American combat troops to take part in D-Day. Classified as an anti-aircraft unit, it was the only U.S. unit of its type in the European theater. In addition, black Private Warren Capers contributed to the D-Day landing by helping to establish a dressing station where he treated more than 330 soldiers. His devotion to duty won him a Silver Star.

June–July 1944 The first African American Marines to be decorated by the 2nd Marine Division—Staff Sergeant Timerlate Kirven and Corporal Samuel J. Love, Sr.—won purple hearts for wounds received in the assault on Saipan. Ironically, these men were part of the Marine Corps' black service units and were not specifically trained for combat. Unlike the Marines in the two black combat battalions, men in the USMC's depot and ammunition companies frequently came under fire during World War II; 9 were killed in action, while another 78 were wounded.

July 1944 The *PC 1264* was the first submarine chaser with an all-black crew. About six months after *PC 1264* was initially commissioned with white officers and petty officers, the latter were replaced by African Americans. The U.S. Navy's first black officer was assigned to the submarine chaser in 1945. In addition, Ensign Samuel L. Gravely, Jr., who also served aboard *PC 1264*, eventually became the Navy's first African American flag officer.

6 July 1944 Army Lieutenant John Roosevelt Robinson, one of the 761st "Black Panther" Tank Battalion's few black officers, refused orders to sit in the back of a military bus at Fort Hood, Texas. He was subsequently court martialed, but was acquitted because the order was a violation of War Department policy prohibiting racial discrimination in recreational and transportation facilities on all U.S. Army posts. After the war, Jackie Robinson went on to break the "color line" in baseball by being the first black to play for the Brooklyn Dodgers.

15 July 1944 The first unit of the 92nd Infantry Division, the 370th Regimental Combat Team, sailed for Europe. There it joined the Fifth U.S. Army in the Mediterranean Theater of Operations on 30 July 1944. The combat team included the 370th Infantry Regiment, the 598th Field Artillery Battalion, and a detachment from each support unit. After it became part of the Fifth Army's IV Corps, the team saw its first combat action when it repulsed two enemy patrols near the Arno River on 27 August 1944. The 92nd's other units—the 371st and 365th Infantry Regiments—arrived in-theater in October and November 1944, respectively.

17 July 1944 The worst home front disaster of World War II occurred when two ships—the *E.A. Bryan* and the *Quinalt Victory*, docked at Port Chicago, California— exploded one night while African American sailors were loading ammunition for use in the Pacific theater. Both ships and the loading pier were destroyed, while many of the nearby town's buildings also suffered severe damage. Of the 320 men killed, 202 of them were black enlisted men; the blast also injured 390 men. The worst military loss of life in the continental United States during World War II, this one incident involved 15 percent of all African Americans wounded or killed in this conflict. Despite the extensive casualties, however, sailors were ordered to resume loading on 9 August 1944 with no training or procedural changes to help safeguard against another such catastrophe. Because they were afraid of another explosion, 258 African American sailors refused to comply with orders. The U.S. Navy court martialed 50 men for mutiny and tried the other 208 on lesser charges. Those convicted of mutiny were sentenced to 15 years in prison, but after the war they were granted amnesty. However, their original convictions were not overturned. Ultimately, though, this incident did result in changes affecting racial relations in the Navy, because ammunition loading ceased to be a "blacks only" assignment. The Navy also adopted safer procedures for loading ammunition.

August 1944 Secretary of the Navy James V. Forrestal approved the Special Unit's recommendation that up to ten percent of the crews assigned to 25 auxiliary ships be African Americans who were integrated with whites. This experiment ultimately led to the integration of black sailors on all fleet auxiliary ships.

25 August 1944 The Red Ball Express began operations. Crucial to the defeat of Nazi Germany, this massive supply effort ran until 16 November 1944 and involved over 6,000 trucks and trailers. Red Ball drivers transported 412,193 tons of materiel to American troops as they advanced through France from Normandy to the German border. About 75 percent of all drivers on the segregated Red Ball Express were African Americans.

October 1944 During fighting along the Gothic line in Italy, the 92nd Infantry Division lost momentum and was forced into a disorderly retreat by the experienced German troops defending this series of fortifications across the peninsula. The division commander, Major General Edward M. Almond, and his staff resorted to racist remarks to explain the division's initial combat failure. Actually, though, problems such as lack of communication, a poorly organized plan of attack, missing white officers, conflicting orders, untested troops, and the confusion of battle were to blame. The basic problem, however, was a serious lack of unit cohesion and trust between white officers and black soldiers. In fact, most of the latter blamed Almond's racism, claiming that the division commander was so prejudiced that he hoped the episode would discredit the entire race. Truman Gibson, who had replaced Judge Hastie, issued a report in 1945 that attributed most of the 92nd Division's problems to the U.S. Army's policy of racial segregation. Unfortunately, the white press focused on certain phrases in the report that seemed to imply that black soldiers did not perform well in combat. Despite their subsequent combat successes, the division's reputation (like that of the 93rd in the Pacific) remained unfairly sullied by this incident.

October 1944 The USMC's second all-black combat unit—the 52nd Defense Battalion—arrived in the Pacific. The battalion served in the Marshall Islands and on Guam, Eniwetok, and Kwajalein, but it never saw combat since these areas had already been secured.

13 October 1944 Lieutenant General George S. Patton presented a Silver Star to Private Ernest A. Jenkins for his "conspicuous gallantry" during the fierce fighting that liberated Chateaudun, France.

18 October 1944 The USS *Mason* and her crew proved their mettle during the "ordeal of Convoy NY-119." Plagued by bad weather for its entire crossing, the convoy was caught by an even worse storm within sight of the English coast. The fierce weather had already claimed three tugboats, eight car floats, and five cargo barges during 30 days of incessant wind and waves. As the convoy neared Falmouth Bay, England, the wind increased to 40 knots, with gusts up to 50–60 knots. The *Mason* was ordered to escort 20 of the smaller vessels to safety, which it did successfully. Despite suffering serious structural damage when its deck split, the *Mason*'s crew not only repaired the deck, pumped out the engine room, and replaced the lost antennae but returned to aid the remainder of the convoy still floundering at sea. The destroyer escort spent 3 more days assisting another 12 ships to reach port, then continued on to France, where the *Mason*'s crew salvaged barges off the continental coast. Despite the efforts of the *Mason*'s white captain and the convoy commander, these black crewmen never received any commendations for their heroic actions.

19 October 1944 After intense pressure was placed on the voluntary organization, the WAVES accepted its first 72 black women, two of whom became officers. Bessie Garret was the first African American woman admitted into the WAVES, while the first black women commissioned by the WAVES were Lieutenant Harriet Ida Pickens and Ensign Frances Willis, who completed their training on 13 December 1944.

20 October 1944 The SPARS, the Coast Guard's women auxiliary, began enlisting qualified African American women. Yeoman Second Class Olivia J. Hooker was the first black woman to enlist. Although the officer training program was closed to civilians by this time, six previously enlisted black nurses did attend Officers Candidate School and received their commissions as ensigns before World War II ended. There are no records available of the total number of black SPARS who enlisted before recruiting began shutting down in December 1944.

November 1944 The 92nd Infantry Division's mortar company wiped out numerous enemy machine gun emplacements during the U.S. Army's Italian campaign. Although elements within the military establishment tried to keep them in a labor support role, African American combat troops made notable contributions in both the European and Pacific theaters.

November 1944 Elizabeth B. Murphy Moss (Phillips) was the first black woman certified as a war correspondent during World War II, but she never filed any reports before she became ill and had to return to the United States.

REFERENCE SOURCE: *Excerpt from "History of Black Military Service," Redstone Arsenal Historical Collections, http://www.redstone.Army.mil/history/integrate/CHRON3.html*

APPENDIX II

Operation Detachment: The Battle for Iwo Jima

Introduction

"Victory was never in doubt. What was in doubt in all our minds was whether there would be any of us left to dedicate our cemetery at the end."—Major General Graves B. Erskine, Commander, 3rd Marine Division

Towards the end of 1944, the Allied forces were successfully pushing the Japanese back from their earlier conquests. In Burma, the British 14th Army had advanced across the Burma-India border and was pushing the Japanese Army down the Irrawaddy River, while the American advance across the Pacific had brought it to the inner ring of Japanese defenses before the mainland. General Douglas MacArthur had advanced across the Solomon Islands and New Guinea and had invaded Leyte in the Philippines in October. The U.S. Navy and Marine Corps under Admiral Chester Nimitz had continued their "island hopping" campaign that had begun at Guadalcanal in 1942 and continued through Tarawa (1943), the Mariana Islands (1944), and Peleliu (1944) and was to reach its climax at Okinawa (1945).

After the capture of the Mariana Islands, the U.S. 20th Air Force could mount a large-scale campaign against the industrial centers of Japan. The only obstacle to this was the strategically important island of Iwo Jima that housed two airfields, with a third under construction, as well as a radar station that could give up to two hours warning of an impending raid. The Air Force needed to eliminate the fighter threat to their bombers and neutralize the radar station there. The island would also be useful as a refuge for damaged aircraft returning from raids, as a base for air-sea rescue flying boats and for P-51 long-range fighters to escort the B-29 bombers. On 3 October 1944, the Joint Chiefs of

Staff issued a directive to Admiral Nimitz to take Iwo Jima. The battle, which was described as the "most savage and costly battle in the history of the Marine Corps" (Lt. Gen. Holland M. Smith), pitted three Marine divisions against 21,000 well-entrenched Japanese defenders.

The Americans Prepare

"It was an operation of one phase and one tactic ... until the mission was completed it was a matter of frontal assault maintained with relentless pressure."—Lt. General Holland M. Smith, Commander, Fleet Marine Force Pacific

The U.S. invasion force would consist of the 3rd, 4th and 5th Marine Divisions from the U.S. V Amphibious Corps under Major General Harry Schmidt with over 70,000 men, many of whom were veterans of previous battles. The 3rd Marine Division sailed from Guam, which it had taken from the Japanese garrison in August 1944, while the 4th and 5th Marine Divisions sailed from Hawaii. While the invasion had been delayed twice by the huge requirements of General MacArthur's Philippines campaign, it had to be completed as quickly as possible to release resources for the invasion of Okinawa (Operation Iceberg), which was scheduled to begin on 1 April 1945. On February 15th, the invasion force left Saipan and was soon spotted by Japanese naval patrol aircraft, which alerted the Iwo Jima garrison.

The American landings would take place on a two-mile stretch of beach between Mount Suribachi and the East Boat Basin on the southeast coast. The beaches were divided into seven landing zones, each of 550 yards (503 meters). Moving northeast from Mount Suribachi the beaches and the initial assault forces were:

> Green Beach—1st and 2nd Battalions, 28th Marine Regiment
> Red Beach 1—2nd Battalion, 27th Marine Regiment
> Red Beach 2—1st Battalion, 27th Marine Regiment
> Yellow Beach 1—1st Battalion, 23rd Marine Regiment
> Yellow Beach 2—2nd Battalion, 23rd Regiment
> Blue Beach 1—1st and 3rd Battalions, 25th Marine Regiment
> Blue Beach 2—None

As Blue Beach 2 lay directly under known enemy gun positions in the Quarry, it was decided that both the 1st and 3rd Battalions, 25th Marine Regiment should land on Blue Beach 1. The 28th Marines would attack straight across the island from their landing zone and after reaching the northwest coast, turn southwest and isolate Mount Suribachi. They would then assault and secure it. The 27th Marines coming ashore on the Red Beaches would also drive northwest to the opposite coast but then turn northeast. The 23rd Marines would attack inland to capture Airfield No. 1 and then move northeast towards Airfield No. 2 while the 25th Marines would land and almost immediately move northeast to attack the high ground around the Quarry (see historical note below).

The Japanese Prepare

"I don't know who he is, but the Japanese General running this show is one smart bastard."—Lt. General Holland M. Smith, Commander, Fleet Marine Force Pacific

The Japanese High Command had astutely noted the strategic importance of Iwo Jima as early as March 1944. They started to reinforce the island and diverted the 145th Infantry Regiment (Colonel Masuo Ikeda) that was originally intended to reinforce Saipan to the island before the American attack. They also sent the 109th Division, which consisted of the 2nd Mixed Brigade (Major General Sadasue Senda), 26th Tank Regiment (Lieutenant Colonel [Baron] Takeichi Nishi), 17th Mixed Infantry Regiment (Major Tamachi Fujiwara), divisional artillery brigade (Colonel Chosaku Kaido) as well as additional combat support battalions (anti-aircraft, artillery and machine gun). The naval force consisted mainly of anti-aircraft, communications, supply and engineering units, and was commanded by Rear Admiral Toshinosuke Ichimaru (who also commanded the 27th Air Flotilla). The total garrison strength at the time of Operation Detachment was 21,060.

Lt. General Tadamichi Kuribayashi had been assigned to command the garrison of Iwo Jima in May 1944. He had served in the United States as a deputy defense attaché and considered the USA the "last country in the world that Japan should fight." When he arrived he immediately began to reorganize the chaotic defenses that were in place and with the arrival of additional troops and Korean laborers began a huge construction program that included tunnels, caves, gun emplacements, pillboxes, bunkers and command posts, many of which were mutually supporting and linked by a vast underground communications system. Many were so well constructed that the intensive naval shelling and aerial bombing in the weeks before the attack simply failed to damage them. A lot of these fortifications were dug into the soft, pumice-like volcanic rock, which mixed well with cement to provide additional reinforcement. Supply areas, ammunition stores and medical facilities were all constructed within the underground tunnel system and when the fighting was at its height, many Marines reported hearing voices emanating from the ground below them. The tunnel system was so extensive that many of the troops that were defending Mount Suribachi managed to escape to the north before the volcano fell. Kuribayashi had studied traditional Japanese defensive tactics that emphasized halting the invader on the beach and realized that they had usually failed and that the traditional "banzai" charge, unless unleashed with care and precision, was a waste of men and resources. He looked at the tactics used by Lt. General Sadae Inoue at Peleliu, who had abandoned the old style, and concentrated on a battle of attrition in order to wear down the enemy. Kuribayashi decided he too would adopt these tactics—the Americans would eventually take the islands but he would extract a fearful price. As the geography of Iwo Jima virtually dictated where the Marines would have to land (the only possible landing site being that already described), Kuribayashi set his defenses accordingly. In addition, he acted on advice from his staff officer, Major Yoshitaka Horie, to use the majority of anti-aircraft guns in the ground role as the Americans were bound to have such overwhelming air superiority that any guns that revealed themselves would be quickly destroyed. Many of his staff officers seem to have objected to this and used their anti-aircraft guns in both roles and many were put out of action quickly.

D-Day: 19 February 1945

"This is going to be a rough one, we could suffer as many as fifteen thousand casualties here."—Lt. General Holland M. Smith, Commander, Fleet Marine Force Pacific

Before the invasion commenced, the commander of the V Amphibious Corps, Major General Harry Schmidt, had requested ten days of continuous shelling from Rear Admiral William Blandy's Task Force 52 (the Support Force) but was turned down by Admiral Harry Hill as there would be insufficient time to rearm the ships before D-Day. Schmidt requested nine and was offered a mere three, with Spruance commenting, "I know that your people will get away with it." This was to have a hollow ring about it as the battle went on. In fact, Lt. General Holland M. Smith was to be scathing about the support afforded by the Navy in many of the amphibious assaults throughout the Pacific Campaign after the war. Two of the three days (the first and the third) allotted to gunfire support were marred by poor weather and on the second day as frogmen of the underwater demolition teams were reconnoitering the beach, both the USS *Pensacola* and the USS *Leutze* were hit by shore batteries, as were all 12 gunboats which were part of the support screen for the frogmen. D-Day however, dawned bright and clear with unlimited visibility. The U.S. Navy task force off Iwo Jima was joined by Task Force 58 under Admiral Marc Mitscher, which had just conducted a series of raids against the Japanese mainland and consisted of 16 aircraft carriers, eight battleships and 15 cruisers, as well as Admiral Raymond Spruance in his flagship USS *Indianapolis*. The battleships and cruisers started to pound the island and were augmented by carrier-based aircraft mounting air strikes. At this point, thousands of Marines began to disembark from troopships and LVTs. They were to be covered by 68 LVT(A)s that were well-armored amphibious tracked vehicles that mounted a 75mm howitzer and three machine-guns. Despite the reconnaissance and beach samples from the frogmen that indicated the assault forces would have some trouble getting off the beach, the planners had considered that it would provide a minor obstacle only. Unfortunately, the initial assault wave encountered 15 foot high terraces of soft volcanic ash that were to frustrate their advance inland and so the advance by the Marines, tanks, and LVTs ground to a halt on the shoreline. These were being followed by successive waves every five minutes or so, and the situation quickly deteriorated. Added to that, the Marines came up against the island's hydrography, which, on the steep beach, consisted of a plunging surf and strong undertow. Such forces soon seriously damaged many Higgins Boats. Admiral Hill and his chief Beachmaster, Captain Carl E. "Squeaky" Anderson, had adopted the experimental "Marston matting" (used to fabricate expeditionary airfield runways) to improve trafficability off the beach, but while it worked well initially, it soon became chewed up as hundreds of tracked vehicles tried to maneuver off the beach. Added to that, the Japanese had not mined the beach itself but had spared no effort in mining the beach exits, which again hindered the assault forces.

By late morning, Admiral Harry Hill had some 6,000 men ashore and the bulldozers that had arrived with the early waves were battling with the terraces. Some elements had indeed managed to get off the beach and start to work their way inland, but it was at this point that Kuribayashi, despite his initial plan to wait until the Marines had reached Airfield One, decided to unleash the full fury of his concentrated artillery fire on the tempting targets struggling on the beach. Added to this, a sizeable element of beach defenders had survived the Navy's rolling barrage and added their weight to the fire. As one Marine battalion commander remarked, "You could've held up a cigarette and lit it on the stuff going by."

Despite this, the Marines kept themselves in good order and started to move off the beaches in force. On Green Beach, the extreme left hand landing zone, the terrain was not so difficult here and Colonel Harry B. Liversedge's 28th Marine Regiment (5th Marine Division, commanded by Major General Keller E. Rockey) started their advance across the island to isolate Mount Suribachi. They were watched by Colonel Kanehiko Atsuchi and over 2,000 men in the independent command that defended Mount Suribachi in well-concealed positions all the way from the lower slopes to the mount. The 1st Battalion (1/28) pressed on towards the opposite coastline but ran straight into the 312th Independent Infantry Battalion under Captain Osada and fierce fighting erupted in and around a complex of pillboxes and bunkers. Some were destroyed but many were bypassed in the dash to isolate Mount Suribachi, and at around 10.35 the leading elements of B Company reached the coast. To their right on Red Beaches 1 and 2, the 27th Marines under Colonel Thomas A. Wornham (5th Marine Division) were having great difficulty in moving off the beaches and were being hampered by the Japanese artillery fire. To their right, the 23rd Marines under Colonel Walter W. Wensinger (4th Marine Division under Major General Clifton B. Cates) had run into a series of blockhouses and pill-boxes manned by Major Matsushita's 10th Independent Anti-Tank Battalion and Captain Awatsu's 309th Infantry Battalion. It was here that Sgt. Darren Cole became the first of 27 Marine Corps Medal of Honor recipients by single-handedly knocking out five pillboxes armed with just a pistol and grenades, before he himself was killed by a hand grenade. Finally, on the extreme right, Colonel John R. Lanigan's 25th Regiment (4th Marine Division) advanced straight ahead to avoid the immediate danger from the high ground of the quarry to their right.

As the day wore on, the Marines continued to advance slowly with a number of tanks from the 4th Tank Battalion pressing inland, only halting after they had reached a large minefield. The 3/25 (Lt. Col. Justice M. Chambers) turned right and began their assault on the quarry in the afternoon. Japanese resistance was strong and casualties were heavy. The 28th Marines continued to consolidate their positions at the base of Mount Suribachi and were reinforced by a number of Sherman tanks that gave invaluable help in destroying a number of pillboxes and by evening, Mount Suribachi had been securely isolated from the rest of the island. An assault on the volcano would come soon enough. The 27th and 25th Marines gradually extricated themselves from the beaches and started to make their way towards Airfield No. 1 while Seabees (from CB—Construction Battalion) performed miracles on the beaches clearing away the debris to allow the following waves to continue landing (Turner had had to halt the landings as the beaches had become too congested) and carving routes out of the terraces.

Most of the Seabees were volunteers from the civilian construction industry and were in their 40s or 50s—hence the Marine joke: "Protect your Seabees. One of them could be your dad." Despite this, they suffered heavy casualties on D-Day. Eventually the Marines reached the southern perimeter of Airfield No. 1 where the Japanese mounted a fierce defense and settled in for the night. The Japanese, on the other hand, were adept at night-time infiltration tactics and continually sought to probe for weaknesses in the Marine line while keeping a constant barrage of artillery fire.

D+1: 20 February 1945

"...Iwo Jima can only be described as a nightmare in hell."—Robert Sherrod,
Combat Correspondent for Time-Life

Bad weather and strong winds produced a four-foot surf that disrupted the follow-on landings. It became so bad that even the larger landing ships, such as LSTs and LSMs, had difficulty in maintaining position on the beach. Cables tied to wrecked or abandoned equipment such as LVTs or tanks simply snapped under the strain. Smaller craft had an even worse time of it, and as a result, Schmidt's desire to land a regiment (21st under Colonel Hartnoll J. Withers) from the 3rd Marine Division (Major General Graves B. Erskine) could not be accomplished. Meanwhile, the 28th Marines were now faced with the prospect of having to storm Mount Suribachi while the remainder of the assault force looked to continuing the advance to capture Airfields Nos. 1 and 2. The 28th Marines, under the cover of naval gunfire and carrier air strikes, started to advance on a broad front but by noon had only advanced some 75 yards in the face of a fierce defense by the Japanese. Even though a number of tanks had become available to support the advance, the Japanese still held an enormous height advantage in their well-concealed positions. The Marines therefore dug in to await reinforcements and additional support to continue the attack the next day. The Japanese were determined that the Americans should have no respite and commenced an artillery barrage all along the front.

Meanwhile, the other three regiments commenced their attack towards Airfield No. 1 with the right flank anchored on the quarry and the left flank swinging northeast to straighten the line. Additional support arrived in the afternoon in the form of the brand new battleship, the USS *Washington*, which commenced bombardment of the quarry with its 16in guns and caused a number of landslides, which blocked several caves. Despite fierce resistance, the Marines had captured most of Airfield No. 1 by mid-afternoon and had straightened their line out, although they had still not reached the intended D-Day 0–1 line. This was a blow to Kuribayashi who had not expected such a rapid advance, but he took comfort that the Marines had yet to reach his main defensive line and the bad weather was still hampering operations. As the second day drew to a close heavy rain began to fall, adding to the Marines' misery.

D+2: 21 February 1945

"Each man should think of his defense position as his graveyard, fight until the last and inflict much damage to the enemy."—Lt. General Tadamichi Kuribayashi

Despite the weather conditions, which continued into Wednesday, the 28th Marines planned to begin their final assault on Mount Suribachi while the remainder, from west to east, the 28th, 27th, 23rd and 24th Marines, would advance northwards across a broad front. Even such simple plans however, rarely develop as the commander wants and the weather quickly deteriorated to such a point that Admiral Turner was forced to close the beaches down again to everything except emergency traffic. The bad weather also disrupted the Marines' assault, which began at 08.00, as it turned the soft volcanic ash into a sticky glue-like substance that hampered all movement. The 28th Marines launched their attack on Mount Suribachi at 08.45 and were supported by an intense artillery barrage, naval gunfire and air strikes. The advance met heavy opposition as well as the Marines' own barbed wire obstacles as it was assumed that tanks would be available from the start but were delayed due to fuelling problems. The late arrival of tanks and half-tracks mounting 75mm guns helped their progress and the Marines gradually advanced around the base of the volcano. The 4th and 5th Marine Divisions started their advance northward, supported by artillery, naval gunfire and carrier aircraft and ran into a network of well-hidden pillboxes and bunkers. The 5th Marine Division made reasonable progress supported by tanks and finally reached the D-Day 0–1 line but the 4th Marine Division could only advance some 50 yards in the rugged terrain around the quarry and was suffering heavy casualties as it gradually cleared out the Japanese caves, pillboxes, bunkers, tunnels and blockhouses.

General Schmidt once again disembarked the 21st Marines (3rd Marine Division) and with a lull in the weather, they managed to land on Yellow Beach. Late in the day, the ships of the Task Force became the target of one of the earliest kamikaze attacks of the war. Around 50 Japanese aircraft from the 2nd Milate Special Attack Unit (Katori Airbase), having refueled at Hachijo Jima (125 miles south of Tokyo), approached the Task Force from the northwest. They were picked up on radar by the USS *Saratoga*, which could only dispatch six fighters as it was waiting to land aircraft. The fighters managed to shoot down two Zeros but a number continued through the low cloud and ploughed into the *Saratoga* with two hitting the side of the ship turning the hangars into a fireball while another crashed through the flight deck about 100 yards from the bow. Fire control teams battled hard to bring the fires under control and the carrier, under escort, limped back to Pearl Harbor, playing no further part in the Pacific Campaign. Her aircraft were recovered by the USS *Wake Island* and USS *Natoma Bay*. Another aircraft, a "Betty" twin-engine bomber, hit the USS *Bismarck Sea* while its flight deck was crowded with aircraft and the ensuing explosion caused uncontrollable fires. The crew abandoned ship and a few minutes later an explosion blew off the entire stern of the ship. She rolled over and sank. Three other ships (USS *Lurga Point*, USS *Keokuk* and LST 477) were also damaged in the attack and 358 men were killed. It would be a foretaste of the carnage that was to happen off Okinawa, accentuated by the American practice of fitting wooden flight decks on their carriers. The three Royal Navy aircraft carriers of Task Force 57 that participated in the invasion of Okinawa were able to continue operations after such kamikaze attacks despite suffering damage, due to the British use of reinforced steel flight decks, a practice the U.S. Navy took up after their World War II kamikaze experience.

D+3: 22 February 1945

"The Americans are beginning to climb the first terraces towards our defenses. Now they shall taste our steel and lead."—Col. Kanehiko Atsuchi, Cmdr., Mount Suribachi

Thursday saw no improvement in the weather and so the 28th Marines prepared to slog it out with the Japanese defenders (Colonel Atsuchi still having some 8–900 men) as the Sherman tanks were mired in mud and the Navy decided it could not provide close air support. Throughout the day the Marines attacked the Japanese positions on the lower slopes of Mount Suribachi, but there was little room for maneuver and it was difficult to use fire support from tanks and artillery to best advantage as the lines were so close. By mid-afternoon the Marines had surrounded the base after heavy fighting and many Japanese were moving through the Marine lines by means of the extensive tunnel network to join Kuribayashi's forces in the north. Those that remained were moving back up the volcano to the higher slopes. The final assault would have to wait. The advance to the north continued with Schmidt placing the 21st Marines (3rd Marine Division) in the centre of the line between the 4th and 5th Marine Divisions just in front of Airfield No. 2 where Colonel Masuo Ikeda's 145th Infantry Regiment manned the strongest part of the Japanese defenses. The 21st Marines had a baptism of fire as they attacked towards the southern end of the airfield and the day's gains were a mere 250 yards (229m). Many units were now suffering the effects of the bad weather, lack of sleep, a lack of regular hot food and heavy casualties. On the far right of the line, the 3/25 under "Jumpin' Joe" Chambers continued to attack the quarry, utilizing rocket-firing trucks and the Japanese mounted a series of counterattacks that were repulsed with difficulty. The weather continued to get worse as the icy rain and thick mist prevented the Navy from providing any support and so the fighting died down. The weather was also hampering the evacuation of casualties, as LSTs could not land on the beaches. The 4th Marine Division's cemetery was inaugurated near Airfield No. 1. Lt. Gen. Holland M. Smith was counting the cost, meanwhile, of three days of battle with the 4th and 5th Marine Divisions suffering 4,574 casualties and the 0–1 line only now being approached. Although the Americans didn't know it, worse was yet to come.

D+4: 23 February 1945

"Those of us who are left fully realize that our hopes of repelling the Americans or living to return to our homeland and loved ones are out of the question. We are doomed. But we will fight to the last man."—Major Yonomata

The weather improved greatly and so Maj. Gen. Harry Schmidt and Maj. Gen. Clifton Cates moved their headquarters ashore (Maj. Gen. Keller Rockey had come ashore the previous day). They decided to let the 3rd Marine Division maintain the centre with the 5th on its left flank and the 4th on the right flank. The Navy would continue to provide support and the tanks of all three divisions would be combined into a single command under Lt. Col. William Collins (5th Marine Division). A major offensive would be commenced the next day in an attempt to break the stalemate, but for the time being, D+4 would be a day of consolidation and replenishment. The exception to this was around Mount Suribachi. With the improvement in the weather the 28th Marines mounted a final assault and, finding opposition surprisingly light, sent out a 40 man patrol under Lt. Hal Schrier, which moved up the northern slopes towards the summit and engaged a number of Japanese who attacked them with hand grenades. Finally, at 10.20hrs, the Stars and Stripes were raised on a length of pipe with *Leatherneck* photographer Lou Lowery recording the moment. The shout quickly went around the southern half of the island, "The flag is up!" and troops cheered while vessels sounded their sirens. At around noon, a larger flag replaced the smaller one and the moment was recorded by Associated Press cameraman Joe Rosenthal and has since become one of the most famous pictures of World War II (see historical note below).

D+5: 24 February 1945

"This is like fighting on a pool table."—1st Lt. Raoul J. Archambault, K Co, 3/21

The American offensive reopened with a huge barrage all along the front line, which included the battleship USS *Idaho* and the cruiser USS *Pensacola*. The attack was spearheaded by the 21st Marines, (3rd Marine Division) who were located between the two airfields and were to be supported by tanks. But Colonel Ikeda had anticipated this and had laid a large number of mines along the taxiways of both airfields and had covered them with antitank guns. The first two tanks were disabled by mines and so it was down to the Marines to take out the bunkers and pillboxes with explosives and flamethrowers. The Marines charged the high ground in a scene reminiscent of World War I and many of the Japanese rose to meet them in a frenzy of close quarter combat. The Marines gradually overcame Japanese resistance and occupied the high ground, but were dangerously short of ammunition. However, they were resupplied by the redoubtable Seabees who came forward in tractors towing loaded trailers of food, water and ammunition. On the right flank, the 24th Marines (4th Marine Division) were fighting for an escarpment just south of the main runway of Airfield No. 2 called Charlie Dog Ridge. The Marines fought and battled their way to the top, suffering serious casualties in the process. This finally brought the Marines to the 0–1 line, although less than half the island had been captured and the battle would still have a long way to run.

D+6: 25 February 1945

"In the last and final analysis, it is the guy with the rifle and machine gun who wins and pays the penalty to preserve our liberty."—James Forrestal, Secretary of the Navy

Sunday was to be no day of rest for the Marines. The attack to the north across the plateau towards the unfinished Airfield No. 3 and the village of Motoyama would continue to not only split the enemy in two, but put the Marines in a position to clear the western side of the island which had accessible beaches that were desperately needed in order to clear the backlog of supplies and equipment still on transports. With Operation Iceberg (the invasion of Okinawa) only two months off, these transports would be urgently required for that but at the moment could not unload as the Japanese still held the commanding heights near to Airfield No. 2 from which they could shell the western beaches. Despite this, the southern end of the island was now a hive of activity with over 2,000 Seabees rebuilding and converting the runways of Airfield No. 1 so it could handle B-29 Superfortresses, P-51 Mustangs and P-61 Black Widow night fighters. On the coast by Mount Suribachi, a seaplane base was being built to handle the Catalina and Coronado flying boats that would undertake rescue missions between Marianas and Japan, while a huge collection of Nissan huts, tents, workshops, supply dumps and equipment stockpiles had sprung up on ground that had seen bloody combat only a short time ago. The advance in the centre reopened with the 9th Marines, having taken over from the 21st Marines, attacking towards the high ground at one end of Airfield No. 2 supported by some 26 Sherman tanks as well as artillery, naval gunfire and air support. They immediately ran into a fusillade of antitank, mortar and artillery fire and three tanks were quickly knocked out. The 9th Marines were to find out the hard way about the ferocity of the Japanese defense. The main defensive feature was a 360ft rocky ridge named Hill Peter. The 1st Battalion repeatedly stormed the hill but could only advance some 200 yards. The 2nd and 3rd Battalions had better luck and advanced to the north around Hill Peter, which remained in enemy hands. The 5th Marine Division was around 400 yards ahead of the 3rd on the left flank and so could afford to spend the time consolidating its position and wait for the 3rd to catch up. On the right flank, the 4th Marine Division faced a collection of four formidable defensive positions just to the east of Airfield No. 2 that would collectively become known as the "Meatgrinder." The first was Hill 382 (named after the elevation above sea level) that had an extensive collection of pillboxes, caves, dug-in tanks, enfiladed artillery positions and bunkers on it. Four hundred yards to the south lay a shallow depression known as the Amphitheater and just to the east of that was a hill called the Turkey Knob on top of which was a huge blockhouse and an observation post. The fourth obstacle was the village of Minami, little more than rubble-strewn ruins destroyed by naval gunfire and studded with gun emplacements. This area was defended by Maj. General Senda and his 2nd Mixed Brigade that included Baron Nishi's 26th Tank Regiment, now largely fighting on foot. The 23rd and 24th Marines, knowing little of what was up ahead, initially attacked Hill 382 but hardly advanced after fighting all day, even after tank support arrived, as the Sherman tanks were finding it difficult going in the deep volcanic ash.

D+7: 26 February 1945

"Easy Company started with 310 men. We suffered 75 percent casualties. Only fifty men boarded the ship after the battle. Seven officers went into battle with me. Only one—me—walked off Iwo."—Capt. Dave Severence, E Company, 28th Marines.

Monday dawned bright but chilly and the American offensive started once again when the 9th Marines attacked Hill Peter but were once again frustrated in their advance. On the left flank, the 5th Marine Division turned their attention to Hill 362A, which was some 600 yards south of the village of Nishi and surrounded by an extensive system of defenses. Tanks from the 5th Tank Battalion attacked and advanced some 100 yards while the 27th Marines (on the left of the 26th Marines) advanced along the west coast assisted by naval gunfire. The 25th Marines replaced the 24th Marines in the battle for Hill 382 in the Meatgrinder and their initial attack advanced over 100 yards before it was halted by machine gun fire from the Amphitheater and Turkey Knob. The 23rd Marines had moved through a minefield at the edge of the airfield and as they approached a ruined radio station at the foot of the hill they were met by an intense artillery barrage and machine gun fire that stopped the advance in its tracks. It was obvious that the Marines had come up against the Japanese main defensive line and that the Japanese would be retreating no further.

D+8: 27 February 1945

"I am not afraid of the fighting powers of only three American Marine Divisions if there are no bombardments from aircraft and warship. This is the only reason we have to see such miserable conditions."—Lt. General Tadamichi Kuribayashi

Once again, the 9th Marines attacked Hill Peter and Hill Oboe with the 1st and 2nd Battalions advancing against intense machine gun and mortar fire. Elements of the 1st managed to reach the top but were pinned down by fire coming from bypassed position to their rear. Another concerted effort was made in the early afternoon and the beleaguered Marines were relieved, with Hill Peter being taken and the Marines reaching the crest of Hill Oboe. Finally, Airfield No. 2 fell into American hands. On the right flank, the 4th Marine Division seemed to be bogged down against the formidable defenses of the Meatgrinder. Five battalions were committed against Turkey Knob and Hill 382 with support from rocket-firing trucks. The battle seesawed backwards and forwards all day and at one point some Marines managed to make it to the top of the Hill but a shortage of ammunition and vicious enemy counterattacks forced them to retreat. However, the Marines managed to complete an encircling action around the base of the hill after intense close quarters combat and decided to consolidate their gains. Further north, the tanks began to find the going very tough and tankdozers (tanks with bulldozer blades fitted) were constantly in action, but the battle was beginning to turn into an infantry-based war of attrition with casualties mounting by the hour. During the night the Japanese attempted to drop supplies to the garrison. In the only attempt of the battle to support the troops on Iwo Jima a number of Japanese planes dropped some supplies, including ammunition and medical supplies. Three of the aircraft were shot down by carrier-based night fighters, but the attempt was a morale boost for the beleaguered garrison.

D+9: 28 February 1945

"There was nothing spectacular about the day's action, but death was everywhere and heroism was commonplace."—Marine Correspondent

The last day of February saw an upturn in the fortunes of the 3rd Marine Division in the centre of the line. The 21st Marines took over from the battered 9th and under an intense naval and artillery barrage started their attack at 09.00, initially making good progress. At one point they encountered a number of "Ha Go" tanks from baron Nishi's 26th Tank Regiment but they were dealt with relatively quickly by bazookas and supporting aircraft. By the afternoon, the Japanese had recovered and resistance became very heavy. The Marines called a second massive artillery barrage in and were soon underway again. The Marines soon entered and cleared the ruins of Motoyama village and the 3/21 continued the advance and took up position on some high ground overlooking the unfinished Airfield No. 3. Meanwhile the 1st and 2nd Battalions had to contend with a mass of bypassed positions and were soon slugging it out in close quarter fighting with demolitions and flamethrowers. Eventually, however, the flanks were secured.

On the left flank, the 5th Marine Division was still confronted with Hill 362A, a veritable fortress with antitank guns, mortars, machine guns, pillboxes and bunkers. Two battalions of the 27th Marines (1st and 3rd) assaulted the hill with the support of tanks and rocket-firing trucks. While some elements reached the top, they were driven back by counterattacks and the gains for the day were limited to an advance of 300 yards. In an amazing display of pyrotechnics a shell hit an ammunition dump near Airfield No. 1 that lit up most of southern Iwo Jima and meant that the 5th Marine Division lost nearly a quarter of its ammunition supplies.

On the right flank, the stalemate at the Meatgrinder continued with the 4th Marine Division attacking with its 25th Marines against the Turkey Knob. The 1st Battalion tried to sweep around in a flanking maneuver but heavy fire from the Japanese defenders foiled the attempt. By late afternoon the Marines had had to pull back to the very same lines that they had started from.

D+10: 1 March 1945

"Fight the battle with the troops you have."—Lt. General Holland M. Smith to Major General Graves B. Erskine

By this point, the combat efficiency of the three Marine divisions was becoming a matter of grave concern. Many units were suffering badly from the effects of the prolonged exposure to such intense combat and in many instances command at a company level had passed from captain to lieutenant to sergeant. General Erskine was concerned that an entire regiment (3rd Marines) was still on board troopships while the 4th and 5th Marine Divisions had all their combat elements on the island. In fact, the 3rd Marines were never landed on Iwo Jima and it remained a contentious issue between Erskine and Smith for many years. Smith's reasoning has never been properly explained, although reasons for keeping the 3rd Marines back have been floated through the years—such as keeping a reserve in case of a serious reversal, that Smith didn't think there was enough room on the island for another 9,000 men or that he wanted to keep a fresh formation for Okinawa. Another contentious issue was the use of battle replacements, instead of organic replacements. "The great majority of the battle replacements were recruits who had gone through Parris Island in the summer of 1944, where they fired for qualification once" (John Lane, 25th Marines, 4th Marine Division).

After looking down on the unfinished Airfield No. 3, the 3rd Marine Division moved forward at first light with the 21st Marines leading the way, after a short but intense artillery barrage. Resistance was surprisingly light and as the 2nd and 3rd Battalions advanced, the 1st Battalion mopped up the bypassed enemy positions. In the afternoon, tanks moved forward to support the advance and after the Marines had advanced across the airfield they came up against the base of Hills 362B and 362C, two more strongpoints the same elevation as Hill 362A. The Marines decided to dig in and consolidate the gains of the day—some 600 yards for a cost of over 200 casualties. A good day on Iwo Jima.

Meanwhile, on the left flank the 5th Marine Division's 28th Regiment was back in the line and set to attack Hill 362A. After an intense barrage, the 28th stormed the hill and took it, but the Japanese had evacuated it and established a position some 200 yards further on Nishi Ridge. The rest of the day was spent mopping up bypassed positions but the cost to the effort was very high. On the right flank, the 4th Marine Division continued to concentrate their efforts on Hill 382 with the 24th Marines replacing the 23rd. The 24th Marines once again launched themselves into the attack but the advance was stalled by a hail of machine gun and mortar fire. It was helped by an intense artillery and naval gunfire barrage which kept the Japanese in their shelters; but, they quickly re-emerged to continue their defense and the advance stalled once again.

D+11: 2 March 1945

"Oh God, not another Ridge."—Marine, 5th Marine Division

On the right flank, the 25th Marines kept up pressure on both Turkey Knob and Hill 382. The 1st Battalion attempted pre-dawn infiltrations but they were driven back by mortar and machine gun fire. A number of Sherman tanks and flamethrower tanks (nicknamed Zippos) moved up in support and pounded the blockhouse at the top of Turkey Knob, but the Japanese simply retired to the depths of their tunnels to wait out the barrage. The 26th Marines, after some intense fighting, managed to secure a foothold on Hill 382 (2nd Battalion) after a three-pronged attack following a short but sharp artillery barrage. In many instances artillery could not be used due to the closeness of the combatants and the Marines had to use small arms, explosives, grenades and flamethrowers to pry the Japanese out of their positions. In the centre, the 3rd Marine Division's hope of making a rapid dash to the sea were rapidly fading in the face of determined Japanese resistance. The division had still to take Hills 362B and C but pressed forward towards the unfinished Airfield No. 3 and the base of Hill 362B with the support of tanks. The open ground of the airfield gave virtually no cover from the Japanese artillery and the 9th Marines came up against the defenses of Baron Nishi's command and progress remained slow. On the left flank, the 5th Marine Division were encountering fewer and fewer manmade obstacles as the ground became rougher and there were plenty of ravines, canyons, valleys and draws so that this natural defensive cover was all the Japanese needed. Nishi Ridge lay some 200 yards beyond Hill 362A and the 5th Engineers had to come forward and fill an antitank ditch in order for the attack to proceed. The 26th and 28th Marines then had the task of clearing the remainder of Hill 362A, after which they advanced to the base of Nishi Ridge.

D+12: 3 March 1945

"Iwo Jima is the most heavily fortified and capably defended island in the world. It will be a tough fight."—Vice Adm. Richmond K. Turner, Cmndr., Task Force 51

By this point, the Americans were in control of some two-thirds of Iwo Jima but the combat efficiency of many units was becoming an ever more pressing problem. Casualty figures were starting to assume tragic proportions, with some 16,000 casualties on the American side (over 3,000 killed) and some 14,000 casualties on the Japanese side. The campaign had become one more akin to the First World War—a war of attrition. The 5th Marine Division (Maj. Gen. Rockey) realigned its front to include Hill 362B, thus allowing the 3rd Marine Division to concentrate on advancing to the northeast coast and attack Hill 357, some 500 yards to the east. The 9th Marines advanced against an in-depth defense line of caves, pillboxes, bunkers and trenches, which forced the advance to slow to a crawl, but with tank support, the 1st and 2nd Battalions attacked and stormed Hill 357 and spent the rest of the day consolidating their positions. The 2nd Battalion even repulsed a major counterattack after intense close quarter fighting. The 5th Marine Division continued their offensive along the northwest coast with the 26th Marine attacking Hill 362B and the 28th Marines attacking Nishi Ridge. Both regiments suffered heavily (particularly the 26th) but both achieved a measure of success with the 26th reaching the summit of Hill 362B and the 28th Marines taking Nishi Ridge. It was a great boost to the division. The 4th Marine Division renewed its attacks on the Meatgrinder and in an attempt to gain some element of surprise, attacked without the benefit of artillery support. The 24th Marines attacked Hill 382 while the 23rd Marines assaulted the complex formed by Turkey Knob, the Amphitheater and Minami Village.

The 24th Marines managed to advance some 350 yards and surround Hill 382, but both regiments were brought to a halt by fire from the blockhouse on Turkey Knob.

D+13: 4 March 1945

"The minute we land, we're going to be in the middle of it, and we're never going to be out of it until the battle is all over.... There isn't a safe spot on the island."
—Anonymous Marine

The last few days had seen good weather, but as D+13 dawned, a grey mist hung over the island and drizzle filled the sky. The air support and naval bombardments were cancelled due to poor visibility and so the Marines had to see to their own devices. The 4th Marine Division once again concentrated on the Meatgrinder with tanks and rocket-firing trucks taking every opportunity to blast the enemy positions in and around the Amphitheater. The 5th Marine Division continued to attack in the north with the support of flamethrower tanks. The 3rd Marine Division in the centre had taken some nine days of bitter fighting to advance 3,000 yards from the edge of Airfield No. 2 until their current positions. General Erskine even delayed their attack until late morning until fresh troops could be brought up, but their impact was negligible and the lines remained very similar to those at dawn. D+13, however, saw the first B29 Superfortress to land on Iwo Jima—the very reason the battle was being waged. *Dinah Might* was returning from a raid near Tokyo with her bomb bays jammed open and the reserve fuel tank transfer valve malfunctioning. Lt. Raymond Malo had two choices, ditch in the sea or attempt to land on Iwo Jima. The latter option seemed the most attractive. The *Superfortress* circled the island twice and then put down on Airfield No. 1. The aircraft was quickly moved to the Suribachi end of the runway and repairs effected. The arrival had not gone unnoticed by the Japanese, who brought a steady rate of artillery fire down on the airfield.

About half an hour later the bomber was on its way again with a parting goodbye of weak Japanese anti-aircraft fire. The floodgates were opened and very soon, Iwo Jima was taking up to 25 flights each day and the large-scale evacuation of wounded by air began. Lt. General Kuribayashi finally realized that the Americans had firmly gained the upper hand and radioed Tokyo that the result was no longer in doubt. It was just a matter of time. What was apparent, however, was that many American planners had underestimated both the determination of the Japanese and the strength of their defenses, just as they had done in most other Pacific battles.

D+14: 5 March 1945

"Our strongpoints may be able to fight delaying actions for several more days. Even when the strongpoints fall, we hope the survivors will continue to fight to the end."
—Lt. General Tadamichi Kuribayashi

D+14 saw the Marine front line run almost along the position designated for D+1. The Japanese still held an excellent advantage as (even though they were now much smaller in number and short of food, water and ammunition) the terrain to the north was very rough and provided superb defensive cover. The Motoyama Plateau, which was the flat area in the centre of the island where the third airfield had been started, gave way to an almost moonlike terrain of hills, valleys, ravines and canyons. Tanks were finding the going extremely tough and every cave or hillock held a defensive position. Any movement would draw fire from a number of different directions and an advance of a couple of hundred yards was good going. The Seabees continued to work on Airfield No. 1, now secure from the worst of the enemy shelling. Around it lay a collection of huts, shacks, tents and compounds that resembled a shanty town—ground that had been so recently a bloody battlefield on a par with the Somme and Passchendaele. Despite the 5th being a day of rest for the Marines, the Japanese continued their incessant shelling. New supplies were brought up to the front, tanks and vehicles were serviced, replacements absorbed (the veterans doing what they could to prepare them for the coming onslaught) and fresh coffee and doughnuts arrived from the bakery near Airfield No. 1. Even the Army started arriving, being assigned the task of garrisoning the island once it was secure.

D+15: 6 March 1945

"There is a quiet deadly stillness in the air, the tension is strong, everyone is waiting. Some will die—how many, no one knows. God knows, enough have died already."
—Dale Worley (diary)

The day's pre-assault bombardment was one of the heaviest so far in the battle for Iwo Jima, with some 132 guns firing some 22,500 shells in just over an hour. Added to that, a battleship, a cruiser and three destroyers added some 450 shells while Corsairs and Dauntless carried out ground attacks with bombs and napalm. The assault was staggered with the 5th Marine Division in the west attacking at 8.00 A.M. while the 4th Marine Division in the east attacked at 9.00 A.M. Resistance was as strong as ever. The 27th Marines (5th Division) and 21st Marines (3rd Division) attacked in the west but soon ran into trouble despite being supported by flamethrower tanks. An element of the 21st Marines led by

Lt. William Mulvey reached the top of another ridge, to see what General Schmidt had been after for so long—the sea. The ocean was no more than a quarter of a mile away, but the Japanese decided to remind the Americans that a quarter of a mile could still be a long way by pinning them down with mortar and machine gun fire. Although reinforcements tried to get through they were beaten back and Mulvey and his group had to wait until later in the day until they could make their way back to their lines. The day had seen advances of on average, around 200 yards, the best being 350 yards by 3/24. Even the Army joined in, with the 506th Antiaircraft Artillery Gun Battalion shelling enemy positions on Kangoku and Kama Rocks, two groups of small islands situated 1.5 and 0.5 miles off the northwest coast.

D+16: 7 March 1945

"After we had advanced about seventy-five yards, I observed a dark, jagged rock formation directly to our front. All hell broke loose after we had advanced another twenty yards or so. Intense machine gun fire and grenades seemed to be the order of the day."—Lt. O'Bannon, 2nd Battalion, 9th Marines

In order to break the stalemate, General Erskine planned to have the 9th Marines undertake an attack in the early hours of D+16. It would be spearheaded by the 3rd Battalion under Lt. Col. Harold Boehm with the 1st (Major William Glass) and 2nd (Lt. Col. Robert E. Cushman) Battalions making diversionary attacks to their right. The objective was to advance straight ahead and capture Hill 362C, the last obstacle between the 3rd Marine Division and the sea. The Marines moved out at 05.00 (after the Navy had inadvertently fired a starshell) with a smokescreen to cover their movement. All went well for some 30 minutes as the Marines bypassed enemy positions but an observant machine gunner opened up on the left flank. Although he was swiftly dealt with, the Japanese were now aware something was afoot and began to mount increasing resistance. At 06.00, Boehm radioed that his men were at the top of Hill 362C, many enemy positions had been eliminated and casualties were light. Erskine was delighted. The euphoria was short-lived however, as Boehm realized that they were in fact on Hill 331 not Hill 362C, which was another 250 yards further on. He decided to press forward now that their position was known. And, although Japanese resistance was fierce, both in front and from a number of bypassed positions, the Marines burned and blasted their way onwards and by 14.00 elements of K Company had reached the objective.

The other two battalions had also achieved surprise, but by 07.30 Japanese resistance had become so fierce that the two battalions had been cut off. They had unfortunately stumbled across the remains of Baron Nishi's 26th Tank Regiment, a crack outfit. Tanks were brought up to try and extricate the two units but were repeatedly defeated by the terrain. B Co / 1st Btn managed to extricate themselves at dusk with many Marines carrying wounded comrades on their backs. The company commander, Lt. John Leims, rescued many of his men himself in the growing darkness, for which he received the Medal of Honor. Two of Colonel Cushman's companies remained surrounded in the pocket (hence the nickname "Cushman's Pocket") and had to remain in place until the following day.

The 5th Marine Division saw a steady advance with the 26th Marines advancing north of Nishi Village. As the advance elements topped a ridge they were surprised by the lack of resistance that they encountered. At that moment the Japanese blew up their local command post in an explosion that demolished the ridge and was heard clearly as far away as Mount Suribachi. It killed some 43 Marines and wounded many others. The 28th Marines made steady progress in the rough terrain near the coast and managed to advance some 500 yards, supported by gunfire from destroyers. The 4th Marine Division deployed its 23rd and 24th Marine Regiments to the east where they swung to the south moving the enemy towards the 25th Marines. Trapped between them were the 1,500 troops of General Senda and Captain Inouye (Imperial Japanese Navy). Seeing the hopelessness of the situation the two officers led a banzai charge (forbidden by Lt. General Kuribayashi), which managed to reach the Marine lines where fierce hand-to-hand fighting took place into the early hours.

D+17: 8 March 1945

"We cannot hallow this ground—the brave men living and dead, who struggled here have consecrated it far above our powers to add or detract."—Abraham Lincoln

The day saw steady if not spectacular progress. The 3rd Marine Division still had "Cushman's Pocket" to overcome, the 4th Marine Division was still battling for Turkey Knob, while the 5th Marine Division continued its advance northeast. A Japanese rocket found its mark on the 2/23 Command Post, killing the communications officer and wounding six others. Two Marines won the Medal of Honor—Pfc. James LaBelle, who threw himself on a hand grenade to save his comrades, and Lt. Jack Lummus, a former professional football player, who knocked out two enemy emplacements single-handedly. In urging his men forward however, he stepped on a mine and lost both legs. He continued to urge his men on before being taken back to the 5th Marine Division hospital where, sadly, he died from shock and loss of blood. Before leaving Camp Pendleton in California for Hawaii, Jack had been dating Mary Hartman, a Nebraska girl who had moved to Hollywood to work. They planned to marry upon his return. She finally returned to his hometown of Ennis, Texas, in 1987. "I follow a rock road through Ennis Myrtle Cemetery. I spotted a small replica of the Medal of Honor next to a flat tombstone. On the granite was engraved Jack's name and the dates October 22nd 1912–March 8th 1945. Once a year now I visit the grave. A gnarled old elm tree shades me as I sit remembering. When I leave, I place a single rose on the grave marker. I have found Jack at last."

D+18: 9 March 1945

"When you go home, tell them of us and say: 'For their tomorrows, we gave our todays.'"—John Maxwell Edmonds

Finally, the breakthrough came on D+18 when a 28-man patrol led by Lt. Paul Connally reached the northeast coast. The men stood and stared, hardly believing that they had finally split the Japanese into two. Connally filled his canteen with seawater and sent it to his CO, Colonel Withers, who passed it on to General Erskine. The cost to get this far for the 3rd Marine Division had been enormous—over 3,500 casualties. That night, the first major firebombing raid by B29 Superfortresses from the Marianas took place over Tokyo. Around a quarter of Tokyo's buildings were destroyed, just over 1 million people were left homeless, over 83,000 people were killed and almost 41,000 wounded.

D+19: 10 March 1945

"The enemy's bombardments are very severe, especially the bombing and machine gun fire against Divisional Headquarters—so fierce that I cannot express or write it here. The troops are still fighting bravely and holding their positions thoroughly."—Lt. General Tadamichi Kuribayashi

It was now clear that the battle was reaching its finale with the Japanese forces divided but still resisting bitterly in Cushman's Pocket and the Meatgrinder. They were, however, being ground down. But in the northeast, where Lt. General Kuribayashi had made his headquarters, Japanese resistance was still as effective as ever. This was to be the last section of the island to fall and the Marines had already nicknamed the area "The Gorge" or "Death Valley" and some 1,500 Japanese were still deeply entrenched in their positions. Kuribayashi had predicted the battle to perfection and waited for the Marines to come and dig him out.

D+20–D+35: 11 March 1945–26 March 1945

"The fight is still raging. It has developed into hand-to-hand fighting with bayonets and grenades."—Dale Worley

As the final part of the campaign on Iwo Jima began, the War Department released the up-to-date casualty figures in the United States. Needless to say, they caused consternation in America and fuelled the rhetoric of the pro–MacArthur lobby. In an attempt to placate public opinion, the island was declared secure on 14 March 1945 in a ceremony many saw as cynically premature. As one Marine put it, "If this damn place has been secured, where the hell is all this gunfire coming from?" Even the words of General Schmidt's personal officer were drowned out by an artillery barrage directed against Cushman's Pocket. The Japanese had been confined to three areas—Cushman's pocket, The Gorge and the east coast. The bulk of the fighting would be done by Marine infantry with flamethrowers, explosives and small arms against a desperate Japanese defense. The bulk of the Navy left for Guam, while the air support was continued by the P51 Mustangs with their machine guns, bombs and rockets. Airfield No. 1 was very busy with the evacuation of the wounded and transportation of replacements, gradually ceding priority to the landing of damaged B29 Superfortresses. There was even a rumor that the war in Europe had ended, but this was quickly revealed to be a hoax.

The 3rd Marine Division slowly ground down the defenders in Cushman's Pocket during fierce fighting. Baron Nishi, who it is believed had been partially blinded during the fighting, led a determined resistance against the Marines with dug-in tanks and fortified caves until resistance finally ended on 16 March. The fate of Baron Nishi remains unclear as his body was never identified and none of his staff remained alive to tell what happened.

The 4th Marine Division continued to battle General Senda, who held a small area of land between the village of Higashi and the coast with a few hundred men. The Americans tried to arrange for loudspeakers to broadcast to the Japanese to appeal to them to lay down their arms and prevent any more needless bloodshed, but the generators failed to work and the Marines had to dig the Japanese out one-by-one, suffering heavy casualties in the process. The struggle lasted four more days, while the body of General Senda was never found.

Meanwhile, the 5th Marine Division regrouped and prepared to take on the last major bastion of Japanese resistance on the island—The Gorge. On 17 March, Admiral Nimitz issued a bulletin stating that Iwo Jima was now secure and Japanese resistance was at an end. Of course, this didn't go down very well with the Marines—"This morning the island was officially secured. They ran the flag up at the base of Hot Rocks. We are still fighting, but it's called 'mopping up operations'" (Dale Worley). In fact, another nine days of bloody fighting were ahead along with almost 2,000 casualties. The Gorge was in fact only some 700 yards long and 3–500 yards wide but Lt. General Kuribayashi had concentrated the remains of his garrison there (around 500 men) and prepared his last stand.

The 28th Marines took up position on the cliffs overlooking The Gorge while the remainder of the division attacked in the centre and from the east. In brutal fighting, the Marines gradually forced the Japanese back into a smaller and smaller pocket of resistance. The cost was staggering though, with the 1st and 2nd Battalions of the 27th Marines badly mauled (the 2nd was in fact withdrawn) in the struggle. A huge blockhouse barred the way for quite a time despite repeated pounding by tanks and demolition reams and it finally took an explosive charge of some 8,500 pounds to destroy it. On D+32 (23 March 1945), a final message was received by Major Horie on Chichi Jima: "All officers and men of Chichi Jima—goodbye from Iwo."

By the end of D+33, the Japanese had been squeezed into an area of around 50 square yards and the final act in a long and drawn out saga was approaching. The Americans once again tried to persuade the Japanese to surrender, but to no avail. With the fighting gradually coming to an end, the remaining few defenders from The Gorge and positions along the west coast, around 2–300 in number, silently infiltrated the American lines in the early hours of 26 March and headed for the bivouac area not far from Airfield No. 2. Led by sword-wielding officers and armed with an assortment of machine guns, rifles and grenades, the Japanese launched a well-planned and coordinated three-pronged attack, not a last-ditch banzai charge, against a mixture of Marine shore parties, Air Force crewmen, AA gunners and Seabees. The Japanese attacked them with determination and the noise from the confrontation brought Marines from nearby Pioneer Battalions and an all–Negro shore party. Lt. Harry Martin of the 5th Pioneer Battalion organized a hasty defense line, rushed into the fight to rescue wounded men and launched a counterattack that momentarily repelled the attackers. The Japanese, however, returned with an even greater fury and in the confused melee, other American personnel came and joined the frantic struggle. Lt. Martin was also killed, earning him the final Medal of Honor of the battle. By dawn a detachment from the Army's 147th Infantry had arrived on the scene with tanks but by then it was mostly over. The daylight revealed some 44 airmen killed, another 88 injured, 9 Marines killed, another 31 wounded. Of the Japanese attackers, some 262 lay dead with another 18 captured. Even though it was rumored that General Kuribayashi (he had been promoted to full General on 17 March) had led the charge, his body was never found.

As the Marines began to leave Iwo, many felt these emotions: "I stood on the rail of the ship as it pulled out. As we left I thought of my friends that had fallen and were buried there. I felt like we were leaving them back there alone, that we were deserting them. We are Marines, fighting men, that are supposed to be hard, with no feelings, but we have them. We talk of our fallen buddies as though they were transferred—we sound indifferent, but when we are alone we would cry. A buddy is something precious, and to lose that buddy is a hard blow."

Conclusion

"Among the Americans who fought on Iwo Jima, uncommon valor was a common virtue."—Admiral Chester Nimitz, CINCPAC

With the final attack on 26 March, organized Japanese resistance was finally at an end. Fighting would continue in small skirmishes well into June when the last few Japanese were captured (such as Lt. Musashino, commander of the 2nd Mixed Brigade's Pioneer Company) by the U.S. Army. Airfield No. 2 was expanded and the infrastructure of the island greatly improved. In the last few months of the war, the island underlined the reason for its capture as P51 Mustangs joined the B29 Superfortresses on the final leg of their journey to Japan and some 2,400 Superfortresses, with crews totaling over 70,000, landed on the island—crews who might have otherwise have had to ditch in the sea.

The Americans had completely underestimated the timescale and cost of the operation as well as the determination and preparedness of the enemy. What had been envisaged as a short, decisive battle became the costliest battle in the history of the U.S. Marine Corps and the role played by Lt. General Kuribayashi cannot be underestimated in this. He had planned the defense of the island and foreseen how the campaign would unfold to perfection and was the only commander to inflict greater casualties on the Marines than what was suffered by the garrison. The Marines suffered some 23,157 casualties (5,885 killed) and the U.S. Navy suffered some 2,798 casualties (881 killed). For the Japanese, out of an estimated garrison strength of 21,060 personnel, some 216 Navy and 867 Army personnel were taken prisoner, leaving one to conclude that 19,977 were killed. Twenty-seven American personnel (22 Marines, four Navy corpsmen and one Naval Officer) received the Medal of Honor (13 posthumously), a third of the total awarded to the U.S. Marine Corps in World War II. The intensity of the combat on Iwo Jima was a stern warning of what was to come on Okinawa and what may well have awaited the Allies in an invasion of the Japanese mainland. Such an operation was already in its advanced planning stages, had been codenamed Operation Downfall and was due to take place in November 1945, the initial phase of which (itself codenamed Operation Olympic) was the island of Honshu. The enormity of the final casualty lists from Iwo Jima made it a priority that if an alternative means of ending the war could be found, then it should be pursued. That means came in the form of the Manhattan Project and the dropping of the atomic bombs on Hiroshima and Nagasaki. The Japanese formally surrendered on the battleship USS *Missouri* anchored in Tokyo Bay on 2 September 1945. The Second World War had finally come to an end.

REFERENCE SOURCE: *http://www.historyofwar.org/articles/battles_iwojima.html*

APPENDIX III

Task Organization for Iwo Jima

EXPEDITIONARY TROOPS—Lieutenant General Holland M. Smith

CORPS TROOPS

Headquarters and Service Battalion, V Amphibious Corps (less detachments)
Medical Battalion, V Amphibious Corps
Motor Transport Company, V Amphibious Corps
Provisional Signal Group, V Amphibious Corps
    Landing Force Headquarters Signal Section
    Signal Battalion, V Amphibious Corps (less detachments)
    Shore Party Communication Unit
    Detachment, Signal Company, 8th Field Depot
    Detachment, 1st Separate Reconnaissance and Intelligence Platoon
    Detachment, Signal Headquarters Company, VII Fighter Command (USA)
    Detachment, 568th Signal Air Warning Battalion (USA)
    Detachment, 726th Signal Air Warning Company (USA)
    Detachment, 49th Signal Construction Battalion (USA)
    Detachment 44, 70th Army Airways Communications System (USA)
Landing Force Air Support Control Unit
Headquarters, Provisional LVT Group
2d Separate Engineer Battalion
62d Naval Construction Battalion (less detachments)
23d Naval Construction Battalion (Cos A and B)
8th Field Depot (less detachments, plus VAC Shore Party Headquarters)
Corps Evacuation Hospital No. 1
2d Bomb Disposal Company, plus 156th Bomb Disposal Squad
Company B, Amphibious Reconnaissance Battalion (FMFPac)
38th Field Hospital, Reinforced (USA)
Medical Section, Civil Affairs
Joint Intelligence Center Pacific Ocean Areas (JICPOA) Intelligence Team
Joint Intelligence Center Pacific Ocean Areas Enemy Matériel and Salvage Platoon

CORPS ARTILLERY

1st Provisional Field Artillery Group
  Headquarters Battery
  2d 155mm Howitzer Battalion
  4th 155mm Howitzer Battalion
  473d Amphibian Truck Company (USA)

ANTIAIRCRAFT ARTILLERY

138th AAA Group (less detachments) (USA)
  Headquarters Battery, 138th AAA Group (USA)
  506th AA Gun Battalion (USA)
  473d Amphibian Truck Company (USA)

ANTIAIRCRAFT ARTILLERY

138th AAA Group (less detachments) (USA)
  Headquarters Battery, 138th AAA Group (USA)
  506th AA Gun Battalion (USA)
  483d AA Automatic Weapons Battalion (USA)

a. *4th Marine Division* (Reinforced)—Major General Clifton B. Cates
  4th Marine Division
  Companies A and B, plus detachment, Battalion Headquarters, 2d Armored
    Amphibian Battalion
  5th Amphibian Tractor Battalion
  10th Amphibian Tractor Battalion
  1st Joint Assault Signal Company (JASCO)
  Marine Observation Squadron 4
  4th Marine Amphibian Truck Company
  476th Amphibian Truck Company (USA)
  7th War Dog Platoon
  1st Provisional Rocket Detachment
  Detachment, 8th Field Depot
  Detachment, 726th Signal Air Warning Company (USA)
  Detachment, Signal Battalion, V Amphibious Corps
  442d Port Company (USA)
  Joint Intelligence Center Pacific Ocean Areas Intelligence Team
  24th Replacement Draft
  30th Replacement Draft

b. *5th Marine Division* (Reinforced)—Major General Keller E. Rockey
  5th Marine Division
  5th Marine Amphibian Truck Company
  5th Joint Assault Signal Company
  471st Amphibian Truck Company (USA)
  11th Amphibian Tractor Battalion

3d Amphibian Tractor Battalion
Companies C and D and detachment, Headquarters Battalion, 2d Armored
 Amphibian Battalion
Marine Observation Squadron 5
3d Provisional Rocket Detachment
6th Marine War Dog Platoon
592d Port Company (USA)
31st Naval Construction Battalion
27th Replacement Draft
31st Replacement Draft
Detachment, 726th Signal Air Warning Company (USA)
Joint Intelligence Center Pacific Ocean Areas Intelligence Team
Detachment, Signal Battalion, V Amphibious Corps
Detachment, 8th Field Depot
Liaison Group, V Amphibious Corps
Liaison Group, Fleet Marine Force, Pacific V Amphibious Corps Reserve

c. *21st Marines*

d. *3d Marine Division* (Reinforced)—Major General Graves B. Erskine*
 3d Marine Division (less 21st Marines)
 3d Joint Assault Signal Company
 Marine Observation Squadron 1
 3d Marine War Dog Platoon
 Joint Intelligence Center Pacific Ocean Areas Intelligence Team
 Detachment, Signal Battalion, V Amphibious Corps
 28th Replacement Draft
 34th Replacement Draft

e. *Garrison Forces* (Assault Echelon)—Major General James E. Chaney, USA*
 Detachment, Island Command Headquarters
 Detachment, 147th Army Infantry Regiment
 Detachment, Headquarters, VII Fighter Command
 Detachment, Headquarters, 15th Fighter Group
 47th Fighter Squadron
 78th Fighter Squadron
 548th Night Fighter Service
 386th Air Service Group, Special
 1st Platoon, 604th Quartermaster Graves Registration Company
 223d Radar Maintenance Unit (Type C)
 Detachment, Administrative Unit, Group Pacific 11
 Port Directors Detachment
 Garrison Beach Party

*REFERENCE SOURCE: http://www.ibiblio.org/hyperwar/USMC/USMC-M-IwoJima/
USMC-M-IwoJima-V.html*

APPENDIX IV

Strategic Location of Iwo Jima to Mainland Japan

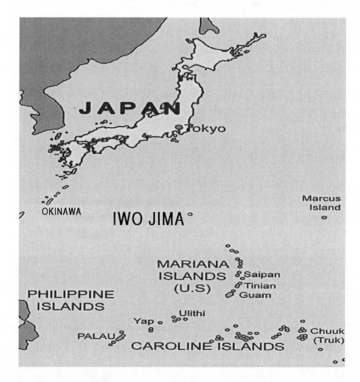

The strategic importance of Iwo Jima to the invading forces and the Japanese is shown in this map. With each victory, a very successful island hopping campaign by U.S. forces in the Pacific was moving ever closer to the Japanese-controlled island of Iwo Jima. Located 650 miles off the coast of the island of *Honshu*, which was the seat of the Imperial Japanese Government (http://en.wikipedia.org/wiki/File:Iwo_jima_location_mapSangredo.png).

APPENDIX V

476th Amphibian Truck Company

APO 86 C/O Postmaster
San Francisco, California

COMPANY HISTORY—1945

1. The 476th Amphibian Truck Company was organized in accordance with TO and E 55-37, dated May 22, 1944.

1. a. On 1 January 1945, the company strength consisted of one captain, three first lieutenants, two second lieutenants and 177 EM.

b. On 28 February 1945, the company strength consisted of one captain, three first lieutenants, two second lieutenants, and 174 EM. There was a decrease of three EM.

c. On 31 March 1945 the company strength consisted of one captain, three first lieutenants, two second lieutenants and 173 EM. There was a decrease of one EM.

d. On 30 April the company strength consisted of one captain, five first lieutenants and 173 EM. Second Lieutenant JOHN B. GREEN, O-1535465, was promoted to first lieutenant, persuant [sic] to paragraph 5, Special Order 94 Headquarters United States Armed Force Pacific Ocean Area dated 4 April 1945, Second Lieutenant ANDREW I. MEDITZ, Jr., O-1946571, was promoted to first lieutenant persuant [sic] to paragraph 6 Special Order 91 Headquarters United States Armed Forces Pacific Ocean Area dated 1 April 1945.

e. On 31 May the company strength consisted of one captain, five first lieutenants and 171 EM. There was a decrease of two EM.

f. On 30 June the company strength consisted of one captain, five first lieutenants and 172 EM. There was an increase of one EM.

g. On 31 July the company strength consisted of one captain, five first lieutenants and 168 EM. There was a decrease of four EM.

h. On 31 August the company strength consisted of one captain, four first lieutenants and 163 EM. There was a decrease of five EM. First Lieutenant JOHN B.

GREEN, O-1535465, was transferred to the 473 Amphibian Truck Company, effective 8 August 1945.

i. On 30 September the company strength consisted of one captain, four first lieutenants and 149 EM. There was a decrease of 14 EM.

j. On 31 October the company strength consisted of one captain, three first lieutenants and 169 EM. There was an increase of 20 EM. First Lieutenant JOHN F. WILLIAMS, O-1946639, was released from assignment and attached unassigned to Western Pacific Base Command Personnel Center and Casual Depot for processing under current readjustment regulation.

k. On 30 November the company strength consisted of one captain, three first lieutenants and 144 EM. There was a decrease of 25 EM.

l. On 31 December the company strength consisted of one captain, three first lieutenants and 150 EM. There was an increase of six EM. First Lieutenant GILBERT M. HOOKER, O-2511953, was released from assignment and attached unassigned to Western Pacific Base Command for processing under current readjustment regulation effective 24 December 1945. First Lieutenant LOUIS M. COHEN, O-1945556, was released from assignment and attached unassigned to Detachment of Patients, 232nd General Hospital, APO 86, dated 28 December 1945. First Lieutenant JOHN B. GREEN, O-1535465, assigned and joined from 473rd Amphibian Truck Company persuant [sic] to Special Order 121, Headquarters 43rd Transportation Corps. Amphibian Truck Battalion, dated 13 December 1945. First Lieutenant RALPH M. BLEAK, O-535664, assigned and joined from 3753rd Quartermaster Truck Company, persuant [sic] to Special Order 133, Headquarters 43rd Transportation Corps. Amphibian Truck Battalion, dated 31 December 1945.

[No number 2 in original document.]

3. From January 1 to 6 January 1945, the company was stationed at Kihauli Bay, Maui, Territory of Hawaii. On 7 January 1945, 44 EM and one officer embarked aboard *Landing Ship Tank 763*, in port at above station. On 11 January 1945, 55 EM and two officers embarked aboard Landing Ship Tank *1031*, and 61 EM and two officers embarked aboard Landing Ship Tank *1032*, both in port at Kihauli Bay, Maui, Territory of Hawaii. On 17 January 1945, the company left Maui, Territory of Hawaii, for Oahu, Territory of Hawaii, aboard Landing Ship Tank *763, 1031, 1032*. Company arrived at Oahu on 18 January 1945. On 22 January the officers and men aboard the Landing Ship Tank *1031* changed to Landing Ship Tank *648*. The *648, 763*, and *1032* left Oahu at 1000 en route to IWO JIMA, Volcano Islands. The company arrived at Iwo Jima on D-Day, 19 February 1945. The company was attached to 43rd Amphibian Truck Battalion persuant [sic] to paragraph 4 General Order 3, Headquarters Army Garrison Force, APO 86 effective 16 March 1945.

4. In January 1945 the company was training with the Fourth Marine Division at Maui, Territory of Hawaii. LST maneuvers occupied the latter part of the month. En route to Iwo Jima the unit stopped at Eniwetok, Marshall Islands, from 3 February until 5 February, and at Saipan, Mariannas Islands, from 10 February to 15 February. The company, consisting of five officers and 159 EM arrived at Iwo Jima

on 19 February. The unit participated in the combat action as a component of the Fourth Marine Division, the primary mission being the landing of artillery pieces and the supply of ammunition. On 16 March the unit was attached to the 43rd Transportation Corps. Amphibian Truck Battalion and assumed garrison duties, operating the amphibian truck on a 24 hour basis, 7 days per week.

5. On 20 February, Technician Fifth Grade THOMAS U. TAYLOR, 33750082, and Technician Fifth Grade WALTER HEATLY, 38500563, were wounded in action by enemy fire. On 21 February, Technician Fifth Grade PETER W. PUGH, 38520724, and Private GEORGE W. PAGE, 38522469, were wounded in action by enemy fire. Technician Fifth Grade WILLIAM R. DRAYTON, 33749957, and Technician Fourth Grade ORA BRIDGES, 38521883, were hospitalized because of exposure to water. On 23 February, Private First Class WILLIE PAGE, 38557519, was drowned in action. Pfc. ARTIE COLEMAN, 38522004, was wounded in action from enemy fire. On 25 February, Technician Fifth Grade EMERSON MANESS, 33749848, was wounded in action from enemy fire. On 28 February, Technician Fifth Grade CONRAD KYLES, 38544057, was injured in action at the shipside. On 4 March Technician Fifth Grade ULYSSES G. WALKER, 33750086, was injured in action shipside. On 8 March Private WALFORD E. RALEIGH, 33749973, was injured in action at shipside.

6. During the combat operations 29 amphibian trucks were lost to enemy action and to extremely rough surf conditions. Two were lost on 20 February, eight on 21 February, nine on 22 February, four on 23 February, three on 24 February, one on 2 March, one on 5 March, and one on 6 March.

7. All personnel of the company were authorized the award of a Bronze Service Star persuant [sic] to paragraph 1, General Order 17, Headquarters 43rd Transportation Corps Amphibian Truck Battalion.

Other awards are as follows:

a. Silver Star Medals

(1). Technician Fifth Grade HORACE TAYLOR, 34659655, General Order 99 Headquarters, Army Garrison Force APO 86, dated 22 October 1945.

(2). Private First Class WILLIE L. PAGE, 38557519 (posthumous), General Order 99 Headquarters, Army Garrison Force APO 86, dated 15 October 1945.

(3). First Lieutenant ANDREW I. MEDRITZ, JR., O-1946571, General Order 95 Headquarters, Army Garrison Force APO 86, dated 15 October 1945.

(4). Private First Class LEWIS H. ANDERSON, 33750088, General Order 95 Headquarters, Army Garrison Force APO 86, dated 15 October 1945.

(5). First Lieutenant JOHN B. GREEN, O-1535465, General Order 93 Headquarters, Army Garrison Force APO 86, dated 10 October 1945.

b. Bronze Star Medals

(1). Technician Fourth Grade RUDOLPH DeMARY, 34041417, General Order 95 Headquarters, Garrison Force APO 86, dated 15 October 1945.

(2). Staff Sergeant ARTHUR L. PETERSON, 33749954, General Order 95 Headquarters, Army Garrison Force APO 86, dated 15 October 1945.

(3). First Lieutenant GILBERT M. HOOKER, O-251953, General Order 91 Headquarters, Army Garrison Force APO 86, dated 2 October 1945.

(4). First Lieutenant JOHN F. WILLIAMS, O-1946639, General Order 91 Headquarters, Army Garrison Force APO 86, dated 2 October 1945.

(5). Technician Third Grade GEORGE E. BROOKS, 33750139, General Order 91 Headquarters, Army Garrison Force APO 86, dated 2 October 1945.

(6). First Sergeant WILLIAM H. MAIDEN, JR., 32958-438, General Order 91 Headquarters, Army Garrison Force APO 86, dated 2 October 1945.

(7). Technician Fifth Grade CHARLES B. BLACK, 33749895, General Order 93 Headquarters, Army Garrison Force APO 86, dated 10 October 1945.

(8). Captain JULES BLAUSTEIN, O-1575761, General Order 93, Headquarters, Army Garrison Force APO 86 dated 8 January 1946.

(9). Technician Third Grade THOMAS H. PERRIN, 33750064, General Order 93 Headquarters, Army Garrison Force APO 86, dated 10 October 1945.

(10). Staff Sergeant JESSE C. FLETCHER, 34654517, General Order 93 Headquarters, Army Garrison Force APO 86, dated 10 October 1945.

(11). Staff Sergeant WILLIAM D. ORANGE, 37369019, General Order 93, Headquarters, Army Garrison Force, APO 86, dated 10 October 1945.

(12). Technician Fifth Grade MAURICE W. PARIS, 33750056, General Order 93, Headquarters, Army Garrison Force, APO 86, dated 10 October 1945.

(13). Corporal CLARENCE COLEMAN, 33899168, General Order 93, Headquarters, Army Garrison Force, APO 86, dated 10 October 1945.

(14). Private First Class ANTHONY THORNTON, 3389168 General Order 93, Headquarters, Army Garrison Force, APO 86, dated 10 October 1945.

(15). Private First Class JAMES M. WOODSON, 34013987, dated 10 October 1945.

(16). Technical Sergeant HERMAN McSEARS, 34747869, General, 10 October 1945.

(17). Sergeant ROBERT S. BARBER 33707516, Recommended for the award but at the time this history was submitted, it had not been awarded.

Duties of Officers are as follows:

Captain JULES BLAUSTEIN O-1575761
    Commanding Officer from 1 January to 31 December 1945.

First Lieutenant LOUIS M. COHEN O-1945556
    Executive Officer from 1 January to 31 December 1945.

First Lieutenant GILBERT M. HOOKER O-2511953
    Motor Officer from 1 January to 23 December 1945.

First Lieutenant JOHN F. WILLIAMS O-1946639
    Platoon Leader and Operation Officer from 1 January to 7 October 1945.

First Lieutenant ANDREW I. MEDITZ O-1946571
   Platoon Officer from 1 January to 23 December, Motor Officer from 24 December to 31 December 1945.

First Lieutenant JOHN B. GREEN O-1535465
   Platoon Leader from January 1 to 8 August 1945, from 13 December to 31 December 1945.

First Lieutenant RALPH M. BLEAK O-535664
   Executive Officer from 31 December 1945.

> Ralph M. Bleak
> 1stLtT.C.
> Commanding

REFERENCE SOURCE: *National Archives*

APPENDIX VI

43rd Amphibian Truck Battalion

Chronology of Service
for "Operation Detachment"

05 July 1944—43rd Amphibian Truck Battalion activated at Camp Gordon Johnston, Florida.

21 October 1944—43rd Amphibian Truck Battalion departs from Camp Gordon Johnston, Florida, by train at 0845, for Ft. Lawton Port of Embarkation, Seattle, Washington.

26 October 1944—Arrive at Fort Lawton Staging Area, Seattle, Washington, at 1000 hours.

29 October 1944—Boarded Transport (Sea Partridge) at 1930 hours. Transport departed 2200 hours.

05 November 1944—Arrived at Oahu, Territory of Hawaii, at 1000 hours. Attached to Waimanelo.

04 February 1945—Left Hawaii aboard troopship *Sea Runner* at 1220 hours for the West Pacific.

11 February 1945—Passed International Date Line (10 February 1945–11 February 1945) at 2236 hours.

14 February 1945—Arrived at Eniwetak

17 February 1945—Left Saipan for Japanese-held Iwo Jima.

19 February 1945—D-Day at Iwo Jima.

23 February 1945—Old Glory raised on top of Mt. Suribachi.

04 March 1945—43rd Amphibian Truck Battalion digs in on Iwo Jima and prepares to stay.

05 March 1945—First B-29 landed on Iwo Jima—we watch it land.

06 March 1945—First land-based fighter arrived at Iwo Jima.

30 April 1945—43rd Battalion DUKWs brought in 20,175 tons of supplies.

REFERENCE SOURCE: *National Archives*

APPENDIX VII

History of Montford Point Marines

As a result of President Franklin D. Roosevelt's Executive Order #8802 (June 25, 1941), African Americans entered the United States Marine Corps for the first time in its history on June 1, 1942. Alfred Masters and George O. Thompson were the first to enlist on that date.

Because of the racial climate, African American recruits were not trained at the traditional boot camps (Parris Island and San Diego). They were trained and garrisoned at a segregated facility which had been designated for all African American Marines. This facility was part of that sprawling complex at Camp Lejeune, North Carolina, Camp Montford Point.

The first recruits to report to Camp Montford Point in August 1942, included Howard Perry of Charlotte, North Carolina. Approximately 19,000 African Americans served in the Marine Corps during World War II, with over 11,000 serving in the Pacific in units such as the 51st and 52nd Defense Battalions, the Stewards Branch, Ammunition and Depot Companies. Many of these units and individuals distinguished themselves in combat.

June 15, 1944—The 7th Field Depot (3rd Ammunition Company, 18th, 19th and 20th Depot Companies) land D-Day at Saipan. They are included in the award of the President Unit Citation to the 4th Marine Division for its combat role on Saipan and Tinian.

July 21, 1944—The 2nd and 4th Marine Ammunition Companies land on D-Day at Guam. The 4th Marine Ammunition Company and the 4th Platoon of the 2nd Company are included in the award of the Navy Unit Commendation to the 1st Provisional Marine Brigade for its actions on Guam. The Brigade Commander, Brigadier General Lemuel C. Shepherd, Jr., became the 20th Commandant of the United States Marine Corps.

September 15, 1944—The 7th Ammunition Company and the 11th and 16th Marine Depot Companies, at Peleliu with the 1st Marine Division, received letters of commendation from General William H. Rupertus, Commanding General, 1st Marine Division.

January 11, 1945—PFC Luther Woodward received the Bronze Star, subsequently upgraded to the Silver Star, for his combat actions on Guam.

February 19, 1945—Units of the 8th Field Depot (8th Ammunition Company and the 36th Depot Company) land D-Day at Iwo Jima.

February 24, 1945—Remaining units of the 8th Field Depot (33rd and 34th Depot Companies) land at Iwo Jima.

Note: The 8th Field Depot (8th Ammunition Company, 33rd, 34th, and 36th Marine Depot Companies) were cited with the rest of the support troops of the V Amphibious Corps in the award of the Navy Commendation, awarded for their part in the furious, month-long battle for Iwo Jima.

March 26, 1945—Privates Whitlock and Davis were awarded Bronze Star medals for heroic achievements in connection with operations against the enemy at Iwo Jima.

April 1, 1945—The 1st, 3rd, and 12th Ammunition Companies, the 5th, 18th, 37th, and 38th Marine Depot Companies, arrive at Okinawa on D-Day.

April 03, 1945—Depot and Ammunition Companies land at Okinawa in support of the 1st and 6th Marine Divisions.

September, 1945—V-J/Victory in Japan.

Occupation Duty

Japan—The 6th, 8th, and 10th Ammunition Companies and the 24th, 33rd, 34th, 42nd, and 43rd Depot Companies of the 8th Service Regiment (redesignated from the 8th Field Depot) and part of the V Amphibious Corps, arrived and disembarked at Sasebo between September 22 and 26, 1945. The 36th Depot and the remaining troops of the 8th Service Regiment arrived in Sasebo in late October.

North China—The 7th Service Regiment (Old 7th Field Depot) supported the 3rd Amphibious Corps in the Tientsin area of Hopeh Province with Corps Headquarters and the First Marine Division. Two Companies, the 12th Ammunition and the 20th Depot, helped support the 6th Marine Division at Tsingtao in Shantung Province. On September 30, 1945, the 1st Ammunition and the 38th Depot Companies went ashore with the first troops to land at Tangku, the port town of Tientsin. The 5th and 37th Depot Companies landed a few days later.

The Marine Depot and Ammunition Companies garnered the battle credits and took most of the casualties suffered by African American Marines during World War II.

African American Marine Units of the Fleet Marine Force (FMF) World War II

51st Defense Battalion
52nd Defense Battalion
51 Marine Depot Companies
12 Marine Ammunition Companies

November 10, 1945—Frederic Branch, formerly with the 51st Defense Battalion, was commissioned a Second Lieutenant in the Marine Corps Reserve. Thereby, becoming the first African American Officer in the history of the United States Marine Corps.

REFERENCE SOURCE: *Reference Source: http://www.geocities.com/nubiansong/briefhistory. htm*

APPENDIX VIII

8th Marine Ammunition Company Roster

C.O. Captain John R. Blackett, USMC
E.O. 1st Lieut. William E. Offut, Jr., USMCR

Adams, Frank Pfc
Alexander, Frank L. Pfc
Alexander, Harry T. PhM2/c
Alexander, Robert Pvt
Alford, Burch Pfc
Alit, William J. Cpl
Anderson, Ambrose Jr. Cpl
Anderson, Richard T. PhM2/c
Andrews, James R. Pvt
Baker, Earl O. Pfc
Balance, William E. Pfc
Barr, James W. Pfc
Barry, John D. GySgt
Berkley, Lawrence H. Sgt
Betrea, Julius Pvt
Betts, Frank M. Pfc
Black, Odell Pfc
Branch, Emil Pfc
Brooks, Walter B. Pfc
Brown, Franklin E. PlSgt
Brown, James E. Pfc
Bryant, Albert Sgt
Bryant, David Pvt
Briggs, Jerome F. Pfc
Burnett, Alex J. ACk
Burnett, Charles Pvt
Bush, John A. Pfc
Campbell, Edward A. Pfc

Campbell, Hugh W. TSgt
Canty, Nelson Jr. Pfc
Carter, Franklin J. Cpl
Christopher, Odell Pfc
Cooper, Cubeit L. Pfc
Crayton, Edward L. Pvt
Cunningham, Ellis Pfc
Dandy, Alphonse Sr. Pfc
Davis, Marvin Pfc
Dawkins, Forest Pfc
Deering, David J. MTSgt
Devergee, Winston W. Pvt
Dismuke, Lenard Jr. Pfc
Durr, Lawyer I. Pfc
Ealara, Ralph G. Cpl
Emmons, Justin M. QMSgt
Erisley, Joseph B. Pfc
Farley, William A. FCk
Fields, Moses T. Jr. Pfc
Foreman, Wauldron Pfc
Frazier, Charles E. Pfc
Freeman, Calvin Cpl
Gesston, Clifton O. Cpl
Graham, Kenneth J. 2ndLt
Greener, Vernon F. PlSgt
Greer, Robert Pvt
Guidry, Cefus Pfc
Hall, Thomas A. Sgt

Hansell, James ACk
Harris, Alan M. 2ndLt
Harris, Clenton Cpl
Harris, James Pvt
Harrison, George O. Cpl
Haslam, Charles B. IstLt
Hayes, James Pfc
Henry, Otis E. Sr. Cpl
Hill, Harrison Pfc
Hill, John H. Sr. Pfc
Hinton, Roosevelt Jr. Pfc
Hodge, William E. Pfc
Holmes, Robert L. Jr. Pfc
Huff, Johnnie C. Pfc
Hunter, Fred S. Pfc
Jackson, Algenon Pfc
Jackson, J. W. Pfc
Jackson, Johnnie R. Cpl
Jackson, Thomas J. Pfc
Jasmin, Calvin J. Pfc
Jennings, Eugene T. Pfc
Johnson, Desmond H. GySgt
Johnson, Ericher Pvt
Johnson, Hiram E. Pfc
Johnson, Ray Pfc
Johnson, Stone W. Pvt
Johnson, William H. Pfc
Jones, Joe T. Pvt
Jones, Leon F. Pfc
Jones, Shelby O. GySgt
Jones, William L. Pfc
Jordan, Arthur A. Pfc
Jordan, Charles H. Pfc
Jordan, Johnnie Pfc
Jordan, William Jr. Pvt
Kelly, James Jr. Cpl
Keys, I. T. Pfc
King, Willie L. Pvt
Lecoq, Morris V. Sgt
Lewis, Isiah Jr. Cpl
Lewis, Limmie D. Pfc
Lightner, Ernest Cpl
Litaker, Harry K. Pfc
Luther, Clark J. Pfc
Mack, Willie J. C. Pvt
Manns, James L. Pvt
Martin, Milton Jr. FCk

Mazych, Christopher J. Pfc
McArtis, Walter Pfc
McArtis, Wilbert Pfc
McDaugherty, Warren J.
McGiver, Harding W. Pvt
McLean, John L. Pvt
McPhatter, Thomas H. Sgt
Means, Henry Jr. Pfc
Meehan, Howard T. PlSgt
Miller, Samuel Cpl
Milton, Arthur Cpl
Mincey, Simon Jr. Pfc
Mitchell, Joseph Jr. Pfc
Montgomery, Samuel III Pfc
Morris, Wilbert Pfc
Morrison, Allen Cpl
Mote, Herbert F. 2ndLt
Murphy, Aujsiah H. FCk
Murrell, Henry A. Pfc
Nelson, Joseph L. Pfc
Nicholson, Thomas G. Jr. Cpl
Norris, Emmet Pfc
Nutall, Willis L. Pfc
Ogletrew, Arthur Cpl
Onley, Stanley L. ACk
Parker, Frank S. Pfc
Parker, Guy C. Pfc
Parks, Robert Pvt
Patten, Sims Pfc
Peoples, Willie C. Pfc
Poulson, Randolph Pfc
Pritchard, Sheldon L. Jr. Pvt
Putemy, Frank Jr. Cpl
Ramsey, English Pfc
Randolph, George R. Pfc
Ratliff, Edward ack
Rice, Charles E. 2ndLt
Richardson, Jamee Pfc
Rule, Willie E. PTc
Russell, Calvin. J. Cpl
Rutherford, Charlie A., Pvt
Sapf, Solomon Cpl
Samons, Stanley Pvt
Sellers, Samuel Pfc
Shaw, Phill Pfc
Singletary, William J. Pfc
Smith, Algernon C. Pfc

Smith, Charlie M. Pfc
Smith, Joe V. Pfc
Smith, Lewell E. GySgt
Smith, Warnell Sgt
Smith, William C. Pfc
Smith, William J. Pfc
Spain, Clifford R. V. Pfc
Spears, Haskell Pfc
Stephenson, William L. Pfc
Steward, Charles T. Pfc
Stiles, Joseph R. Pfc
Strayhorn, Calpernia Pvt
Sullivan, Willie J. Sgt
Taylor, William Jr. Pfc
Teague, Bolden Pfc
Thomas, Edward Pfc
Thompson, Casper Jr. Pfc
Tillman, Robert Pfc
Tracey, Charles D. Pfc
Triplett, Frank Pfc
Trueman, Moses D. Pfc
Turner, Will A. Jr. Pfc
Tyson, Eddie L. Pfc
Villars, Roy L. 1stSgt
Wade, Ben W. Pvt
Wadlington, Wilbert Pfc
Walker, Woodrow Pfc

Washington, George R. Pfc
Waytes, George R. ACk
Weber, Woodrow Cpl
Wells, David J. Sgt
Wells, Norman Pfc
Weston, James Pvt
Wheeler, Alphonse Pvt
Wheeler, Van B. Cpl
Whetstone, Artis Pfc
White, Frank Pvt
Williams, Hezekiah C. Pfc
Williams, Johnnie B. Pvt
Williams, Lawrence Pfc
Williams, Leon N. Pfc
Williams, Matthew Pvt
Williams, McKinley Pvt
Williams, Orie Pfc
Wilkins, Willie J. Cpl
Wilson, George Jr. Pvt
Wilson, Patrick J. 2ndLt
Wilson, William D. Pvt
Wilson, Willie J. Pfc
Woods, Joseph A. Pvt
Woolfork, Fred L. Pvt
Wrathersby, Joseph B. Pfc
Wright, David C. Cpl

REFERENCE SOURCE: *Muster of the Eighth Field Depot for February 1945, U.S. Marine Corps Historical Center, Quantico, Virginia*

APPENDIX IX

33rd Marine Depot Company Roster

C.O. 1st Lieut. Elmer G. Fremont, Jr. USMCR
E.G. 2nd Lieut. Robert J. Schrank, USMCR

Acker, George B. PhM2/c
Aitchison, Henry M. PhM3/c
Albritton, Howard C. Pfc
Anderson, Fred Pvt
Aught, Vector Sr. Pvt
Baldke, Alonso, Pfc
Barnett, John L. Pvt
Baugh, Howard Sgt
Bishop, Clarence T. Pfc
Bonner, John L. Pvt B
Boyd, John H. Pvt
Braithwaite Ralph R. HAl/c
Brave, Charles Pvt
Bruce, Archie L. A. Cpl
Burton, John W. Pvt
Cannon, Willie G. Pvt
Carey, Milton G. Pfc
Christmas, Francis J. Pvt
Clayton, William N. Pfc
Cleveland, Mack M. Sgt
Coleman, Joseph Pvt
Coleman, Percy Pfc
Colvin, Ed. Jr. Pfc
Connerly, Wilton D. Pvt
Croner, Wilburn A. Pvt
Dawson, Herbert Pfc

Dawson, T. C. Pvt
Douglas, Eugene C. Pfc
Douglas, Lucius H. Pvt
Durden, Roland B. Pfc*
Easterling, James A. Pfc
Edwards, Louis G. Pvt
Ellis, John A. Sgt
English, William Pfc
Erion, John H. Pfc
Field, Oscar R. Pvt
Floore, Henry P. Pfc
Freeman, Arthur R. Pvt
Freeman, Rodney Pvt
Frye, William F. Jr. Cpl
Gaskin, George L. Pvt
Gibson, John Pvt
Goodman, Ernest Pfc
Green, James Sr. Pfc
Greenard, Jewel Pfc
Greer, Garland E. Pfc
Greer, Obie Pfc
Preston, Charlie Jr. Pvt
Prootch, Alfred Jr. Pvt
Redmond, Louis K. Pvt
Reed, Lyman Jr. Pvt
Reed, Wilson Pvt

Editor's note: The official roster incorrectly lists Roland Durden as "Durien."

238

Rena, Vincent Pfc
Richmond, Lester Pfc
Roberts, George Pfc
Robertson, Harvey L. Pvt
Robinson, Charlie Pvt
Rollins, Vernan L. Pvt
Rosk, Paul S. Pfc
Ross, Ernest R. Jr. Pfc
Sampson, Alfred Pvt
Sampson, Joseph Pvt
Sanders, William H. Pfc
Savage, Corris C. Pvt
Scott, Bobby L. Pfc
Scott, Sheppard C. Sr. Pfc
Semper, George R. Cpl
Seward, Junior Pfc
Shamberger, Mordecai Pfc
Sims, Wesley F. Sr. Pfc
Smith, Leon W. Pvt
Smith, Robert J. Sr. ACk
Smith, Robert L. Pvt
Smith, Talmage Pvt
Strait, Frederick D. Pfc
Strickland, Obie Pvt
Taylor, Nelse, Jr. Pvt
Taylor, Sylvester Pvt
Thigpen, Edward Pvt
Thomas, Edward Pvt
Thomas, John S. Pvt

Thomas, Leveron Pvt
Thompson, Gary Pvt
Thompson, Hilton Pvt
Toliver, Charles Jr. Pfc
Tomlinson, Roy M. WO
Tonek, Ellie Pfc
Turner, Robert J. Pfc
Tynes, Nathan B. Pfc
Waddell, Samuel Pvt
Walker, Everett S. Cpl
Ward, Terner A. Pvt
Ward, William I. Pvt
Washington Daniel W. FMl/e
White, James C. Pvt
White, Kermit A. PISgt
Wicis, John N. Pvt
Wiggins, Archie P. Pvt
Williams, Donald C. Pvt
Williams, John H. Pfc
Williams, John L. Pvt
Williams, Robert L. Pvt
Wishfton, Robert E. Pfc
Witherspoon, Willienus Sr. Pvt
Wortham, Floyd E. Cpl
Wright, Elmer Jr. Pfc
Wright, Samuel W. Pvt
Wyatt, Edward C. Pvt
Yancy, Luke Pvt
Young, Leroy Jr. Pfc

REFERENCE SOURCE: *Muster of the Eighth Field Depot for February 1945, U.S. Marine Corps Historical Center, Quantico, Virginia*

Appendix X

36th Marine Depot Company Roster
C.O. Captain John B. Harvie, USMCR
E.G. 2nd Lieut. James Myers, Jr. USMCR

Allbritton, Charles G. Pfc
Allen, James S. Pfc
Allison, James L. Pvt
Aplin, Jimmie L. Pfc
Austin, William E. Pvt
Baldwin, James H. Sgt
Bannister, Ernest H. Sr. Pfc
Betle, Mathew B. Sr. Pvt
Blackmon, Willie J. Pvt
Brady, James Pfc
Britton, Jimmie Pfc
Brooks, Cyril R. Cpl
Brown, Edward Pvt
Brown, Horry Pvt
Brown, Jack ACk
Brown, James Sr. Pvt
Brown, Lloyd D. Sr. Pvt
Brown, Thomas K. Pvt
Bullock, Ike Pvt
Bunch, Louis Pvt
Burnett, Charles R. Pvt
Carter, William R. Pvt
Chesson, Thomas G. Pvt
Clayton, Carroll S. Pvt
Coley, Charlie W. Pvt
Colson, Lester M. Jr. Pfc
Cook, James E. Pfc
Cooper, Edward J. Pvt

Cooper, James J. Pfc
Copeland, Robert Pfc
Cox, Leamon T. Sgt
Cox, Mortimer A. GySgt
Crumb, John Pvt
Crumes, Alonzo B. Pfc
Culver, Walter Pfc
Davis, Charles Pvt
Davis, James Pvt
Davis, Wilbert Cpl
Dawson, Troy S. HA1/c
Dean, George Pfc
DeLoach, Robert Pvt
Donaldson, Vardell Pvt
Doughty, Eugene Cpl
Dove, Clayton Pvt
Dukes, John A. Pvt
Dunbar, Paul L. Pfc
Durham, John H. Pfc
Edwards, Johnnie Pvt
Flowers, Oazie Pfc
Ford, Bernal V. Pvt
Franklin, Charlie L. Pvt
Fryson, Charlie Pfc
Gary, William P. Jr. Sgt
Goode, James H. Pfc
Goodman, Norman W, PhM3/c
Goodwin, Laumerion Cpl

240

Hackings, Thomas Pvt
Hairston, John J. Cpl
Hardin, McDuffie Pvt
Harris, James A. Pfc
Harrison, James P. Pvt
Henderson, Benjamin C. Jr.
Henry, Earnest Pfc
Hilliard, Vandy Pvt
Hoffman, Willie W. HAl/c
Holland, Nathaniel Pvt
Holman, George W. Cpl
Hopkins, Paul Jr. Pvt
Hughes, William Pvt
Ivory, Printist Pfc
Jackson, Emmet D. Pfc
James, Adolphus Pvt
Jennings, Willie E. Pvt
Jiggets, William A. Pvt
Johnson, Charles J. Pfc
Johnson, Earnest Pvt
Johnson, Floyd Cpl
Johnson, Randolph Pvt
Johnson, Warren J. Sr. Pfc
Johnson, Wilbert Pvt
Jones, Bobby E. Pfc
Jones, David Pvt
Lane, Hadley P. Pfc
Leake, Hardie Cpl
Lee, William Pfc
Legette, Roosevelt Pvt
Lewis, LeRoy Sr. Pfc
Lindsay, Ellis R. Pvt
Locke, John J. WO
Lyons, Marshall E. Pfc
Martin, William Pvt
McClendon, Sunnell Pvt
McCord, Arthur A. Sgt
McCormick, Max Pfc
McLain, Willie Pfc
Meekins, Andrew Pvt
Mercer, Astor G. Pfc
Mosley, Archibald S. B. Jr. Pfc
Nelson, Robert W. Cpl
Nesbitt, Eugene Jr. Pvt
Newson, Harold P. 2ndLt
Nichols, LeRoy G. Pfc
Oliver, Richard Pvt

Patterson, Henry R. Pvt
Payne, Frederick Cpl
Pearson, James E. Pvt
Pelman, James W. Pvt
Peterson, Lewis M. Pfc
Porter, Otis Pvt
Price, John Jr. Pfc
Rabb, George W. Pfc
Ragland, Lee Pvt
Ranee, James R. Pfc
Redman, Edward B. Pvt
Reid, James M. Sgt
Rhea, Nerus Pfc
Rice, J. D. Cpl
Rickerson, Carey Pvt
Riley, Lester M. Cpl
Riley, Matthew Pfc
Sammons, Gardner M. Jr. Pvt
Sanders, Oscar H. Cpl
Saunders, Crofton T. Pfc
Seay, Abraham Pvt
Sheaffer, Andrew A. Pfc
Skinner, Wilbert ACk
Smalls, John H. Pvt
Smith, Covert L. Pfc
Smith, Luru Pvt
Smith, Wilbur A. Pfc
Smott, Willie R. Pvt
Sneed, Ralph E. Cpl
Spencer, Sidney Pvt
St. Claire, Buford Cpl
Stewart, James A. Pfc
Stith, Judge H. Pvt
Sutton, Felton Pvt
Taylor, James Jr. Pfc
Thompson, William N. ACk
Tolliver, John G. Pfc
Toney, James Pfc
Tousant, David E. Pvt
Tucker, Cassell Pvt
Waddell, Ellis Pvt
Ward, Willie T. Pvt
Warren, Stanley E. Pvt
Weber, Peter J. Pfc
White, Gordon A. Pfc
Whitlock, James M. Pvt
Wilkie, Horace S. Pfc

Williams, David Pvt
Williams, LeRoy Pvt
Willis, Arthur Jr. Pfc
Wilson, Neal Pfc
Wingate, Dave Jr. ChCk

Woods, Bennie C. Pfc
Woods, Thomas J. Pfc
Worth, Miles Pvt
Young, Robert Sr. Pvt

REFERENCE SOURCE: *Muster of the Eighth Field Depot for February 1945*, U.S. Marine Corps Historical Center, Quantico, Virginia

APPENDIX XI

Executive Order 8802

Executive Order 8802—Reaffirming Policy of Full Participation in the Defense Program by All Persons, Regardless of Race, Creed, Color or National Origin, and Directing Certain Action in Furtherance of Said Policy

WHEREAS it is the policy of the United States to encourage full participation in the national defense program by all citizens of the United States, regardless of race, creed, color, or national origin, in the firm belief that the democratic way of life within the Nation can be defended successfully only with the help and support of all groups within its borders; and

WHEREAS there is evidence that available and needed workers have been barred from employment in industries engaged in defense production solely because of consideration of race, creed, color, or national origin, to the detriment of workers' morale and of national unity;

NOW, THEREFORE, by virtue of the authority vested in me by the Constitution and the statutes, and as a prerequisite to the successful conduct of our national defense production effort, I do hereby reaffirm the policy of the United States that there shall be no discrimination in the employment of workers in defense industries or government because of race, creed, color, or national origin, and I do hereby declare that it is the duty of employers and of labor organizations, in furtherance of said policy and of this Order, to provide for the full and equitable participation of all workers in defense industries, without discrimination because of race, creed, color, or national origin;

And it is hereby ordered as follows:

1. All departments and agencies of the Government of the United States concerned with vocational and training programs for defense production shall take special

measures appropriate to assure that such programs are administered without discrimination because of race, creed, color, or national origin;

2. All contracting agencies of the Government of the United States shall include in all defense contracts hereafter negotiated by them a provision obligating the contractor not to discriminate against any worker because of race, creed, color, or national origin;

3. There is established in the Office of Production Management a Committee on Fair Employment Practice, which shall consist of a Chairman and four other members to be appointed by the President. The Chairman and members of the Committee shall serve as such without compensation but shall be entitled to actual and necessary transportation, subsistence, and other expenses incidental to performance of their duties. The Committee shall receive and investigate complaints of discrimination in violation of the provisions of this Order and shall take appropriate steps to redress grievances which it finds to be valid. The Committee shall also recommend to the several departments and agencies of the Government of the United States and to the President all measures which may be deemed by it necessary or proper to effectuate the provisions of this Order.

Franklin D. Roosevelt
The White House
June 25, 1941

REFERENCE SOURCE: http://www.eeoc.gov/abouteeoc/35th/thelaw/eo-8802.html

APPENDIX XII

Executive Order 9981

Executive Order 9981—Establishing the President's Committee on Equality of Treatment and Opportunity in the Armed Services

WHEREAS it is essential that there be maintained in the armed services of the United States the highest standards of democracy, with equality of treatment and opportunity for all those who serve in our country's defense:

NOW, THEREFORE, by virtue of the authority vested in me as President of the United States, by the Constitution and the statutes of the United States, and as Commander in Chief of the armed services, it is hereby ordered as follows:

1. It is hereby declared to be the policy of the President that there shall be equality of treatment and opportunity for all persons in the armed services without regard to race, color, religion or national origin. This policy shall be put into effect as rapidly as possible, having due regard to the time required to effectuate any necessary changes without impairing efficiency or morale.

2. There shall be created in the national Military Establishment an advisory committee to be known as the President's Committee on Equality of Treatment and Opportunity in the Armed Services, which shall be composed of seven members to be designated by the President.

3. The Committee is authorized on behalf of the President to examine into the rules, procedures and practices of the armed services in order to determine in what respect such rules, procedures and practices may be altered or improved with a view to carrying out the policy of this order. The Committee shall confer and advise with the Secretary of Defense, the Secretary of the Army, the Secretary of the Navy, and the Secretary of the Air Force, and shall make such recommendations to the President and to said Secretaries as in the judgment of the Committee will effectuate the policy hereof.

4. All executive departments and agencies of the Federal Government are author-

ized and directed to cooperate with the Committee in its work, and to furnish the Committee such information or the services of such persons as the Committee may require in the performance of its duties.

5. When requested by the Committee to do so, persons in the armed services or in any of the executive departments and agencies of the Federal Government shall testify before the committee and shall make available for the use of the Committee such documents and other information as the Committee may require.

6. The Committee shall continue to exist until such time as the President shall terminate its existence.

Harry S Truman
The White House
July 26, 1948

REFERENCE SOURCE: http://www.trumanlibrary.org/9981.htm

Bibliography

General World War II Background and History

Alexander, Joseph H. (Colonel USMC [Ret]). "Marines in World War II Commemorative Series." *www.ibiblio.org*, 1994 <http://www.ibiblio.org/hyperwar/USMC/USMC-C-Iwo/index.html>. Transcribed and formatted by Emily Brickhouse for the HyperWar Foundation.

Antill, P. "The Battle for Iwo Jima." *www.historyofwar.org*, 6 April 2001 <http://www.historyofwar.org/articles/battles_iwojima.html>.

"Battle of Iwo Jima." *www.battle-fleet.com* <http://www.battle-fleet.com/pw/his/Battle-of-Iwo-Jima.htm>.

_____. *Wikipedia, the Free Encyclopedia*, Wikimedia Foundation, Inc., 10 Aug. 2004 <http://en.wikipedia.org/wiki/Battle_of_Iwo_Jima> (26 February 2009).

Bradley, John H. "The Land Battle." Iwo Jima, Inc., 2005 <http://www.iwojima.com/battle/battlec.htm>.

Brown, Otis L. II (Lieutenant Colonel). "USAWC Strategy Research Project: Universal National Service Policy." United States Army.

"Camp Plauche: Pictures and History," *Geocities.com* <http://www.geocities.com/twincousin2334/NO_Camp_Plauche.html>.

"A Chronology of African American Military Service from WWI through WWII." *Redstone. Army.mil* <http://www.redstone.Army.mil/history/integrate/chron3c.htm>.

Dattilo, Matt. "The Invasion of Iwo Jima, February 19, 1945." 18 February 2008 <http://mattstodayinhistory.blogspot.com/2008/02/invasion-of-iwo-jima-february-19-1945.html>.

"G.I. Bill." *Wikipedia, the Free Encyclopedia*, Wikimedia Foundation, Inc., 10 Aug. 2004 <http://en.wikipedia.org/wiki/GI_Bill> (22 February 2009).

"Iwo Jima: The Battle, Reasons, and Strategy." *World War II: Battles with No Boundaries*, Oracle Thinkquest Education Foundation, 2002 <http://library.thinkquest.org/CR0215466/iwo_jima.htm>.

MacGregor, Morris J., Jr. "Chapter 4. World War II: The Marine Corps and the Coast Guard," in *Integration of the Armed Forces 1940–1965* by Morris J. MacGregor, Jr. Washington, D.C.: Center of Military History United States Army, 1985<http://www.history.Army.mil/books/integration/IAF-04.htm> (21 June 2001).

Naval Analysis Division. "Chapter 13: The Iwo Jima Campaign," in *The Campaigns of the Pacific War, United States Strategic Bombing Survey*, United States Government Printing Office, 1946 <http://www.ibiblio.org/hyperwar/AAF/USSBS/PTO-Campaigns/USSBS-PTO-13.html>. Transcribed and formatted by Patrick Clancey, HyperWar Foundation.

Overton, Richard E. *God Isn't Here: A Young Man's Entry Into World War II, and His Participation in the Battle for Iwo Jima.* Clearfield, Utah: American Legacy Media, 2007 <http://books.google.com/books?id=Yd9Qrtf4p8gC>.

Shaw, Henry I. Jr. *Opening Moves: Marines Gear Up for War.* Washington, D.C.: Marine Corps Historical Center, 1991 <http://www.nps.gov/archive/wapa/indepth/extcontent/usmc/pcn-190-003115-00/sec2a.htm>.

Smith, Charles R. *Securing the Surrender: Marines in the Occupation of Japan.* Washington, D.C.: Marine Corps Historical Center, 1997, <http://www.nps.gov/archive/wapa/indepth/extContent/usmc/pcn-190-003143-00/sec5.htm>.

Smith, Holland M. (Lieutenant General). "Appendix V, Task Organization, Expeditionary Troops," in *Iwo Jima, Amphibious Epic* by Lt. Col. William L. Bartley, USMC, Historical Section, Division of Public Information Headquarters, U.S. Marine Corps, 1954 <http://www.ibiblio.org/hyperwar/USMC/USMC-M-IwoJima/USMC-M-IwoJima-V.html>. Transcribed and formatted by Patrick Clancey, HyperWar Foundation.

Sullivan, John L. "Appendix IX Navy Unit Commendation," in *Iwo Jima: Amphibious Epic* by Lt. Col. William S. Bartley, USMC, Historical Section, Division of Public Information Headquarters, U.S. Marine Corps, 1954 <http://www.ibiblio.org/hyperwar/USMC/USMC-M-IwoJima/USMC-M-IwoJima-IX.html>. Transcribed and formatted by Patrick Clancey, HyperWar Foundation.

United States Department of Veterans Affairs. "Born of Controversy: The GI Bill of Rights." *www.gibill.va.gov,* 8 January 2009 <http://www.gibill.va.gov/GI_Bill_Info/history.htm>.

"WWII Terms & Definitions." Wilson School District, *www.wilsonsd.org,* 2002–2008, Schoolwires, Inc. <http://www.wilsonsd.org/770271111693348/lib/770271111693348/20070126111712924.pdf>.

Youmans, John B., M.D. "Malnutrition and Deficiency Diseases," in *Preventive Medicine in World War II,* edited by Col. John Boyd Coates, Jr., MC. Washington, D.C.: Office of the Surgeon General, 1955, *history.amedd.Army.mil* <http://history.amedd.Army.mil/booksdocs/wwii/PrsnlHlthMsrs/chapter5.htm>.

African Americans in the Military

"African Americans, World War II," in *Americans at War. www.bookrags.com,* 2006, Macmillan Reference USA, an imprint of the Gale Group, <http://www.bookrags.com/research/african-americans-world-war-ii-aaw-03/>.

Converse, Elliott Vanveltner. *The Exclusion of Black Soldiers from the Medal of Honor in World War II.* Jefferson, NC: McFarland, 1997.

DeClouet, Fred. *First Black Marines: Vanguard of a Legacy.* AuthorHouse, 2000 <http://books.google.com>, Path: Black Marines Iwo Jima.

Flynn, George Q. "Selective Service and American Blacks during World War II." *The Journal of Negro History,* Vol. 69, No. 1 (Winter 1984), pp. 14–25 <http://www.jstor.org/pss/2717656>.

Frazier, John W., and Eugene Tettey-Fio. *Race, Ethnicity, and Place in a Changing America.* Global Academic Publishing, 2006 <http://books.google.com/books?id=zKHu-LRhpRUC>.

Lee, Ulysses. "Service Units in the Combat Zone: An Overview of Black Quartermaster, Transportation, Air Defense, Medical, Chemical and Engineer Inits That Were Involved in Combat during World War Two," in *Service Units Around the World Special Studies: The Employment of Negro Troops* by Ulysses Lee. Washington, D.C.: U.S. Center of Military History, 1966 <http://www.qmfound.com/black_service_units_in_combat.htm>.

MacGregor, Morris J., Jr. *Integration of the Armed Forces, 1940–1965.* Washington, D.C.: Center of Military History, United States Army, 1985 <http://www.history.Army.mil/books/integration/IAF-fm.htm> (2 May 2001).

McLaurin, Melton Alonza. *The Marines of Montford Point: America's First Black Marines.* Chapel Hill: University of North Carolina Press, 2007 <http://books.google.com/books?id=fekFdJae62cC> Path: Black Marines, Sasebo, Japan.

"Minorities Playing Major Roles in the Government: Diversity in Bush's Cabinet." *Diversityworking.com* <http://www.diversityworking.com/generalDiversity/ww2diversity.php>.

Moskos, Charles C. "Success Story: Blacks in the Military." *The Atlantic*, May 1986 <http://www.theatlantic.com/doc/198605/blacks-military>.

Nalty, Bernard C. *The Right to Fight: African American Marines in World War II*. Darby, PA: Diane Publishing, 1995.

Osur, Alan M. *Blacks in the Army Air Forces during World War II: The Problems of Race Relations*. Darby, PA: Diane Publishing, 1976 <http://books.google.com/books?id=9_HDePlKlMsC&printsec=frontcover>.

Payne, Richard J. *Getting Beyond Race: The Changing American Culture*. Boulder, CO: Westview, 1998 <http://books.google.com/books?id=vM5NeBBhXBEC>.

Putney, Martha S. "A Historical Overview of African Americans and the Military." Remarks delivered at Ford's Theater at a National Park Service ceremony for the Civil War Soldiers and Sailors System, July 17, 1998, <http://www.itd.nps.gov/cwss/history/aa_militaryhistory.htm>.

Randall, Vernellia R. *Race, Racism and the Law: Speaking Truth to Power!* (Examples of Jim Crow Laws) <http://www.academic.dayton.edu> (24 February 2009).

Silver, Christopher and John V. Moeser. *The Separate City: Black Communities in the Urban South, 1940–1968*. Lexington: University Press of Kentucky, 1995 <http://books.google.com/books?id=hZYGqOZbWcoC>.

Simkins, Chris. "African American Soldiers in World War II Helped Pave Way for Integration of US Military." *Voice of America News*, 10 May 2005, <http://www.voanews.com/english/archive/2005-05/2005-05-10-voa47.cfm>.

Westheider, James E. *The African American Experience in Vietnam: Brothers in Arms*. Lanham, MD: Rowman & Littlefield, 2007 <http://books.google.com/books?id=VHEL34ALzO4C>.

_____. *Fighting on Two Fronts: African Americans and the Vietnam War*. New York: New York University Press, 1999 <http://books.google.com/books?id=IS_MgHE35BIC>.

Coming Home

Lee Woodman Media, Inc. "Coming Home." 10 November 2003, <http://www.loc.gov/vets/VHPComingHomeScript.pdf>.

Dukw

"Amphibious Vehicle." *Wikipedia, the Free Encyclopedia*, Wikimedia Foundation, Inc., 10 Aug. 2004 <http://en.wikipedia.org/wiki/GI_Bill> (9 February 2009).

Commander in Chief, United States Fleet. *Amphibious Operations, Capture of Iwo Jima, 16 February to 16 March 1945*. Washington, D.C.: Department of the Navy, 1945 <http://www.history.Navy.mil/library/online/iwojima_cap.htm#index> (6 March 2006).

Land Ship Transportation

"House Resolution 1316" (H. Res. 1316 in the House of Representatives. U. S.). United States L.S.T. Association, 1 August 2008 <http://www.uslst.org/Docs/HRES1316EH.pdf>.

Priolo, Gary P. "Tank Landing Ship (LST) Index." *NavSource Naval History*, 2005 <http://www.navsource.org/archives/10/16/16idx.htm>.

Troop Statistics

Samz, Robert W. "Some Comments on Engel's 'A Verification of Lanchester's Law.'" *Operations Research*, Vol. 20, No. 1 (Jan.–Feb., 1972), pp. 49–52 <http://www.jstor.org/pss/169337>.

Flag Raising Photo

Leary, Kevin. "Joe Rosenthal: 1911–2006: Photo was his fame—his pride 'My Marines.'" *San Francisco Chronicle*, Monday, August 21, 2006, <http://www.sfgate.com/cgi-bin/article.cgi?file=/c/a/2006/08/21/MNGEJKM9VH1.DTL>.
Wright, Derrick. *Iwo Jima 1945: The Marines Raise the Flag on Mount Suribachi*. Oxford, UK: Osprey, 2001.

Index